The Innovation War

The Innovation War

Christoph-Friedrich von Braun

Prentice Hall PTR
Upper Saddle River, NJ 07458
http://www.prenhall.com

Library of Congress Cataloging-in-Publication Data

```
Braun, Christoph-Friedrich von.
   [Innovationskrieg. English]
   The innovation war / Christoph-Friedrich von Braun.
       p.    cm.
   Translation of: Der Innovationskrieg.
   Includes bibliographical references and index.
   ISBN 0-13-268178-1 (alk. paper)
   1. Research, Industrial.    I. Title
T175.B7313   1996
658.5'7--dc20                                    96-9352
                                                    CIP
```

Editorial/production supervision: *design•in—sync*
Cover design director: *Jerry Votta*
Cover design: *Bruce Kenselaar*
Manufacturing manager: *Alexis R. Heydt*
Acquisitions editor: *Bernard M. Goodwin*

©1997 by Prentice Hall PTR
Prentice-Hall, Inc.
A Simon & Schuster Company
Upper Saddle River, New Jersey 07458

The publisher offers discounts on this book when ordered
in bulk quantities. For more information, contact:

> Corporate Sales Department
> Prentice Hall PTR
> One Lake Street
> Upper Saddle River, NJ 07458
>
> Phone: 800-382-3419
> Fax: 201-236-7141
> E-mail (Internet): corpsales@prenhall.com

Printed in the United States of America
10 9 8 7 6 5 4 3 2 1

ISBN: 0-13-268178-1

Prentice-Hall International (UK) Limited, *London*
Prentice-Hall of Australia Pty. Limited, *Sydney*
Prentice-Hall Canada Inc., *Toronto*
Prentice-Hall Hispanoamericana, S.A., *Mexico*
Prentice-Hall of India Private Limited, *New Delhi*
Prentice-Hall of Japan, Inc., *Tokyo*
Simon & Schuster Asia Pte. Ltd., *Singapore*
Editora Prentice-Hall do Brasil, Ltda., *Rio de Janeiro*

*To my three children Johanna, Daniel
and Kaspar, who failed to prevent the
publication of this book.*

Contents

Introduction

This book emerged as the result of gradually growing doubts: doubts as to whether progress is really always progress, and not in fact a "progression" away from the real needs of markets or societies; doubts as to whether an action generally viewed as beneficial will not prove to be harmful instead; doubts as to whether certain routes to the future will not turn out to be dead ends; and doubts as to whether our steady striving for greater technical improvement will not in the end achieve exactly the opposite.

This is not to suggest a questioning of civilization in general, perhaps coupled with some back-to-nature fancies. That option has long ceased to exist. It already slipped away when the first of our ancestors decided to slide down the tree trunk and to walk henceforth on his hind-legs. There is no way back up the tree, any more than there can be a return to the flint, the battle-axe, the galley, or the stagecoach. Technology and technical development cannot be undone. They are one-way streets. Their turnoffs and the speed at which we drive on them can be decided. But there is no turning back.

The doubts about the turnoffs and the pace of technical research and development (R&D) are the subject of this book. Its attention focuses primarily on the R&D in corporate laboratories. This is by far the greatest share of total R&D, and its object is the development of new products or industrial processes. From modest beginnings towards the end of the 19th century and the early years of the present century, industrial R&D has grown into a formidable apparatus. Hundreds of thousands of chemists, electronics and genetic engineers, computer scientists, linguists, aviation and mechanical engineers, materials specialists, microbiologists, pharmacologists, physicists, software developers, process engineers, and a host of scientists and humanities scholars from many other disciplines are employed worldwide in the relentless further development of existing products and the conception of new ones. All of them have undergone long years of schooling and training. Many have received prestigious academic degrees and have accumulated extensive research experience. Every year, many billions of dollars, yen, deutschmarks, francs and pounds are spent on their salaries, for the construction and equipment of laboratories, experiments, manufacturing process adoptions, computer times, raw materials, conference trips, and scientific literature.

The number of specialized scientific journals reporting on R&D work now measures in the hundreds of thousands. A few hundred on-line magazines have already appeared on the Internet and other computer communication networks. Store window displays, newspaper articles, and advertising are continuously signaling the availability of myriads of newer, bigger, faster, cheaper, and better products. The most popular term in Japanese television commercials is *"shin hatsubai"* ["new on the market"]. Things which only yesterday were beyond technical reach have become the discount warehouse items of today. Tomorrow, they will be replaced by products still deemed impossible today. At the same time, national and international patent offices are drowning in a flood of patent applications and documents. We live and breathe technical innovation. The new has occupied the place once held by the constant and the permanent. Even more, newness has become the *only* constant.

Yet even today it is still not clear where it all originates. What exactly is R&D? What constitutes the relationship between research and technology, and just what is the meaning of the much vaunted term "innovation"? The goal of *Chapter 1*, therefore, is first to equip the reader with a number of tools for comprehension. It begins with the work of T. A. Edison, the father of any systematically-conducted industrial R&D. It goes on to describe how inspired do-it-yourselfers as of the end of the last century were gradually replaced by full-time professional R&D specialists. This is followed by a discussion of the innovation process. The discussion shows that in spite of this century's wealth of innovative experience, the successful market introduction of new products is still a very risky undertaking. Neither do we know exactly how best to go about it, nor can we determine in advance whether an innovation will in the end prove to be successful.

Chapter 2 is dedicated to the historical development of industrial R&D. It provides a rough sketch of where the beginnings of large-scale industrial R&D lay prior to World War I. It charts the course of the development of R&D between the wars, and finally traces its development in the postwar era, particularly since the 1960s. The objective here is not a detailed, complete survey of everything that industrial or quasi-industrial R&D has encompassed or still does now. Particularly for earlier decades, such comprehensive statistics are at best partial in nature. They would also have far outstripped the possibilities of the author, and are thus best left—along with many other related uncertainties and estimates—to more competent agencies such as the Organization for Economic Cooperation and Development (OECD) and economic research institutes. The goal is rather to point out that, in monetary terms, investment in R&D has today reached orders of magnitude which are no smaller than the revenues of entire industries and would even suffice to finance a midsize war.

As early as 1988, the United States, Japan, West Germany, Great Britain and France were spending a total of approximately $630 million on R&D *per day*. By comparison, the 8-year-war of the 1980s between Iran and Iraq, according to expert opinion, cost about $500 billion, or $170 million per day, a little more than 25% of that. Nor has R&D spending stopped there. In 1992/93 total daily R&D expenditures in the large industrial western economies had already grown to approximately $1 billion.

These R&D efforts are unequally distributed, both in terms of geography and industrial sectors. By far the greatest portion is conducted in only a very few countries. There, R&D is heavily concentrated among certain branches of industry such as pharmaceuticals, industrial equipment, electronics and aerospace. On the company level, the lion's share of R&D volume is found among the large multinational corporations. In terms of sales, however, it is often the small and medium-sized companies that are characterized by the highest R&D ratios. R&D spending in some industrial companies already surpasses expenditures on other traditional cost items, such as marketing or sales, and at times even exceeds total revenues.

For many years, the rise in total R&D expenditures substantially exceeded the growth rates of the respective economies. Only recently has a weakening tendency become apparent in a number of sectors and industries. Correspondingly, a large share of economic activity in the developed countries goes into researching new phenomena or into developing new products and processes. Since World War I, Governments are also playing an increasingly large and active role in R&D, not only by performing regulatory tasks, but also through direct or indirect financial support of R&D work performed in industry- or government-owned facilities. Meanwhile, many less developed countries are threatening to fall hopelessly behind in yet another area of economic endeavor.

Chapter 3 looks at questions immediately resulting from these developments: Are the enormous R&D efforts really worth while? It attempts an answer based on hard numbers. R&D spending, net profit, and revenues of thirty major corporations from the electrical and electronics industry in the United States, Japan, and Western Europe are compared over a 13 year period. It is shown that R&D spending among the thirty companies outstripped corresponding profits by far. Revenue growth also failed to keep pace with the growth in R&D expenditures. Even the identification of any *delayed* effects on sales growth from expanded R&D spending several years earlier proved to be difficult. Drawing the conclusion from all this that R&D is superfluous would be overhasty. But it does raise a number of critical questions. These focus primarily on whether the long-term survivability of a company can be assured simply by perpetually maintaining or even increasing high rates of new technology development.

A fundamental cause *and* result of the growing importance of R&D in corporate activities is the increasingly swift succession of new or improved products on the market. On the one hand, increased R&D spending leads to an increasing and/or speedier development of new products. On the other hand, the faster succession of new products forces companies to spend more money developing new products just to keep up with the competition.

Chapter 4 therefore examines the processes occurring within a company that is exposed to a continuous acceleration of product life cycles. It shows that companies and industries which seek to ensure their long-term survival by an increasingly faster succession of new product introductions can find themselves caught in the so-called "Acceleration Trap." The inherent danger of the acceleration strategy is that at first it appears very attractive. As long as product life cycles become shorter, revenues will rise. But maintaining this acceleration becomes increasingly difficult. It requires more and more R&D resources. Simultaneously, the capacity of the market to absorb a faster succession of product innovations is gradually exhausted. Sooner or later acceleration comes to a halt. This produces a decline in sales, where the extent of the decline depends on the degree of previous acceleration. There is a growing suspicion that in a number of industries a lower limit of reasonable cycle lengths has already been reached or soon will be.

Chapter 5 discusses the real-world impact of the Acceleration Trap on competition and companies' behavior. The way in which corporations think and operate under conditions of decreasing cycle times is explained. It is also shown how R&D management, planning, and strategy-formulation find themselves confronted with new and increasingly risky parameters. Procurement, training and management of R&D personnel become more difficult. Capacity and utilization rates are affected, as are manufacturing, quality, marketing, and customer relations. Not least of all, an unduly rapid succession of new products entails the wasteful use of macroeconomic resources and raw materials, in spite of recycling efforts. It may further be assumed that with faster acceleration and further calls for rising R&D budgets, the competitiveness and competitive behavior of industry will change, not only in degree, but also in quality. These changes include the willingness and the need to enter into strategic partnerships and joint ventures, to acquire other companies, invest capital and pursue specific patent policies. At the same time, classic instruments of industrial management are proving to be blunt when applied to R&D. Versatile new ones are not in sight. No one profits from this development, least of all the customer.

Chapter 6 deals with the question of why companies are prepared to face such risks and participate in a research race in the first place. It shows that the mechanisms governing an industrial R&D race are in many respects similar to those operating in a classic arms race between enemy nations. Projects, plans, and new programs are taken up less with an eye to the long-term survival of the company (to national security), but rather in response to R&D measures taken by the competitor (to the armament efforts of a potential or actual enemy). The—correct or erroneous—perception of what the competitor (the enemy) is either doing, or planning to do, becomes a prime determinant of one's own actions. Since such thinking occurs on all sides, a process of escalation takes hold in which all participants are driven to ever-greater R&D (armament) efforts, even though the market (the political state of affairs) may no longer warrant this. The typical result is obvious: overkill by orders of magnitude. This dynamic inter-action is further encouraged by the fact that the management of R&D today is essentially a matter of R&D itself. Effective management tools and external controls, such as they exist for all other areas of corporate activity, are still notably absent in the field of R&D.

The escalation of R&D can be brought to a halt only with great difficul-ties. As a rule, it is only when resources are exhausted that companies are willing to cut specific R&D programs or overall budgets. However, a short-age of cash so acute that a pain threshold is crossed is a very poor, and per-haps the worst form of R&D management. This is true not only because the level of pain becomes unbearable only at a very late stage, but also because the successful reassignment of R&D personnel and resources is possible only under great impediments and costs. In the majority of cases, R&D investments in people and equipment are of a long term nature. They can not easily be put on hold or switched on and off. In the process of "restruc-turing," therefore, major outlays are irretrievably lost.

Chapter 7 attempts two things: For one, it shows implicitly what is *not* the intention of *The Innovation War:* to give a set of tools and directions on how to win the R&D race. Its aim is rather to sow scepticism among R&D policy makers, corporate managers, and strategic planners whether the race itself makes sense. For another and explicitly, it summarizes the doubts expressed in the preceding chapters in the form of individual hypotheses. Central to these hypotheses are the two key concepts developed in Chapters 4 and 6, the Acceleration Trap and R&D Escalation. Several R&D selection guidelines are derived. Of primary importance among these are thoughts on how best to bring the R&D escalation to an end. Experience shows that strategies exist which permit a gradual reduction of R&D output without endangering the future of the company. At the same time, they allow industry to furnish the market with those innovations for which there is a true need.

The chapter contains a number of further recommendations that serve this purpose. These include the need to develop a frame of mind that sees R&D in a proper perspective. This perspective involves focussing R&D bud-gets on the *right* program, rather than on spending the maximum amount the company can afford. Key to this move is to define the R&D program in the light of the overall corporate setting. It includes not only company spe-cific aspects, but also the incorporation of exogenous factors such as global-ization and long-term social issues even if they go beyond immediately recognizable market trends. It also implies the definition of an R&D program that is properly balanced, for example, between product and process technologies. All this requires thorough preparatory work that makes ample use of all available information resources and environmental scanning techniques. Due to the long-term commitment and the major risks involved in any R&D project, what is required above all are extensive planning, careful decision-making processes and a correspondingly close control of results. From this, it follows that R&D projects which R&D management and corporate management cannot agree upon should not be worked on "just to be on the safe side."

None of this will happen on its own if the R&D function is left to its own devices or is not subject to adequate accountability. Today, the R&D function has matured sufficiently for it to be able to justify itself in the same manner as other functions in any industrial enterprise have been doing for many decades. Where it *does* supply adequate justification, however, R&D must be able to rely on the type of long-term support that its work requires.

Acknowledgments

Proper acknowledgment of all those whose ideas, advice and comments have contributed to *The Innovation War* is difficult. The main reason for this is that the book raises questions which could only partly be adequately addressed using the standard sources that report on R&D and innovation issues. For the greater part, therefore, the book's findings are not based on a few major pillars, but on a whole host of small, sometimes inconspicuous, mosaic pieces gathered on three continents. Only when taken together, are they capable of rounding out the picture presented here. Occasionally, such pieces consisted merely of a casual remark in a discussion through which a series of individual facts coalesced into a line of argument. Elsewhere, it might have been a newspaper clipping which underscored or clarified a connection. For reasons of space, many of these comments, ideas, contributions, and examples could not be included in the text or in the footnotes. Nevertheless, even if unused, they were not unwelcome since they supported the author in his conviction of being on the right track. Listing every suggestion, opinion, or instance of assistance, and their origins, would have vastly exceeded this space. The author's appreciation of them, though, is no less sincere.

Among this number, however, there are several sources of support without whose collaboration *The Innovation War* might never have received its name. Among these, particular thanks must go to Hartmut Gero Fischer, who participated in the project from its very start, critically questioning every sentence and train of thought, and yet maintaining his perspective throughout. The author also wants to mention thankfully the men and women of the Central Research and Development Department, the Strategic Planning unit, and the Corporate Archives of Siemens AG in Munich, who generously provided facilities, documentation and insights, particularly concerning the historical development of R&D. Their kind support was as gratefully received as that of the senior staff of the Research and Technology, Economic and Finance Departments of Henkel KGaA in Düsseldorf, and that of Henkel Corp. in Pennsylvania. Particularly helpful in researching the Japanese R&D experience were Mitsubishi Petrochemical and Nippon Electric Companies (NEC), as well as the Industrial Science and Technology Agency of the Ministry of International Trade and Industry. In his travails to update and translate *The Innovation War* into English while allowing for different metaphors, idioms, cultural contrasts and national settings, invaluable help and a plethora of useful suggestions were received from Prof. Carey C. Curtis of Connecticut State University and Julianne C. Smith of The American University. Any Germanisms that might have eluded their unfailing sense of proper language are entirely the fault of the writer. Finally, the author is indebted to Prof. Thomas J. Allen of the Massachusetts Institute of Technology for a wealth of ideas and explanations, advice and encouragement.

Christoph-Friedrich von Braun

Munich, Germany

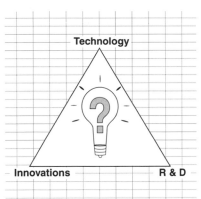

1

The Foundations of Industrial Research and Development

Edison, The Founding Father

Thomas Alva Edison, it is often said, was the greatest inventor of all time. More than any other person before or since, he understood how to turn newly devised products and processes into prosperity and prestige. There was certainly nothing to indicate that Edison's path was in any way foreordained. He was born in Ohio in 1847 as the youngest of four children.[1] At the age of seven he had the benefit of the only three months of formal education he would ever have, at the end of which his teacher classified him as "retarded," excluding him from further instruction. But Edison—and with him the world, which among his 1,093 patents owes him the invention of the microphone, the light bulb, the phonograph, the nickel-iron battery and the film projector—was lucky: His mother was a former teacher. In the years to follow, she not only taught him to read, and write and do arithmetic. She also instilled in him a lifelong thirst for learning and knowledge. Even in the ninth decade of his life, Edison was still working on producing rubber latex from domestic plant species. Little wonder that he achieved world renown in his own time. To this day, he is considered a technical genius and the personification of Yankee ingenuity.

---

1   Died 1931. Most of the information on the life and work of T. A. Edison is based on
    Josephson, 1979, p. 308.

But Edison was more than just a passionate technician and gifted inventor. In the assessment of his superiors at Western Union (in the late 19th century one of America's leading electrical companies) he was characterized as a "fiend for work," by "obsessive diligence," "dogged persistence," and "unfailing self-confidence." In addition to his technical work, he was also responsible for a number of inventions of an organizational, financial and institutional nature. These too, are of great significance in industrial research and development to this day.

Thus, when Edison left Western Union in 1876 to establish his own commercially oriented research laboratory at Menlo Park, New Jersey, he was already a well regarded and reasonably well-to-do inventor. His intention in Menlo Park was to create an "all-purpose laboratory," an "invention factory" that would introduce a minor innovation on the market every ten days and "a big trick" every six months. Inventions were to be made "on order," i.e., in direct response to customer demand.

Equipping the laboratory cost $40,000. It included measuring devices, induction coils, copper wire, a steam engine, a supply of various chemicals and metals, and even a small library of scientific publications and technical journals. In terms of size and equipment, it was rivalled only by the leading university laboratories, which at the time where the only organizations doing systematic research work. About twenty precision mechanics, clockmakers, machinists and metalworkers worked for Edison, joined after some time by an academically trained mathematical physicist.

The laboratory at Menlo Park was an outstanding success. Up to 40 projects were pursued at the same time and in some years as many as four hundred patents were applied for. Inventions were produced like goods on an assembly line. A special feature of the laboratory was teamwork, although all instructions came from the master inventor Edison himself, then still in his twenties. One of his most important achievements was to have replaced the lonely and talented do-it-yourselfers and their unpredictable, occasional hits with a systematic, commercially oriented R&D company. "Anything that won't sell I don't want to invent," was his business principle. It was perhaps Edison's greatest and most enduring invention. But there was more:

- In 1878 Edison announced his intention to invent a cheap, safe, and mild source of electric light, which would replace millions of dangerously inflammable gaslights as well as the glaring brightness of the electric arc. This was a project that had unsuccessfully been worked on for fifty years. However, the shrewd announcement alone was sufficient to convince leading financiers, among them the Morgans and the Vanderbilts, to advance the famed inventor Edison $50,000, well before a technical approach had even been clearly defined, let alone the actual invention completed—*the first case of technical venture financing.*

- This occurred under the corporate cloak of the Edison General Electric Company, the later corporate giant General Electric—*an early, perhaps the first example of entrepreneurial spin-off.*

- In 1887, the laboratory moved from Menlo Park to a facility ten times its size in West Orange, also in New Jersey. In very short order, Edison's prestige and the productivity of his laboratory sufficed to attract factories producing an extremely wide variety goods and employing more than 5,000 people—*the first technology park.*

- It was due to Edison's influence as an advisor to the U.S. Congress that the Naval Research Laboratory was founded in 1920—*the first military research facility.*

- Edison was not a scientist. Indeed, as a self-educated and outstanding experimenter he often joked about the "long-haired" fraternity of theorists. Nevertheless, there were a number of academically trained scientists among his employees, among them such a well-known name as that of Nicola Tesla (1856–1943).[2] Even Edison himself made a contribution to pure science: the discovery of the thermionic emission of electrons from an electrode. What later was to be called the Edison-Effect lay beyond the grasp of contemporary scientific explanation, although it eventually became the basis of the electron tube and thus laid the foundation for the television industry.—*This showed that applied and practical engineering work could also precede and stimulate fundamental research on natural phenomena.*

---

2   Tesla discovered the rotating magnetic field, the foundation of practically all alternating-current machinery, and made a number of other important inventions.

And even when it came to failures, Edison was characterized by the stubbornness of the passionate inventor: Everything he had earned in inventing the light bulb ($4 mill.) he invested in the futile attempt to develop a process for the magnetic extraction of iron ore from low grade deposits. When he finally gave up, it was with the words: "Well, it's [the money] all gone, but we had a hell of a good time spending it."

Do-it-yourselfers, Inventors and Scientists

Up to of the Second World War and even beyond, the conviction reigned in many places that a company rested first and foremost on two pillars: one of them, a technical and organizational facility for manufacturing products, and the other, some form of capacity for the marketing and distribution of these products. Of these two, the manufacturing function, i.e., the factory, was invariably the more important, at least during the early decades of industrialization. In addition, there were a number of other organizational units such as legal and personnel departments, whose primary mission was the support of the two core corporate functions.

Today, in practically all large industrial corporations, as well as in many small and medium-sized companies, research and development (R&D) has established itself—largely undisputed—as an additional pillar of corporate activity. Even service sector corporations (e.g. some banks and insurance companies) have begun to set up R&D departments. Not all companies call it by this name, of course. Occasionally it is referred to as the Department for New Products or the Department for Product Development/Process Technology, or the Development Department, the Engineering Department, the Technical Department, etc. Sometimes it has no name at all and cannot even be found in any organization plan. That does not mean that it does not exist, however. Even where it does not lead an independent existence, one can usually find it integrated in the company's production activities in one form or another. Apart from historical reasons, there are also sound, practical grounds for this. Often, the larger (and more important) share of innovations in a company stems from work occurring between development and production. In today's optimized production facilities there is rarely time—or space—to try out new product ideas. R&D departments that operate in organizational and physical isolation from the rest of the company, on the other hand, come up with new inventions far less frequently, even though these inventions may occasionally be of a more fundamental nature.

Irrespective of structures or labels, all of these more or less formalized organizational decisions are based on one fundamental realization: that to sustain a company's long-term survival, it must look after not only today's products and production methods, but also those of tomorrow. Although it had not yet entered the minds and corporate practice everywhere, this realization was not entirely new even in Edison's days. As early as 1776, Adam Smith (1723–1790) in his classic work *An Inquiry into the Nature and Causes of the Wealth of Nations* had attributed great importance to mechanical improvements. Similarly, Karl Marx (1818–1883) a few decades before Edison, had granted technical innovation a central role in the development of the capitalist system.[3] What was new, however, was the garb in which research and development increasingly began to appear at the beginning of the 20th century.

In the mid-19th century the improvement of existing products or the development of new ones was still left largely to those who were directly involved in the production process. With the help of mechanical tinkering, limited trials, but primarily on account of their own experience and observations, they were able to contribute to technical progress more or less in a sideline function. In those years, it was the practitioners of the present who laid the foundation stones of the future.

Beginning with Edison, this task was increasingly taken over by specialized full-time employees. Their exclusive task was to create the appropriate scientific and technical prerequisites for the innovations demanded in the competitive arena. The concept of the division of labor spread to, and seized hold of, R&D just as it had already done decades, if not centuries, earlier in the field of production. Hand in hand with the general specialization of functions and professions that had become the hallmark of the industrial age, the execution of research and development was thus also entrusted to experts and became "professionalized."

Simultaneously, it attained a scientific character in two completely different ways. Firstly, it became the object of scientific scrutiny, primarily of the economic sciences. Although the economists of the late nineteenth and early twentieth centuries had generally considered "technical progress" to be important for the process of economic development, they tended to treat it as an exogenous factor. This meant, it could neither be influenced nor subjected to rigorous analysis. Simply stated, technical progress was viewed as

---

3   Cf. Freeman, 1982, p. 3, gives numerous further sources.

somewhat akin to the weather: As far as possible it was included in one's plans, but one could not influence it. In whatever form, it was going to happen anyway. Nobody had any doubts that economic development depended among other things on a continuous flow of technical ideas and improvements. But whether this flow would take the form of a wide stream, a sluggish trickle or a dry river bed was at best God- *and* engineer-given.

It was only the Austrian-American economist and social scientist Joseph Alois Schumpeter (1883–1950) who in the beginning of the twentieth century first subjected the process by which new technologies emerged to a more rigid analysis. Building on the teachings of the marginal utility school, he elaborated a theory of economic development that was characterized by "dynamic entrepreneurs" whose deliberate (rather than coincidental) innovations led to economic growth. Schumpeter made it clear that there could be no growth without pain. Companies and industries, nations and peoples, rose and fell, and technology could be a decisive factor in this. There were not only winners, but also losers. To large degree, it was the entrepreneur's determination to win, or his fear of losing, that formed the driving force of free market economies.

Schumpeter was also the source of the crucial differentiation between invention and innovation which has now been generally accepted. An *invention* is an idea, a drawing, or model for a new or improved device, product, process or system. Inventions can be patented (but do not have to be), and do not necessarily lead to marketable goods and services. In fact, most of them do not. This only occurs through *innovation*. More specifically, the innovation process adds the economic dimension to the technical one. An innovation only comes about when the first commercial transaction relating to the new device, product, process or system has taken place.[4] It is often the far more difficult part of the overall process than the actual invention.[5] Simply stated, an invention is the technical solution to a question or a problem, while an innovation is the economic implementation of an invention.[6] In this sense both terms will also be employed here.

---

4   Freeman, 1982, p. 7.

5   A useful recommendation from an experienced inventor to would-be followers: "My advice to anyone coming up with a new invention is: think about it, enjoy thinking about it, and then throw the idea in the bin." quoted by Fischer, Andrew, 1993.

Secondly, R&D in Edison's time received a scientific flavor in the sense that it was increasingly performed by engineers, scientists and technicians who had received their training and education in universities or equivalent institutions of learning. It is no coincidence that during the same period, i.e. the second half of the nineteenth century, the first technical academies, colleges, and ultimately, technical universities were founded in Europe and North America.

In modern industry, the rule that R&D work is conducted exclusively by trained specialists is true with almost no exception. At the very minimum, all employees engaged in actual R&D work have undergone professional training for supporting or assisting functions (laboratory workers, pharmaceutical technical assistants, librarians etc.). This is not to say that gifted do-it-yourselfers and private inventors, whose active participation at the inventor fairs actually result in business deals, no longer exist. They (hopefully) always will. At the 1991 Geneva Inventors' Fair, for example, contracts totalling SFr 30 mill. (ca. $20 mill.) were signed. One also cannot dispute the fact that the unprejudiced approach and the tremendous determination of independent inventors contributes enormously to stimulating innovations. It is precisely these attributes which have often led to the establishment of successful companies, and indeed still do. Today, however, even these successful inventors-innovators-entrepreneurs are as a rule also academically trained engineers or scientists. Only very rarely are they autodidacts like Edison.

Moreover, whenever the R&D function is not the work of a lone inventor, but is performed in any mid-sized or indeed large-scale industrial setting, it is exclusively in the hands of technically and scientifically trained specialists. Others are not even considered for the job.[7] Today's exclusive reliance on technically-trained specialists is largely due to the sheer complexity associated with any kind of technical development work. This is true not only of relatively new scientific fields such as bioengineering, but also of

---

6   The OECD has suggested the following definition: "Technological innovations comprise new products and processes and significant technological changes of products and processes. An innovation has been <u>implemented</u> if it has been introduced on the market (product innovation) or used within a production process (process innovation). Innovations therefore involve a series of scientific, technological, organizational, financial and commercial activities." Source OECD, 1992, p. 28, emphasis from the original.

7   Some years ago, only software development seemed to be an exception to this rule. But that period has also passed.

more conventional areas of business endeavor such as the steel industry. In today's world, technical understanding—and even more importantly—the ability to creatively enhance this understanding and to arrive at new solutions and applications invariably requires a correspondingly long and thorough period of previous schooling and training.

In earlier times such lengthy training was not always necessary, Edison himself being the best example. On his 21st birthday he bought an old edition of Michael Farraday's (1791–1867) laboratory journals, *Experimental Researches in Electricity*. The 4,000 pages and 20,000 entries of these journals he read in one sitting. They were to be a decisive stimulus in his life as an inventor. The meticulous descriptions of Farraday's experiments (who himself had also not attended a university but was a bookbinder by training) as well as his work in the field of chemistry and electricity,[8] were still comprehensible to Edison. Due to his general education and talent he was able to profitably analyze and evaluate them. He could not have done so, however, with the theoretical work of the English physicist James Clerk Maxwell (1831-1879) who expressed Farraday's original concept of the electromagnetic field forty years after him in mathematical terms.[9]

A Few Definitions

It would be beyond the scope of this book to trace the entire development of technology since Edison. This is not only due to the sheer volume of developments and events. The difficulty of separating the essential from the nonessential as well as the distorting filter of contemporary and recent experience, which tends either to overlook or overestimate present events, also places narrow constraints on any unprejudiced assessment. Whatever the "greatest" (?) invention of this or the last century may be—the airplane, the computer, the contraceptive pill, the telephone, interplanetary spacecraft, nuclear power, the automobile, antibiotics, the laser beam, genetic engineering—or edible underwear, the question may rest unanswered. More important is the realization that during this short period of history almost every branch of technology has advanced further and faster than in mankind's entire previous experience. This advancement continues unabated.[10]

---

8   Euler, 1981, p. 10.

9   Solla Price, 1975, p. 127; Mowery and Rosenberg, 1989, p. 23.

The next chapter will provide an idea of the orders of magnitude to which industrial and state-sponsored R&D has grown in this century. It will also show that this magnitude is occasionally on a par with the production volumes of entire industrial sectors. Before doing so, however, and in the interest of a better understanding of this development, it will be useful to explain a few terms and interrelationships.

Technik and Technologie, technique and technology

For thousands of years, mankind has engaged in one form or another of technological development. Its effects encompass every region and every aspect of human life. Except perhaps in the very remotest corners of this planet, there is probably no one who can claim to have remained untouched by the impacts of modern research, science and technology—even if only as butcher or baker or candlestick maker. Nevertheless, in more than one language it is not always clear just what these terms really mean. Germany's small (but praiseworthy) Brockhaus encyclopaedia of 1977, for instance, defines *research* (Forschung) as "the scientific activity, to the extent that it strives to attain new knowledge." Conversely, "*science*, (Wissenschaft) is primarily the process of methodically conducted research...," a classic example of a circular definition, which is at least helpful in that it underscores the nebulous nature of the terms.[11]

Moving from this most general to more specific levels, definitions become a little less hazy. Thus, in the same encyclopaedia, *natural science* (Naturwissenschaft) is defined as "the science of natural phenomena and natural laws." This definition one could live with. New difficulties arise, however, when facing the term *Technik*. In German, Technik has several

10 For an in-depth account of the more recent history of technology with numerous sources, see Buchanan, 1979. p. 24, particularly p. 45.

11 A very lucid discussion of the term "science", is contained in Staal, 1995, p.7 (quote): "For 'science', even in English, does not denote a single and stable concept. There exist confusing differences in usage between English (American as well as British) and other European languages. English *science* refers primarily to the physical and life sciences, although it includes mathematics which is not about physical or living things. French *science*, spelled the same but pronounced differently, like German *Wissenschaft*, Dutch *wetenshap* or Russian *nauka*, applies also to human, social, natural and other domains. In English there is confusion about human sciences, humanities, letters and even arts. In Dutch and German, the terms *geesteswetenshap* and *Geisteswissenschaften* are used, although no one agrees or even knows what *geest* or *Geist* refers to. The French incorporate these same disciplines among the *sciences humaines*, which in German or Dutch suggest anthropology, in French a *science sociale*."

meanings. When used in a procedural sense it refers to "the knowledge and mastery of the rules and practices of an activity." As such it is not limited to activities which are of a scientific nature, (for instance, the driving technique of a race car driver or the amorous techniques of a Don Juan). However, when used in the context of a field of activity, "Technik" can also refer to "the measures, processes and facilities used in the control and purposeful exploitation of natural laws, energy and resources," making it akin to the definition of *natural science* mentioned above.

The confusion does not cease here. Aside from "Technik" there is also *"Technologie,"* just as one finds both "technique" and "technology" in English. The combination of the Greek words "techne" (art, craft) and "logos" (word, language, knowledge) would literally indicate a meaning equivalent to the "science of crafts." Eighteenth century sources[12] in fact do imply the existence of a technology science. However, in today's industrial usage, for example, the way the word is employed internally at Siemens AG, technology as such is not a science in itself, but only *"the practical application* of scientific or technical possibilities for attaining performance characteristics of products and processes."

Other companies use similar definitions. This has not led to a shism in definitions, though. The Brockhaus encyclopaedia simply offers a second definition of Technologie: "The study and application of technical production processes." Though not quite the same as the industrial definition, it does come quite close. Just to be on the safe side, the Brockhaus finally tosses yet a third definition into the pot: *Technologie* is *Technik*.

Some of this confusion also exists in English. While the English term "technique" does not have the same ambiguity as its German counterpart "Technik," it does correspond to a whole spectrum of concepts including "process," "method," "skill," or even "aptitude." Likewise, the term "technology" has undergone a considerable expansion in content since its original inception in the 17th century. Having shed its original meaning of "a discourse on the arts" (the fine arts as well as the crafts), by the middle of the

---

12 *"Technology is the science* which teaches the use of natural resources or the knowledge of skilled trades. Instead of merely issuing instructions in the workshops on how wares are to be produced by adhering to the rules and customs of the master, technology provides, in systematic fashion, fundamental guidance on how, based on true principles and reliable experience, the resources necessary for precisely these ends are to be found, and how phenomena occurring during production shall be explained and exploited." Beckmann, 1780, p. 17; author's translation, emphasis added.

twentieth century it came to include "the means or activities by which man seeks to change or manipulate his environment."[13] Increasingly, the German word *Technologie* is also used in this sense.

Research and Development

As is so often the case, when a purely verbal definition is of little help, a brief glance at actual practice can contribute to clarity. In scrutinizing the process of governmental and industrial R&D a little more closely, one can distinguish a series of distinct and sequential steps in the realization and transformation of new knowledge into new products and processes. In many ways, this sequence is similar to the chain of value-added steps in industrial production. Expanding on the work of the Organization for Economic Cooperation and Development (OECD),[14] in the economic sector these steps together are referred to as *research and experimental development*. Their definition[15] is as follows:

"Creative work undertaken on a systematic basis in order to increase the stock of knowledge, including knowledge of man, culture, and society and the use of this stock to devise new applications."

At first glance, this looks like a two-part definition: on the one hand, the expansion of knowledge, and on the other, the application of this expanded knowledge. The OECD, however, breaks the term research and experimental development into three parts by distinguishing between *basic research*, *applied research*, and *experimental development*, where

Basic research is defined as:

"Experimental or theoretical work undertaken primarily to acquire new knowledge of the underlying foundations of phenomena and observable facts without any particular application or use in view."

---

13 Anon. {1}, p. 21

14 OECD (Organization for Economic Cooperation and Development), headquartered in Paris, France. The 25 member countries are the industrialized countries of Western Europe incl. Turkey and Iceland, plus Australia, Canada, Japan, Mexico, New Zealand and the U.S. For an overview of the OECD's activities and the compilation of the so-called Frascati Manual see, Young, 1993.

15 OECD, 1984, Annex 2.

Applied research becomes:

"Original investigation undertaken in order to acquire new knowledge directed primarily towards a specific practical area or objective."

Experimental development finally is:

"Systematic work drawing on existing knowledge gained from research or practical experience directed towards producing new materials, products and devices, to installing new processes, systems and services and towards substantially improving those already produced and installed."

While these differences are accepted in principle in all the Western industrialized countries (where the lion's share of worldwide R&D activities are financed and conducted), they still provide generous scope for interpretation. Above all, even with the most conscientious efforts by companies to organize their R&D activities into the three stated categories—and many companies in the industrialized world do so—one is still a long way away from a reliable source of R&D statistics. On the one hand, there are some generic types of R&D activities that are difficult to subsume under one of the stated categories. Software development is an example of this. On the other hand, definition problems can also occur in individual cases. For instance, the manufacture of the prototype of a new device could be regarded as experimental development at one company, while it would already be considered pre-production, or even production itself at another. This can have significant impacts. For example, in a Siemens-internal analysis of a Japanese competitor, the German company determined that its competitor's spending on R&D was triple the amount reported by that company if its R&D activities were defined in exactly the same way as they were at Siemens.

A further source of uncertainty has to do with differentiation of R&D activities by goals ("..undertaken in order to...", "..directed towards...") In order to say whether a certain measure or specific R&D project is still part of basic research or already constitutes applied research, it would, strictly speaking, be necessary to determine the exact objective of the project. Is the aim simply the acquisition of "new knowledge of the underlying foundations of phenomena and observable facts"? Is "a specific practical area or objective" being pursued? Or is scientific knowledge to be "directed towards producing new materials, products and devices, to installing new processes, systems and services (or) towards substantially improving those already produced and installed"? No doubt, the simple description of specific activities will frequently suffice to answer such questions, though by no means always. Even if the content and sequence of two activities are absolutely identical, one can still be characterized by a specific, practical objective, and the other be aimed purely at obtaining knowledge. An autopsy, for instance, can be performed for the sake of epidemiological research or simply to determine the cause of death. In both cases, the goals are different but the actions are the same.

Also, the individual parts of a specific project can serve different objectives. Moreover, an individual researcher will not always be willing or able to answer questions about the purpose of his work. It may be secret or the researcher does not know himself. For example, among the many tens of thousands of people participating in the Manhattan Project probably only very few knew what its ultimate goal was. But even in the far more regular case where they do know the goal, there may be differing views on this among the researchers and financiers involved in a project. Finally, the objectives of a project that would have initially fallen under basic research may change during the course of the work, thus altering the character of the project.

For these reasons, it is not surprising that confusion reigns even in places where one might expect a certain amount of competence concerning such matters. For instance, in 1992, the Agency of Industrial Science and Technology, an affiliate of Japan's Ministry of International Trade and Industry (MITI), announced a wide-ranging "Basic Research Program" in six as yet little-researched fields, among them femtosecond technology (1 femtosecond= 1×10^{-15} seconds).[16] In the same announcement, the Agency contradicted itself by naming applications where the knowledge gained in this "basic" research could be put to commercial use (e.g., in communications and measuring technology).[17] As indicated above, research with a goal of practical application is *not* basic research.

Of course, there have been various proposals to break away from this goal-oriented division of R&D activities and to concentrate on the boundaries between science and technology instead. One suggestion has been not to look at the *intentions* of the researchers and institutions involved, but at the achieved *results*. Thus, if the result of an R&D project is essentially knowledge, i.e. something that must be published to be recognized, it is sci-

---

16 Anon. {6}, 1992.

17 Solla Price, 1975, p. 125.

ence and/or research. If, on the other hand, the result is essentially a thing, e.g. a chemical reaction or a technical process, something which can be bought and sold, then "technology" has been created.

At first glance, this seems like a very useful differentiation. In practice, however, it also runs into difficulties. A neat separation of science and technology is simply not always possible. Why should, for example, an R&D project not end with both a patent (i.e. technology) and an article in a scientific journal (i.e. science)? Apart from this, the differentiation assumes that there will really always *be* a result. A failed or cancelled project would then be neither science nor technology. But what would it be then?

In one sense, however, the differentiation is useful: it introduces economic aspects. One must bear in mind that only very little research activity today is conducted purely with the aim of expanding the horizons of human knowledge and nothing else. In an encompassing sense, this claim can at best be made for such fields as astrophysics and only for the simple reason that the objects under observation there have yet to come within technological grasp. To give an example, presumably so far nobody has given serious thought to the use of a black hole as a weapon or for other purposes (for instance, radioactive waste disposal). So the quest for really pure knowledge without any practical goal is perhaps still possible there. In quantum physics, however, or in genetics, this has long since ceased to be the case.[18]

In the overwhelming majority of cases, a relatively concrete intention lies behind each and every R&D project, the most frequent case, of course, being the intention of a company to enhance revenues or to preempt the competition with a new product introduction. But the intention can also lie with the government wishing to ensure the long-term well-being of the country by creating technologically sophisticated jobs or by improving the state of its military hardware. Whatever the situation, any spending on such application-oriented R&D projects must always be linked to some corresponding yield, whether in a monetary or non-monetary form. As far as industry is concerned, therefore, one might reasonably expect that R&D resources will only be made available if there is a credible likelihood that they will lead to one or more profitable innovations. The fact that such thinking is not neccessarily always practiced in real life will be shown below, primarily in Chapter 6.

18 Jopp, 1991.

No matter what the final outcome of this conceptual discussion may be, we will not conclude it at this point. It may suffice to have indicated its existence. For our own purposes, it will be enough to bear in mind the following simplified, but convenient rules of thumb:

- Research is the transformation of money into knowledge.
- Technology is the transformation of knowledge into money (or other utility units).

The Innovation Process

From the preceding considerations, a frequent notion of the innovation process has emerged which combines the individual parts of the process mentioned above into a mental model summarized in the cycle shown in Figure 1–1. According to this, basic research, occasionally also referred to as *pure research*, is usually not quite so pure. Under normal circumstances, it is aimed at some vaguely defined area of concern and produces knowledge which at least in general terms relates to the problems and questions of particular industries. For example, a scientist investigating magnetic phenomena will at least know that his findings can have ramifications for industries such as communications or data processing where switching speeds are relevant. Applied research transforms the knowledge gained in basic research to a point where it can be used for the solution of specific technical problems. Finally, during experimental development, the steps required for turning the new process or product into reality are taken. An invention is completed.[19]

19 A similar mental model seems to have already existed in the industrial practice of earlier decades. For example, an internal notice of Siemens AG dated August 22, 1944 on the basic differences between research and development states:

"The object of 'development' is a device or the application of a device for which the required knowledge base already exists. *Thus any development is founded on research activity that has been largely completed.*

The object of 'research' is something that is basically an as-yet-unknown, something that exists as a more or less vague idea, as an as yet unproven consequence of a natural law or as a concept for a clarification attempt in the mind of a researcher.

'Applied research' ('Zweckforschung') differs from general research—or to put it better—forms a special, delimitable subset of general research whose purpose is the identification of an as yet unknown usefulness of a basically understood phenomenon or process for a desired purpose or a certain application.

The result of successful (general) research is increased knowledge which can be employed, for example, in applied research or directly for a certain development.

The result of successful applied research is the technical development of a device or the application of a device for a technical purpose..." (translated by author, emphasis added)

As the process continues, the breadth of the field under observation becomes increasingly narrower and the commitment of manpower and resources more and more focused. At the end of the process stands the innovation and the market which determines the commercial success of the innovation and, in turn, generates resources for the development of future products and processes.[20]

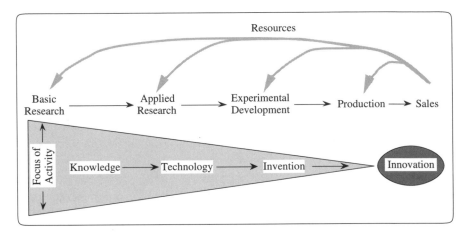

Figure 1–1   Simple Model of the Innovation Process

So much for the simplified model. Unfortunately, reality is a little more complicated. Although the relationship illustrated in Figure 1–1 is not fundamentally wrong, it shows only part of the story. That is, innovations *can* come about in this way, but do not have to. A new piece of scientific knowledge is not always the father or mother of a young innovation, nor even the midwife. Probably only a minority of all innovations can be traced directly or indirectly to scientific breakthroughs or new technologies that have been developed independently of ideas about later applications.

On the other hand, the opposite, (i.e., that demand for improved technical performance will stimulate innovations) is also not *always* true either. Markets can, of course, express certain needs and set research and development efforts into motion which will aim to produce a new product to meet this demand. A treatment for the HIV-Virus would be a particularly poi-

---

20 Similar models of the innovation process also seem to influence thinking on government levels, see for instance MITI, 1992, p. 9-14.

gnant example of this. Here, the wish for a solution of a global and urgent problem is abundantly clear. However, one should be aware that a specific demand for a product is not really conceivable in the absence of an equally specific, i.e., existing, supply of such a product. It is only when a new product has been sufficiently well defined and when its characteristics are reasonably well known or believed to be known (in the case of a pharmaceutical product, for instance, its success rate, price, side effects, safety, etc.), that any demand can really arise. Strictly speaking, before this point one can only make more or less justified assumptions of a future market for a potential product at best. As Lawrence Ellison, CEO of Oracle Corp. remarked, "If you are ahead of the game, if you are delivering a technology before anyone else, then by definition there is no market."[21]

Wherever completely new products, technologies or services are involved which go beyond only gradual improvements of existing supply and offer something radically new, then conventional market research on what consumers really want is extremely difficult. Imagine, for example, a facial cream whose one-time use will inhibit any beard growth for a period of six months, thereby eliminating the need for a morning shave. What would its chances of success be? Many men may regard the five daily shaving minutes as a nuisance. Conversely, they might also value them as a confirmation of their masculinity. They might even do both. Perhaps Italian men would view things differently than Danish men (and Italian women differently than Danish women), to say nothing of the price they would be willing to pay for such a product.

In such situations, the significance of an innovation from the perspective of the customer, and sometimes even of the supplier, is often difficult to determine. The usefulness of a telephone for a potential user, for example, is hard to judge if one has never seen or used one. Even if potential users could somehow sense the true implications of the instantaneous transmission of the spoken word for everyday life and business, it is highly unlikely that they would also envisage the transmission of written texts and images (fax). Similarly, a casual observer of Marconi's experiments with wireless telegraphy at the beginning of this century would not have had visions of stereophonic radio and color television transmissions in every home and automobile (or horse drawn carriage, for that matter). Likewise, the enormous breadth of personal computer applications ranges light-years beyond anything Steve Jobs and Stephen Wozniak might have had in their minds

21 Gradyl, 1995.

when they were assembling the first Apple computer for home use in 1976. Evidently, technical and scientific breakthroughs for which there is no readily discernible commercial market initially, later often result in the stimulation of quite specific and completely unexpected demand structures. Indeed, in looking at the history of technology it is striking that the dispersion of a new technology is not just slow but extraordinarily uncertain even after its first commercial applications have been realized.[22]

Not every scientist is an inventor, let alone an innovator. Nor, conversely, are new products and new technologies always the result of scientific research. The path that leads from scientific discovery to practical technical application is frequently beset with long delays, and often enough leads to a dead-end. It has been said, for instance, "that most (of today's) advances in the technological state of the art are based on no more recent advances than Ohm's law (1827) or Maxwell's equations (1873)."[23] If that is true then the scientific discoveries of today will still nourish technology intensive industries many years in the future.

On the other hand, there are numerous examples of how practical development work by technicians and engineers has provided the impetus for *later* scientific work to explain previously discovered phenomena. The discovery of thermionic emission by T. A. Edison (Edison-Effect) has already been mentioned. Even today, we employ many and highly varied technical processes with no real or in-depth scientific understanding of why and how they actually work. In our cars, for example, we have been using high performance engines for decades without really comprehending the combustion processes that keep them running. Any fundamental research in this direction is fairly recent and was probably only sparked by the energy and environmental awareness of the last two decades. Much the same is true of aviation. From the very beginning, aviation technology lay in the hands of practitioners like Otto Lilienthal (1848–1896), who set to work with passion, intuition and gradually growing experience, but who had no academic or theoretical underpinnings of a "science of flight." Orville and Wilbur Wright (1871–1948 and 1867–1912, respectively) were also by no means flight theoreticians, but bicycle mechanics. At the risk of confirming any reader's fear of flying, this basic understanding of the principles of flight is lacking to this day. Whatever computer simulations or wind tunnel experiments reveal, how well an airplane really flies can only be seen when it is in the air. Or

22 For many instructive examples of this, see Rosenberg, 1995; Anon.{17}, 1994.

23 Allen, 1988, p. 14, with further references.

was. Although the equations describing laminar flows are known, advanced aircraft wing profiles still have to be optimized empirically. We simply do not know enough about turbulences and aerodynamics to determine their shapes beforehand. For this reason, Lilienthal undertook more than 2,000 glider flights before his fatal crash in 1896. To this day, it is the tedious and endless series of tests and alterations which are chiefly responsible for the enormous development costs of modern aircraft.[24]

From all of this it is clear that the innovation process can draw on many sources. An initial spark

- can arise from scientific knowledge

- or from the recognition of a need for new or improved products or processes

- or can result from a technical breakthrough which renders specific characteristics of a technology economically attractive in one or more application fields.

Whatever its origin, this initial spark in and of itself is insufficient for the final success of an innovation. Turning an idea into a commercially viable product requires the strong and effective combination of a whole range of other influential factors. The OECD has named a number of them that do not belong directly to the realm of R&D proper.[25] This leads to a view of R&D not as a source of inventive ideas, but rather as a form of problem solving, to be called upon at any point in the innovation process. Research thus becomes "an adjunct to innovation, not a precondition for it."[26] This becomes clearer when we view the interplay of the three driving forces of the innovation process in Figure 1–2:[27]

- Science explains phenomena and creates new knowledge, thereby opening new technological potentials.

24 Rosenberg 1982, p. 143; Hermann, 1991. This also holds true of more recent developments like the Boeing 777. Even the massive use of computer modeling did not render flight tests unneccessary. Only in the more distant future can one possibly expect mathematical tools like computational fluid dynamics to allow at least partial forecasts of air flow patterns on untested wing profiles, see Dash 1992, p. 48.

25 OECD, 1992, particularly p. 17-19.

26 Ibid. p. 19.

27 Taken from Allen, 1988, p. 16.

- *Technology*, on the one hand, draws on science by pointing to unexplained phenomena or revealing the frontiers of current knowledge. On the other hand, it reacts to market demand signals by improving existing products or processes or by outlining new ones.

- The *market* formulates demand signals by defining the economic and technical performance characteristics for which buyers are prepared to pay a certain price, or for which a specific need is perceived.

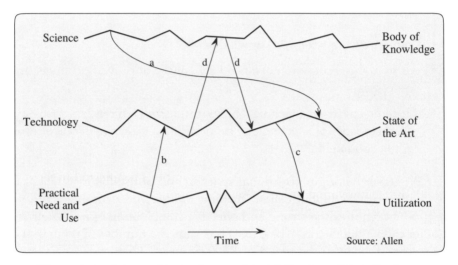

Figure 1–2   Science, Technology and the Utilization of their Products, Showing Communication Paths Among the Three Streams. ([a] The normal process of assimilation of scientific results into technology. [b] Recognized need for a device, technique, or scientific understanding. [c] The normal process of adoption of technology for use. [d] Technological need for understanding of physical phenomena and its response.)

   Although there is interaction between them, all three driving forces are on-going, continuous processes. Their progress over time leads to a permanent succession of new constellations and configurations of performance characteristics, i.e., to innovation opportunities in the market. The signals indicating such opportunities are not always properly read or interpreted by the technicians, scientists, business people, and market researchers involved in the innovation process. In these cases, the consequences are products with the wrong characteristics (e.g. wrong price, too large or too small, inappropriate features) or wrong timing (too late, sometimes too early). Their product lives are generally quite short. If, however, one combines the right resources and tools at the right time and uses them in the right way one will—as so often in life—see one's efforts crowned by success. That is how trivial, and how complicated, it is.

Summary

Chapter 1 begins with a description of Edison's (1847–1931) pioneering work as an industrial innovator. It shows how R&D gradually came to be seen as an important element of industrial success. Increasingly, R&D changed from an activity performed by craftsmen and hobbyists whose success depended on experience, ideas, obstinacy or sheer luck into a systematically organized and specialized discipline. At the same time, R&D received scientific attention (by the natural and social sciences) in two ways. On the one hand, it became the object of scientific scrutiny. On the other, it was increasingly performed by specialists with scientific training.

The debate surrounding exactly what constitutes Research and Development or Science and Technology also began more than a century ago. It has not ended yet. The lack of conclusive definitions is reflected in the complexity of the innovation process. A successful innovation depends on many factors. These can be of an economic, technical or organizational nature. They must all converge at the right time, in the right way and under the right circumstances. The process of innovation has not been mastered yet. Its success can be guaranteed even less.

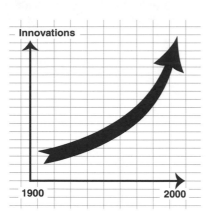

2

On the History of Industrial R&D

Prior to World War I

"A nation's industry will never be able to achieve a dominant position if it is not simultaneously in the vanguard of scientific progress. Achieving this is the most effective means of promoting industry," said the inventor and entrepreneur Werner von Siemens (1812–1892) in 1883.

The institutional and economic framework for such ambitions was particularly favorable at the time. Towards the end of the 19th century, an international system of mutual patent recognition emerged. Since this reduced the risk associated with expensive investments in know-how generation, it represented a major boost to the growth of industrial research and development. Of course, at this time the notion of patents was already centuries old. As early as 1474, the Republic of Venice had introduced an Inventor Statute. England enacted the Statute of Monopolies in 1624. The U.S. and France had passed their first patent laws in 1790 and 1791, respectively. But it was only during the 19th century that patent laws were introduced in virtually all countries which were then undergoing industrialization. They culminated in the Paris Convention for the Protection of Industrial Property of 1883.[1]

1   Source: European Patent Office.

The creation of a suitable framework was not limited to protecting inventors. Other institutions and norms were also altered in ways favorable to R&D. On the national levels, as early as 1887 the Physikalisch-Technische Reichsanstalt was founded in Germany. Its purpose was the establishment of a system of weights and measures that would be valid throughout the country. In 1911, this was followed by the founding of the Kaiser-Wilhelm-Society for the Promotion of the Sciences, the forerunner of today's Max-Planck-Society, which among others maintained facilities for cooperative R&D work by industrial companies. In 1901, the U.S. National Bureau of Standards, the American counterpart of the former, was established. Similar measures were also taken in the U.K. and France.

In private industry, the first hesitant beginnings of industrial R&D centered largely around Edison and a handful of others who had seen the historic writing on the wall earlier than others. The years around the turn of the century witnessed the creation of the first large-scale industrial R&D laboratories. In many respects, the leader in this process was the recently united and economically ambitious German Reich, followed initially on a somewhat smaller scale and a slight delay by the United States. By the year 1900, large companies such as Zeiss, Siemens and others were employing hundreds of people in scientific research and development. Already in 1862, the steel baron Alfred Krupp had had the prescience to establish an "experiment facility" for mechanical materials testing, followed in 1863 by a chemical laboratory, and in 1883 by a "chemical-physical testing facility." In 1909, Krupp's new "research facility" was inaugurated. Within three years the facility created the stainless steels which would carry the reputation of the Krupp company's research around the world.[2]

In the U.S., apart from the laboratory of the Edison Electric Light Co., the first industrial R&D labs were established at Cambria Iron Co. and at Pennsylvania Railroad Co. in 1867 and 1875, respectively. These were still relatively modest facilities, employing only a few handfuls of technicians. In the years immediately prior to the World War I, however, large American corporations such as Du Pont, AT&T, Westinghouse, Eastman Kodak and Standard Oil also began to install R&D capacities which could draw on substantial resources both in manpower and equipment.

Strangely enough, other industrial countries in these years, particularly Great Britain and France, for the time being clung to the classic

2 Anon. {4}, p. 4.

research traditions of the nineteenth century and continued to rely first and foremost on the ideas and inventions of isolated individuals. In Britain, there was a lively public debate around the turn of the century on the danger posed to the country's economic position by the industrial and scientific efforts in Germany. But aside from the foundation of the National Physical Laboratory, no other measures were taken. Also in France, which could look back on an excellent tradition of scientific achievement in the eighteenth and nineteenth centuries, the scientifically-oriented research at the universities only rarely triggered any activities geared toward the foundation of industrial, application-oriented laboratories.[3]

One can speculate why these two nations exercised such restraint, particularly at a time of widespread nationalism. At the turn of the twentieth century, Britain and France with their many colonies were perhaps the two most powerful nations on earth, or at least were regarded as such. Both countries certainly also had the economic and academic infrastructures that would have allowed them to quickly generate a significant industrial R&D potential. Possibly they chose not to do so because the existence of vast colonial empires assured the supply of raw materials to the mother country and thus made large-scale industrial R&D seem superfluous or scarcely even a topic for serious discussion. Perhaps the prevailing system of social values did not let the importance of commercially oriented R&D become sufficiently clear. Especially in Great Britain, which for almost a hundred years had been the leading industrial nation, this period was characterized by a relatively low esteem of engineers and their role in business and society. This was partly reflected in organizational principles, but was partly also a function of the educational system, which led to a conscious tendency for industry and science to maintain their distance.[4]

All this changed fundamentally with the advent of World War I. It quickly became clear, not only to the warring parties but also to the neutral industrialized powers, just how important modern technology could be for the security and prosperity of nations. This realization was not only founded on the many new weapon systems such as aeroplanes, airships, telegraphic communications, tanks, submarines, etc. which entered large-scale service between 1914 and 1918. To the same degree, it was also based on the many so-called "civilian" products, which were either specifically developed for

3   McLeod, 1979, p. 739.

4   Extensively on this point: Mowery and Rosenberg, 1989, p. 98.

peaceful purposes during the war years or which utilized one of the many new defence technologies and extended their applications into peaceful times. The compression engine for heavy petroleum invented by Rudolf Diesel in 1890 even travelled in both directions between military and civilian uses. Originally designed for civilian purposes, it was further developed during the war for use in submarines, and in this improved form was used after the war in tractors, locomotives, harvesting machines and the like.

Occasionally, the First World War has been nicknamed the "War of the Chemists." This label was partly founded on the first-time deployment of weapons based on chemical research, such as high-performance explosives or poison gas shells. Without doubt, these have harmed the reputation of chemists and chemical engineers to this day. But chemical developments that came to fruition in peaceful times and places were at least equally important in proving the significance of chemistry. The Haber-Bosch process which from 1913 on allowed BASF to synthesize ammonia for fertilizer production, and the development of artificial rubber which also occurred during this period, are just two examples of many.

Along with these technical developments, the aftermath of World War I also witnessed a fundamental change in attitudes towards R&D and its institutional and financial framework. More and more often, both government and industry openly began to support R&D, each seeking to encourage innovations deemed important within their own sphere of operations. In this way, the war contributed decisively to an upheaval of the R&D world and its organizational setting. Previously, most work had been done by small and isolated groups of scientists. Now there emerged a system of integrated and partially networked infrastructures in which the lion's share of work was conducted by large research teams in government-owned or industrial laboratories. Occasionally, these groups cooperated with one another. But at least as often they jealously worked alone in order to protect their own know-how.

As an aside, it should also be noted that an even stronger impetus towards the systematization of R&D occurred in the years prior to, during, and after World War II. In the course of this war it became increasingly clear that technologically superior weapons could be of a war deciding significance. The superiority of German tanks during the invasion of the Soviet Union, of British fighter aircraft in the Battle of Britain, of the Japanese Zero fighter in the months following Pearl Harbor, and finally of American nuclear technology in ending the war in the Pacific are but four examples among many.

Teams of scientists and technicians, sometimes numbering in the thousands, worked with no concern for costs on the development of new types of weapon systems. Some 150,000 people—140,000 of them scientists and engineers—worked on America's Manhattan Project. Much the same was true of Germany's efforts to develop long-range ballistic rockets. These enormous technical operations were later also to serve as models for civilian programs such as the Apollo moon project in the 1960s. Their typical organizational structures were even integrated into the R&D programs of private enterprises. Examples of this include the Siemens-Mega(chip)-Project, the development of the Airbus A-300, or the Japanese 5th Generation Computer Initiative.[5]

Between the Wars

Anyone engaging in an even cursory study of research and development in the early decades of this century will quickly become aware of the sparsity of documentation that might help in shaping an accurate impression of the period. Specific references to the increasing importance of R&D on national levels only rarely emerge in the standard historical treatments of the tangled and many-layered political and economic events in Europe and the U.S. during the 1920s and 1930s.[6] Nevertheless, these events were also influenced by the world of R&D and vice-versa. The ramifications are still felt today.

For the first time in its five-thousand-year history, technology moved to the center of public attention during the 1920s. Its members and representatives achieved a status of genuine prestige. Partly, they became objects of hero worship, an adulation previously reserved for great warriors, statesmen and, perhaps, prophet-priests and artists. In contemporary Western society, professors, scientists and inventors—at least the successful ones—are highly revered. Especially in Germany and Austria, anyone discretely indicating the possession of a *Doktor*-title while reserving a table at a fashionable restaurant will attest to its effectiveness. Today, the supreme pinna-

---

5   Occasionally companies came close to betting their very existence on such major strategic projects. An interesting account of such a project—RCA and the Videodisc—is contained in Graham, 1986.

6   There are, of course, numerous and excellent historic accounts of individual industrial enterprises in North America, Europe and even Japan. A number of them also contain information on the R&D efforts of these corporations before World War II. Apart from definitional problems, what is usually lacking, however, is their aggregation to national overviews.

cle of scientific honors, the Nobel Prize—first granted in 1901—is probably considered by a world-majority as the highest honor bestoweable upon a living person residing on this planet. It certainly ranks higher than any medal of Olympian provenance, and is at least equivalent to membership in the elite but largely unknown Association of Space Explorers, the worldwide club of the few human beings who have travelled in space. Some may even view the Nobel Prize to fall only slightly short of sainthood, particularly since the latter is awarded only to the dead.

Scientists and technicians have continued to enjoy this tremendous prestige for the greater part of this century. Streets, units of measurement, asteroids, plant and animal species, and mathematical or physical constants were named after them. It is only in the most recent period of history that doubts and acceptance problems even among scientists themselves have gradually arisen, usually associated with the fears of the dangers and destructive powers of modern technology.

Nevertheless, it is not surprising that standard libraries and archives contain so little aggregate national (as opposed to company-specific) information on the history of research and development. Neither need one wonder why only very recently a few university chairs and research institutes dedicated to the history of R&D have been established. The discussion touched upon in Chapter 1 as to what exactly constitutes research and development, science and technology is still in full swing. It was only in the 1950s that any systematic work on this subject even began. In the absence of any useful or agreed-upon definitions, there was, therefore, strictly speaking nothing to report about. To illustrate: Anyone who either does not know, or does not care, about the difference between crocodiles and alligators will hardly keep separate statistics or make separate reports on both species.

Ever since World War I, of course, there was no disputing the fact *that* R&D existed. There was also some notion what it *consisted* of. But the activity itself was generally not seen as an independent function. It was therefore not a separate accounting or budgeting item. Nobody asked, so nobody reported. In practice, R&D was regularly lumped together with production costs. Since these were normally broken down along different lines, e.g. wages and raw materials, no further conclusions regarding R&D-related expenditures, their objectives, or the application of material and human resources could be drawn. Relative to total production costs they were usually minor anyway. The routine inclusion of a company's R&D spending in its annual report became common only much later. In the United States and Europe it began on an extensive scale only in the 1960s, in Japanese companies not before the 1980s.

For these reasons, any account regarding the scope of R&D activities in the 1920s and 1930s must necessarily be sketchy. It is inevitably based on scattered and isolated sources such as reports and books on individual companies, contemporary publications by professional associations, or newspaper articles. Obtaining an overall picture, a comprehensive statistical base or, indeed, an international comparison of the R&D activities in the industrialized countries at the time is a task still undone. It is perhaps best left to a more ambitious author. Nevertheless, what documentation was gathered by this writer does perhaps provide at least a small notion of the R&D-related activities of the industrialized countries in the years following World War I.

It may be assumed that the greatest upheavals in the R&D world occurred in the United States and Germany. The description will therefore be confined to these two nations. There were, of course, changes in other countries too, particularly in Great Britain, France and Italy. However, these tended to be of a similar, albeit less intensive nature.[7] Even in the newly-founded Soviet Union, the Bolsheviks overcame their distaste for the "bourgeois intelligentsia," as which scientists were regarded, and were

> "enthusiastically committed to the development of science and technology to which they attributed an important role in building a new society. Lenin realized that the scientists and technologists had a vital part to play in the future development of the country; speaking in Moscow in April 1918, he said: 'we need their [the bourgeois specialists', author's note] knowledge, their skills and their labor'." And the Party followed him 'in spite of the fact that they [the scientists, author's note], in the majority of cases, are inevitably impregnated with bourgeois attitudes and habits'.[8]

---

7   For a discussion of the developments in the U.K., see Mowery and Rosenberg, 1989, p. 98.

8   Lewis, 1979, p. 6.

The United States

Among all industrialized countries, the U.S. is the one where studies and statistics regarding research efforts prior to World War II are in best supply. Figure 2–1, for example, shows the number of new industrial R&D laboratories established in the United States between 1899 and 1946.[9] The solid line gives the total number of new laboratories (right scale), the respective columns the distribution of laboratories by industrial sectors (left scale). The role that science and technology played for the course and outcome of World War I probably explains the greater part of this development. Just in the one decade immediately following the war (1919-1928), a total of 660 laboratories were established. Even during the nine-year period between 1937 and 1946 this number barely sank to little under 400.

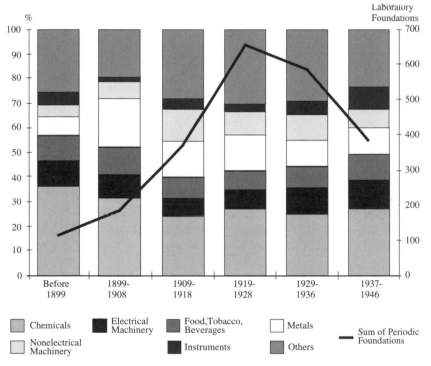

Figure 2–1   Establishments of Industrial R&D Laboratories in the U.S. by Number (right scale) and Industry Sector (%, left scale)

---

9   Unless indicated otherwise, the following account of the developments in the U.S. is based on Mowery and Rosenberg, 1989, Chap. 4, p. 59 with numerous further sources.

One should note that the overall number of laboratories actually in operation cannot be obtained by merely adding the number of newly established R&D labs over the observed timeframe. The source unfortunately provides no information regarding lab closures, of which there must have been at least some. What we do know, however, is that for an extended period the number of newly established laboratories significantly exceeded the number of those closed down. From a different source, we find that the number of industrial enterprises with their own research laboratories in 1921 totaled 462. By 1927, this figure had reached 926, and by 1931, had jumped to 1,520. It took the Crash of 1929 to push the number of laboratories down to 1,462 by 1933, though with the end of the depression (1938) the number had again risen to 1,752.[10]

Breaking down the number of laboratory start-ups by industry, the continuously large share of chemical labs, even without the mineral oil and rubber industries, becomes evident. Throughout the entire period under review, it averaged a little under 30%. The respective shares of laboratories in the electrical and in the food, beverage and tobacco industries remained relatively steady at roughly 10%. The latter category, incidentally, included all research work in the field of agriculture, which prior to World War II was at the center of governments' interest in every industrialized country. The gradual decline in the metal industry's share of lab start-ups was reflected in a corresponding increase in that of the mechanical engineering and machine tools sectors. Thus, some priority shifts between industries do seem to have occurred. All in all, however, it is remarkable that over the course of nearly half a century there were no fundamental, let alone revolutionary, changes. The intensification of R&D was a phenomenon which affected all relevant industries to a roughly constant and equal degree.

Figure 2–1 obviously provides a fairly good impression of the increasing attention enjoyed by the research and development function in the thinking and behavior of U.S. industry in the first half of the twentieth century. Lacking more specific data on the researchers and resources actually employed, however, it does not give any indications of actual R&D volumes or their changes, if any, over this period. Figure 2–2 provides an insight into these developments. The two lower curves (right scale) show the total number of R&D employees in U.S. industry. Of these, a relatively constant proportion of roughly 50% were academically qualified. It is here that the gradual shift of American industry towards more technology- and know-

10 National Research Council, 1930 and 1940.

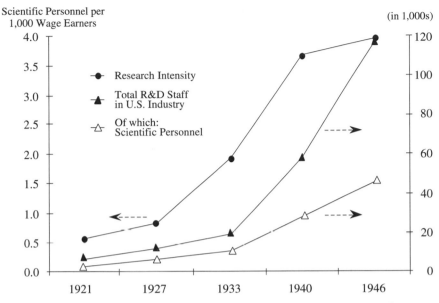

Scientific Personnel per
1,000 Wage Earners

(in 1,000s)

Figure 2–2 R&D Personnel in U.S. Industry 1921-1946, absolute
(right scale) and relative (left scale)

ledge-intensive sectors becomes most clearly apparent. From a total of
approximately 6,700 industrial employees in 1921, the number of persons
engaged in R&D activities rose to nearly 118,000 by 1946.

Relating to overall employment, the growing number of those engaged
in R&D activities appears to have been relatively unaffected by the turbu-
lent, and indeed traumatic, upheavals in the economy and labor market of
the 1920s and 1930s. For instance, the Crash of 1929 reduced the total number of wage-earners in U.S. manufacturing in 1933 by 26.2% below the level
of 1927. During the same period, however, the number of scientists and
engineers in manufacturing *rose* by 72.9%. Likewise, during the period of
economic growth between 1933 and 1940, in which total industrial employment rose by 35%, the number of those engaged in R&D activities soared by
154%. This disproportionate trend in "researcher density" can be read from
the upper curve of Figure 2–2 (left scale): whereas in 1921 there were fewer
than 0.6 persons engaged in scientific work per 1,000 employees in American industry, 25 years later it was 4.0. According to a report to Congress by
the National Research Council nd National Resources Planning Board in
1940, a total 70,033 persons were employed in technical-industrial research

at 2,350 industrial companies. More than half of these had enjoyed academic training, primarily as chemists and engineers.[11]

From all this one can conclude that the resources allocated by U.S. industry to research and development continued to grow throughout the 1930s: In 1930, the figure amounted to roughly $116 mill. By 1940 (in 1930 dollars), the amount had more than doubled to $295 mill. It was only after 1941 and when the U.S. war economy began to pick up momentum, that growth in the number of R&D personnel fell behind that of overall employment.

Neither R&D expenditures nor R&D employees in this period were distributed evenly between large and small enterprises. Table 2–1 shows that between 1921 and 1946 there was a steadily increasing concentration of research activities in the larger industrial laboratories. Towards the end of the 1930s, 150,000 U.S. companies had no laboratories at all, while one third of all research personnel were employed in 13 corporate groups or 140 companies. Even among these 140, there was a strong tendency towards concentration. In 1946, one tenth of all the companies possessing laboratories employed just under two thirds of total research personnel.[12] At the same time, the significance of independent research institutes such as the Battelle Memorial Institute, Arthur D. Little Inc., and Mellon Institute, decreased. Presumably, one of the main causes of this trend was a growing degree of specialization in the individual areas of knowledge and in company-specific R&D requirements. This meant that corporations with R&D capacities of their own would draw on external resources only in exceptional cases. Later, and as they grew in size, industrial laboratories would therefore need the services of external R&D contractors to a declining degree.

Table 2-1   Distribution of R&D Personnel in U.S. Industry, percent

Percentage of R&D Personnel	1921	1927	1933	1940	1946
In the 10% Largest Industry Laboratories	47.4	43.5	47.7	56.8	61.1
In Independent Research Institutes	15.2	12.9	10.9	8.7	6.9

11   Source: Internal notice of Siemens AG referring to a communication of the German Economic Council on Fine Mechanics and Optics, No. 11, End of August 1941, p. 80.

12   National Research Council, 1940.

By the 1930s, a number of U.S. industrial laboratories had taken on impressive proportions, even by today's standards. In 1930, for example, Western Electric's and AT&T's famous Bell Telephone Laboratories had 4,600 employees and a budget of $19 mill. General Electric's Research Laboratories employed 400 scientists, engineers, and support staff with a $2 mill. budget, and General Motors' Research Laboratories had a staff of 500 scientific personnel and mechanics housed in an 11 story-building, five floors of which contained 18,000 m^2 (194,000 ft.^{2}) of laboratories and offices. Among government-owned R&D institutions there were also giants: the National Bureau of Standards, for instance, had a budget of $2.94 mill. and a staff of 1,055 employees.[13]

Only a few short remarks will be made regarding the role of the government in R&D during this period, partly because the reviewed data is contradictory. In the 1930s, the research budget of the U.S. federal government averaged about 0.5% of the total budget. In 1937, for instance, it amounted to $124 mill (for comparison, in 1991 government R&D expenditures in the U.S. were on the order of $80 bill. and corresponded to about 6% of the total budget.). More than one third of government research spending in 1937 was earmarked for agricultural topics and research facilities. A further fifth was dedicated to military R&D.[14] With the growing threat of war in Europe and the Far East, the proportion allocated to military research expanded significantly in the late 1930s, so that in 1940, the last year before the United States entered World War II, agriculture and the military together absorbed 70% of the federal research budget.

In the 1930s, the contribution of the federal government to all R&D spending in the U.S. ranged between 12% and 20% (as opposed to a little under 50% today). Roughly two-thirds was borne by industry, the remainder by foundations, private research establishments, the individual states, and universities. The universities also appear to have concentrated a large part of their R&D on agricultural matters. Thus, out of an approximate total of $50 mill. in university research spending in 1935/36, a share of $16 mill., or 32%, went to so-called "agricultural experimental stations." Just as in industry, the greater part of research occurred in only a few handfuls of top institutions:[15]

13 National Research Council, 1930.

14 Potter, 1939, p. 205.

15 Potter, 1939, p. 207.

- 1,450 universities and colleges in 1935/36 performed R&D for approx. $51 mill.

- of which 150 universities and colleges spent approx. $50 mill.

- of which 19 universities and colleges spent approx. $19 mill.

In a speech shortly before the United States entered World War II, President Herbert Hoover stated the main goals of industrial research and development for the coming years:[16]

1. Greater self-sufficiency.
2. Reduction of inefficient use of raw materials and equipment in industry.
3. A significant increase in abstract and basic research at the universities (to be financed by contributions from industry).
4. Improved coordination of industrial and national research expenditures with the aim of subordinating corporate interests to the strengthening of national and strategic productivity.

Germany

With the end of the First World War, the economic situation of Germany and of German industry was the exact opposite of that in the United States. This was not only due to the immediate impact of the lost war. The provisions of the Versailles Peace Treaty had wrecked the raw material and energy base of the economy and had saddled the country with a crushing debt burden. Heavy industry, then a prime source of industrial R&D funding, was particularly hard hit. Directly or indirectly, the Peace Treaty had led to the loss of some 79.9% of national iron ore extraction, 43.5% of pig iron production, 35.8% of ingot steel production, and 32.4% of rolling mill production capacity. Germany's world market share in exports of manufactured goods had fallen from 22.9% in 1913 to 0% after the end of the war.[17] Looking back and in view of the great role technology had played for all of the warring parties, it almost appears as if the victorious powers neglected by oversight to add a complete ban on scientific and technological research and development to the many other obligations contained in the treaty. A prohibition on R&D existed only for certain industries, e.g. for the manufacture of

16　Anon. {2}; retranslated from German.
17　Herbst, 1989.

munitions or of military aircraft. As a result, German industry was virtually forced to emphasize scientific and technical research and, in the absence of other possibilities, to search for its "raw materials" in the minds of its employees rather than in the soils of home or any former colonies.

In this spirit, the journal *Wissenschaft und Industrie* [Science and Industry] was founded in 1922. Its raison d'être was expressed in its first editorial as the need for the "closest association between science and industry"[18] and stated:

> "Yet if it is to maintain its place among the civilized peoples, Germany depends completely on an even closer alliance of science, technology and industry than it did ten or twenty years ago, or indeed, even if it is to hold on to any form of reasonably profitable work that will enable it to feed its people, still so rich in talented individuals—virtually its very last source of wealth!"[19]

Much as in the U.S., German industrial research policy in the following years aimed at broad national goals and well-being rather than the prosperity of individual firms. After 1933 and with the Nazi regime's conscription of industry into its rearmament policy, this was to become even more apparent. To be sure, similar tendencies were also occurring in other countries, but not to the same all-consuming and totalitarian degree that is revealed in the following quote from the year 1940:

> "When the whole of research coalesces around a single crystallization point, it takes on an aim and achieves the prospect of a uniform goal. This crystallization point is called Germany and the German people. All German research is subordinated to it. Its purpose is to serve its life, its development and its rise; otherwise we are unworthy to call ourselves the 'German people'."[20]

As a matter of course, the German government even before 1933 did not restrict itself to only organizing R&D, but just like other governments, was also involved in its implementation. As an indication, this can be read from the budgets of the three major state agencies and foundations included in Figure 2–3. Within their technical fields they were responsible for measurement standardization, norms and safety engineering and also conducted their own research.[21]

18 Anon. {3}, p. 1.

19 Sudhoff, 1922, p. 34.

20 Hartmann, 1940, p. 10.

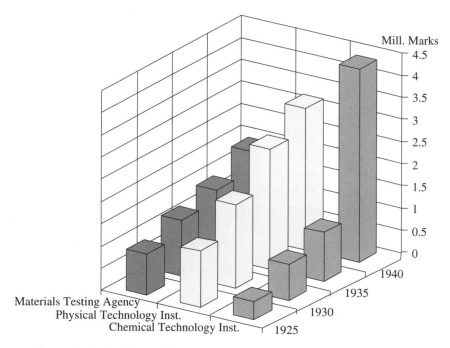

Figure 2–3 Budgets of the National Technical Research and Testing Institutions in Germany, 1925-1940, mill. of marks

A search for the scope of German industrial R&D expenditures during the interwar years (particularly during the Nazi period) reveals relatively little official documentation and individual reports in comparison to the U.S. However, an indirect indication of the growing importance of R&D is provided by the two following figures, which do not focus on R&D expenditures themselves, but rather on their results. If we assume that a growing output of R&D cannot have been achieved without a corresponding input, then the development of two important values—Nobel Prizes and patent applications—permit us to conclude at least indirectly that there must have been a notable R&D effort. One should beware of attaching great statistical or numerical significance to such conclusions, however. We do not know the precise relationship of R&D expenditure and R&D yield and perhaps never will. On the other hand, two basic rules of life also hold for R&D: There is no free lunch, i.e., you cannot get something for nothing; and, regularly at

21 Lundgren et al., 1986, p. 50.

least, an increase in efforts will not lead to a decrease in results. For lack of better data, the two following Figures 2–4 and 2–5 may therefore serve as crude indicators.

Figure 2–4 shows the share of Nobel Prizes for the fields of physics, chemistry and medicine/physiology awarded to the major recipient countries in the two periods before and after the World War I. The figure shows that there were some important shifts, especially with regard to the growing shares of the U.K. and the U.S. Particularly clear, however, is also that in spite of the lost war, Germany's scientific predominance at the time remained largely unbroken.

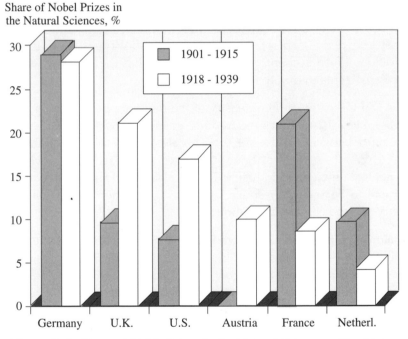

Figure 2–4 Share of Noble Prizes in the Natural Sciences of the Major Recipient Countries, 1901-15 and 1918-39, percent

Now one must bear in mind that, without exception, Nobel Prizes are awarded for scientific achievements in the past, not for on-going research. Their appreciation must be preceded by a period that allows for adequate recognition. Despite the specification in Alfred Nobel's last will and testament that the selection of prize winners was to be based on the scientific achievements of the "last year," in practice such recognition can take many years. Prizes which were awarded in the 1920s or even the 1930s could easily have been based on pre-World War I scientific achievements. To this extent, therefore, one might very well doubt the strength of the evidence contained in Figure 2–4.

Interestingly, however, the period around 1920—only two years after the end of the war—was also the only period in the history of research in which there were more scientific publications in German than in English.[22] Anyone wanting to study chemistry in those years, for example, had to be able to read and speak German. Since scientific publications are based on work only just completed or even still in progress, they have a far greater degree of contemporary relevance than Nobel Prizes do. They are a much better reflection of the emphasis of on-going R&D work and the present state of knowledge. Therefore, taking both indicators—Nobel Prizes *and* publications—into account, strongly suggests that the interwar era was a particularly fertile period for German research.

As an indicator of the intensity of the more application-oriented R&D activities, Figure 2–5 shows the trend in patent applications to the German patent office between 1910 an 1940.[23] This also clearly shows that the lessons of World War I on the strategic importance of research and development were not lost on German industry. Technical skills and scientific knowledge had come to be seen as resources vital to the economic survival of both industry and the country as a whole.

However, it is also clear from Figure 2–5 that during both the Weimar Republic (1918–1933) and the Third Reich (1933–1945) periods, German R&D expenditures were managed on a "procyclical" basis. The trend in patent applications is virtually a mirror image of economic development between the wars. Following the economic decline during the German hyperinflation of the early 1920s and again after the world depression following the Crash of 1929, there were corresponding decreases in patent applications. For whatever reasons, any countermeasures such as an expansion of R&D efforts aimed at overcoming the recession with the introduction of innovative products never took place. Unlike in the U.S. at this time, economic measures led to cuts in R&D spending and thus to a considerable decline in patentable knowledge. The decline in the number

22 Ammon, 1992, p. 117.

23 Statistical Yearbooks for the German Reich 1923-1941/42.

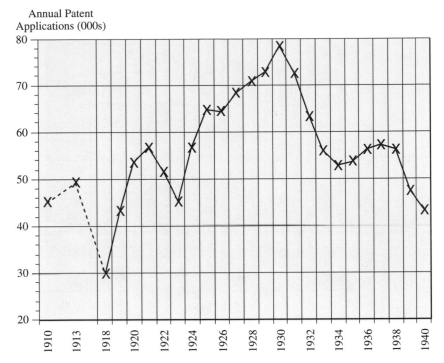

Figure 2–5 Annual Patent Applications in Germany, 1910 to 1940.

of patent applications in the second half of the 1930s (when the economy was picking up again) can presumably be attributed to the gradual shift of industry to accelerated production of war materials for which patent protection is typically less likely to be sought.

What could be observed of Germany as a whole applies equally to individual companies. Figure 2–6, for example, shows the structure of R&D work between 1926 and 1933 at IG Farbenindustrie AG, the result of a six-company merger in 1925 that created one of the world's largest chemical companies of the time. In the German boom years of the late twenties and up to the world economic crisis of 1929, the company's R&D spending remained fairly high. In 1927, it reached a level of 12% of sales, impressive even by today's standards. In the years following the crisis, Farbenindustrie's R&D spending fell in both absolute and relative terms. The decline primarily affected development work in "new areas" where sales were only gradually commencing. Conversely, development work in "older areas"

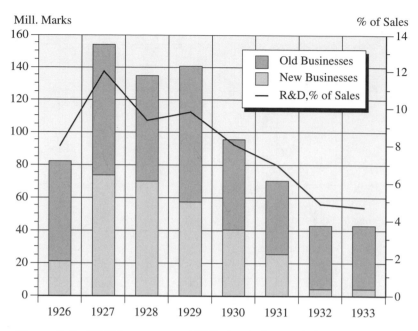

Figure 2–6   R&D Investment of IG Farbenindustrie AG, 1926-1933

where revenues already existed and where costs were thus easier to justify, was subjected to far smaller cutbacks and remained largely intact.[24]

Let us finally turn to the question of research *organization* in the interwar years. As the scope and relevance of a corporation's R&D activities begin to take on greater weight, the question naturally arises as to how the characteristic features of R&D work can be harmonized with the numerous other requirements of a corporation and how R&D can be successfully integrated into the existing organization. The specific requirements and qualities of R&D operations as well as the interests, mind sets and attributes of R&D employees differ in many respects from those working in the classic corporate functions of production and sales.

Today, this subject is at the forefront of the work of academic theoreticians. It is also a growing source of income for consultants with interests and expertise in the areas of R&D management or R&D strategy. Yet the subject is not limited to the present day. One of the dominant issues in the management of complex organizations—centralization or decentralization, production orientation or market orientation, regional or technological structures, indepen-

24 Plumpe, 1990, p. 472.

dence or control, etc. and the proper balance between them—is a question that is perhaps as old as the first organization itself and for which there will presumably never be a final answer. The question was poised anew and with increasing urgency when the first large R&D laboratories were introduced into corporate reality. In the 1930s, there were already extremely complex structures for research organization in individual companies. These sought to meet the needs of a large number of highly qualified specialists working together on the leading edge of science and technology. At the end of the 1930s, Krupp Corporation's research units, for instance, consisted of more than 1,000 employees. As indicated above, a number of U.S. organizations had grown to similar if not larger sizes. Their appropriate organization and control along with the need to ensure their orientation of their work to corporate goals, already posed considerable problems for management.

Figure 2–7 contains a particularly progressive example for its time. It shows the structure of the research and development laboratories at Siemens & Halske AG, one of the largest electrical groups in German industry in 1936.[25] On inspection, it reveals the inverse nature of two fundamental requirements which must be considered in the organization of a large corporation's R&D efforts. On the one hand, there is the need to focus the company's resources and employees so as to ensure close contact among the scientists and technologists cooperating on common projects. On the other, R&D must be closely connected with the other corporate departments and needs to consider the constraints inherent in engineering, manufacture, and sales. As already recognized by Edison, the problem thus lies in sustaining close teamwork among a group of specialists and allowing successful creativity without isolating the rest of the company from the innovation process at the same time. Fulfilling only the first requirement would, in the extreme, lead to the concentration of all laboratory work in a single research unit. This would avoid duplicate work and guarantee the optimal use of laboratory facilities. Conversely, the exclusive pursuit of the second requirement would lead to the distribution of all R&D work away from a central facility to the individual factories or sales units. This would confer upon the scientists and technicians involved a deeper understanding of the needs and problems of both manufacturing and marketing but cut off, or reduce, the important technical discourse among each other.

Figure 2–7 shows that as early as 1936, Siemens & Halske was quite successfully attempting to do one without neglecting the other. All R&D work dedicated to specific applications (which was by far the largest share)

25 Reche, 1937, p. 113.

Laboratories of Siemens & Halske AG

Telecommunication: Plant		Measuring Techn.Pl.	Electrochemistry Department
Central Laboratory	Telephone Department Laboratory / Telegraph Department Laboratory	Measuring Equipm. Lab.	Electrochemistry Laboratory
Main Fields	**Main Fields**	**Main Fields**	**Main Fields**
Low Frequency and Carrier Frequency Telephone Systems	Automatic, Local, Regional and Long-Distance Telephone Exchanges	Technical Measur. Equipm.	Electrometallurgy
AC and DC Telegraph Systems	Extensions + Party Lines	Precision Measur.Equipm.	Electroplating
Communication Transmission on Power Lines	Customer Equipment of all Types	Transducers	Electrooxydation
Radio Interference Elimination	Selectors and Relays	Plotters, Oscillographs	Analytic and Preparatory Chemistry
Wireless Equipment	**Telegraph Department Laboratory**	Remote Indicator and Control Devices	Organic Insulating Materials
Electro-Acoustic Devices, especially Microphones and Telephones	**Main Fields**	Selective Protection Relays	Ceramics
Radio Measuring Equipment	Telegraph Equipment	Medical Measuring Equipm.	Metallurgy
Magnetic Materials (1)	Signaling Devices	Testing Equipment of all Types, incl. X-Ray Materials	Magnetic Materials (2)
Insulation Materials and Condensers	Lightarc Devices	X-Ray Equipment	Lightarcs and Induction Furnaces
Communication Relais and other Components	Fire Alarms	Thermal Testing and Control Devices	
Optical Equipment, especially for 8-mm-Film	Electric Clocks	Gas Analysis Equipment	
Color Film		Volume Measuring Equipm.	

Development Departments of Companies Associated with Siemens&Halske AG

Siemens-Reiniger Werke: Electromedical Equipment

Siemens-Plania Werke: Coal and Silite Products

Siemens Apparate und Maschinen GmbH: Military, Aviation and Maritime Systems

Telefunken (S&H together with AEG): Wireless Communication in the broadest sense

Vereinigte Eisenbahn (4) Signal-Werke: Railroad Safety Systems

Other Subsidiaries and Shareholdings with a Wide Variety of Electrotechnical Systems and Products

(1) particularly iron powder and magnetic layer materials

(2) particularly permanent magnets and sheet metals

(3) excluding the joint laboratories of Siemens & Halske and Siemens Schuckert Werke

(4) in cooperation with Braunschweig AG für Industrie Beteiligungen and AEG

Development Depts. of (3) Siemens Schuckertwerke AG

Main Fields
Generators
Motors
Transformers
Switchgear
Electrical Resistance Furnaces
Elektric Trains
Installation Materials
Household Appliances
Steam Turbines
Porcelain Insulators

Joint Laboratories of Siemens&Halske and Siemens Schuckert Werke

Tube Plant Laboratory	Research Laboratory	Cable Plant Laboratory
Main Fields	**Main Fields**	**Main Fields**
Rectifiers, Modulators	Atomic Physics	Cables and Leads
Technical Amplifier Tubes	Electrical Discharge Physics	Metal Products
Transmitting Tubes	Electrical Transmission Physics	Rubber Products
Photo-Cells	Contact Research	Molding Machinery Materials
Visible Type Fuses, Vacuum Switches	Acoustic Research	Organic Insulating Materials
Special Resistors	Thermics Research	
Control Devices with Tubes	Physical/chemical Development	

Figure 2-7 The R&D Laboratories of Siemens & Halske AG Within the Overall Framework of Technology Development in the Siemens Group, as of 1936

was done in laboratories which were integral parts of major plants. At the same time, however, these labs were sufficiently large to ensure a fruitful exchange of ideas among the engineers and scientists working there. Characteristic of this approach was that the major fields of development work in the individual plant laboratories were defined according to products, product groups or manufacturing techniques, i.e., categories which were related directly to the markets of the respective plants (e.g. "medical measuring equipment", "signaling devices" or "electric clocks").

Only a small part of total R&D efforts were carried out in the joint central "research laboratory" in the lower center of Figure 2–7 which worked both for Siemens & Halske AG (predominantly communications technology) and its sister company Siemens-Schuckertwerke AG (predominantly electrical engineering). The emphasis of the research laboratory was primarily in fundamental scientific work whose practical application, with respect to product groups and process technologies, could not be discerned yet. Correspondingly, its major fields of work did not distinguish between application areas, but between fields of knowledge (e.g. "atomic physics," "electrical discharge physics"). The research laboratory, which belonged to Siemens & Halske but was jointly operated with Siemens-Schuckert, had a work force of nearly 2,000. The logic of this overall R&D structure can still be found today in the R&D set-up of many large corporations whose businesses involves a wide spectrum of different technologies and scientific domains.

After World War II

In the wake of World War I, the greater part of R&D had left its former dusty studies, remote or mysterious laboratories, tinkers' basements or university institutes. Increasingly, it had been transferred to rigorously organized industrial laboratories, often with large staffs and major material resources. Even if it did not seem so to those involved at the time, R&D had become an integral component both of the industrial state and of the industrial corporation. Conceptually, it did not make much of a difference whether new technologies were self-developed or were purchased externally, e.g. through licensing agreements. The investment in technology itself was what counted and by now that had become—in whatever form—a matter of course.

The Second World War did not end this process. Quite to the contrary, the resources available for R&D purposes grew again by orders of magnitude. Of course, this did not happen at once. Europe, which together with the United States had been the most important source of technological innovation up to 1939, was exhausted from six years of war and lay largely in ruins. Germany in particular had been devastated and divided into occupation zones. The aim of all European technological efforts was first and foremost the desire to heal wounds and to regain the pre-war levels of industrial development. Only after this had been achieved could there be any thought of the scientific and technological needs of the future. As a result, very little money was available for research and development in Europe for several years. Only to a certain degree did the United Kingdom form a European exception. As a result of the war, certain high-tech fields such as aeronautics had become highly developed there and continued to expand. Other areas, such as the British nuclear program, were in accordance with the U.K.'s long tradition as one of great powers and were called into existence only after hostilities had ended.

American Technology Leadership

The situation in the United States was the exact opposite of that prevailing in Europe. The U.S. had ended the world conflict as a glorious victor and undisputed world leader. No other country could come even remotely close to competing with America's economic strengths or technological prowess. In 1945, the United States alone accounted for 50% of world GNP. Anyone wanting to buy an aeroplane, a computer (or perhaps more accurately, in those days, a Hollerith machine), a car, a television set, a new refrigerator, or even a light bulb with few exceptions could only find these in the United States, or at best, in domestic brands frequently containing essential components from America. Not only in the military and economic sense, but also in terms of science and technology the U.S. was, by far, the world leader. Due to the long period of reconstruction in other parts of the developed world, the nation was to continue to enjoy this quasi-monopoly in almost every major industry for a number of years to come.

The Second World War altered the domain of technology in another sense as well: during the First World War it had been learned that science and technology could play an important role and contribute decisively to the well-being of a nation. The Second World War also showed that enormous effects could be achieved through massive, government controlled programs. The budget of the Manhattan Project, for instance, amounted to $730 and $859 mill. during the peak years of 1944 and 1945, exceeding the entire U.S. defence budget during these decisive war years by 63% and 67%, respectively. [26] The government had provided the group of scientists around

---

26 Mowery and Rosenberg, 1989, p. 161. The description of the post WWII development of R&D in the U.S. is largely based on this account.

Robert Oppenheimer, Edward Teller, Hans Bethe and others with virtually unlimited funds. It was typical of the American approach that a large part of the government funds devoted to this a task was not spent in government-owned laboratories and research facilities. Instead, it went to the development laboratories of private industry, whose large scientific and technical resources were thus successfully harnessed for the national war effort.

The United States has remained largely true to this model of government-sponsored technology development to this day. Both before and during the war, large government research institutes had been founded, e.g. the National Bureau of Standards, the National Institute of Health, or the nuclear bomb development center at Los Alamos. Various agricultural research institutes had been scattered around individual states. Most of them still exist today and will probably continue to do so. Some of the National Laboratories and Federally Funded Research Centers are of considerable size and have R&D budgets comparable to those of very large industrial enterprises. In practice, many of these government-owned research facilities are run on a contract basis by private sector companies and universities. The telecommunications giant AT&T, for example, manages Sandia National Laboratories (budget: $1.2 bill, 3,600 employees) in Albuquerque, New Mexico on behalf of the Department of Energy. Massachusetts Institute of Technology runs Lincoln Laboratory (budget: $400 mill., 1,350 employees) for the Pentagon. The University of California is in charge of Lawrence Livermore National Laboratory (budget: $1.1 bill., 3,300 employees), and Oak Ridge National Laboratory ($500 mill., 2,100 employees) in Tennessee is operated by the aerospace company Martin Marietta (now Lockheed Martin). In both of these latter cases, the responsible government agency is the Department of Energy.[27]

The special circumstances of these publicly-owned research facilities notwithstanding, the lion's share of U.S. R&D work during the war and ever since has been carried out by private industry. Since 1945, around 75% of U.S. government research money has been spent in the private sector. This is not only true of civil and so-called "dual-use technologies" i.e., with both civilian and military applications. It also applies to various large-scale post-war military programs, including the development of a fleet of nuclear-powered submarines, supersonic jet fighters, and intercontinental ballistic missiles. Even the non-military Apollo moon program adhered to this basic model. Although it was financed by the government through NASA, the greater part of actual development work was carried out by industry.

27 Kaplan and Rosenblatt, 1990, p. 41.

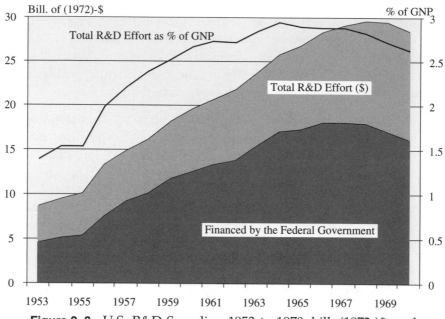

Figure 2–8 U.S. R&D Spending 1953 to 1970, bill. (1972-)$, and percent of GNP

Fig 2–8 shows the long-term trend of U.S. R&D spending after World War II, including work financed by private industry. Its most conspicuous feature is its tremendous growth since the beginning of the 1950s, impressive even by U.S. standards. In the immediate post-war years and with the winding down of the Manhattan Project as well as other military development work, there was a brief decline in overall R&D spending. In the second half of the 1940s, R&D spending in the United States accounted for approximately 1% of GNP, or less than $1 bill. (in 1972 dollars). The shock associated with the first Soviet nuclear tests toward the end of the 1940s, coupled with the Berlin Blockade and the Korean War, however, caused R&D spending to rise again. By 1953, it reached 1.4% of GNP and from thereon continued to climb steadily. By the mid-1960s, following the "Sputnik Shock" and with the moon program moving into high gear, spending on R&D peaked at just under 3% of GNP. Only then did it begin to ebb again.

Other Industrialized Countries Follow the Lead

Comparing U.S. R&D spending development with that of the Federal Republic of Germany between 1949 and 1964 in Figure 2–9,[28] shows the enormous differences between both countries, both in absolute and relative

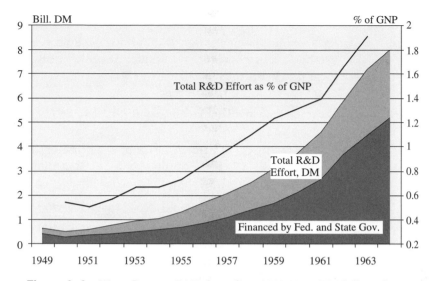

Figure 2–9　West-German R&D Spending 1949-1964, DM bill. and percent of GNP (within this timeframe, $1 = DM 3 to 4, on average)

terms. This is all the more so because German spending statistics include the substantial funds borne by the individual *L*änder (or federal states) for scientific research at the universities. It was not until 1961—by which time the German post-war economic miracle no longer seemed quite so miraculous—that German R&D expenditures reached 1.4% of gross national product, eight years after the United States.[29]

Apart from West Germany, there was also no other country even remotely able to compete with the United States. Table 2–2 compares absolute and per capita R&D expenditures of the most important industrialized countries for 1964.[30] At this time, U.S. expenditures were nearly three times that of the other eight countries *combined*. U.S. per capita spending was 2.8 times that of the closest competitor England. Japan, the future technological giant, still lagged far behind the European countries. Japanese per capita spending was only one third of France's and one twelfth of America's. Although the number of Japanese engineers and scientists was relatively large, spending per scientist and engineer amounted to only $7,800, compared to $43,000 in Germany and $42,500 in the United States. In 1964, of

28　Association of Research Foundations for the German Sciences (Stifterverband für die Deutsche Wissenschaft), 1966, p. 14.

29　For the development of the sciences in post-war Germany, see Michaelis and Schmid, 1983.

30　Rudzinski, 1967.

course, the Japanese economy was still primarily procuring its technological knowledge and skills by licensing foreign know-how. Japan's relatively small scale R&D establishment concentrated above all on adapting these skills to the specifics of the domestic market.

Table 2–2   R&D in Selected Industrialized Countries in 1964, $ and R&D Personnel

Country	R&D Effort, Bill.$	Effort/Capita of the Population, $	Engineers and Scientists
U.S.	21.075	111	496,500
U.K.	2.160	40	59,400
West Germany	1.436	25	33,400
France	1.299	27	32,500
Japan	.892	9	114,800
Canada	.425	23	13,430
Netherlands	.330	27	2,260
Italy	.291	6	19,140
Sweden	.257	34	6,340

Source: OECD

These differences in the spending patterns of the individual countries were to shift in the following years, but only gradually. Even in 1969 (the year of the first moon landing), total U.S. expenditures for R&D were still twice that of France, Germany, Japan, and the U.K. combined.

The Technology Race Begins

Although non-U.S. spending on research and development until the mid-1960s was still quite modest compared with the U.S., other developed countries already had ambitious plans on the drawing board. Industry in these countries—at least the large corporations that had already long-established traditions of R&D in pre-war times—recognized this earlier than the general public. Comparing R&D spending of major European industrial companies with that of their American competitors in 1964 in Table 2–3, for example, gives an impression that is quite different from the comparison between countries in Table 2–2. A number of corporations had reached, and in some cases even surpassed, the ratio of R&D to sales of major U.S. corporations. The R&D intensity at Machines Bull in France (data processing), for example, was second only to the U.S. conglomerate ITT.

Table 2–3 R&D Expenditures of Major U.S. and European Industrial Corporations 1963/64, Local Currencies and Percent of Sales

Company (Country)	Sales	R&D Effort	R&D/Sales,%
AEG (Germany)	3.39 Bill. DM	ca.250 Mill. .DM	6-8%
BASF (Germany)	3.18 Bill.DM	160 Mill. DM	5.0%
Bayer (Germany)	3.62 Bill. DM	202.3 Mill. DM	5.6%
BBC (Switzerland)	541 Mill. Sfr	38-40 Mill. Sfr	7-8%
Elliot Automation (UK)	36 Mill. £	ca. 3 Mill. £	8-10%
General Electric (US)	4.92 Bill. $	300-400 Mill.$	6-8%
Hoechst (Germany)	3.32 Bill. DM	172 Mill. DM	5.2%
IBM (US)	2.06 Bill. $	124 Mill. $	6%
ITT (US)	1.31 Bill. $	170 Mill. $	13%
L.M.Ericsson (Sweden)	1.48 Bill. Skr	ca. 74 Mill. Skr	ca.5%
Lockheed (US)	1.60 Bill. $	27.2 Mill. $	1.7%
Machines Bull (France)	461 Mill. FF	58 Mill. FF	12.6%
Osram (Germany)	302 Mill. DM	ca.21 Mill. DM	7.1%
Philips (Netherlands)	7.74 Bill. hfl.	470 Mill. hfl.	6%
Siemens (Germany)	6.53 Bill. DM	400 Mill. DM	6.1%

Source: OECD

But not only companies, foreign nations as a whole were also determined to catch up. In the first half of the 1960s, for example, Germany was involved in a frenzy of media and parliamentary hand wringing regarding a so-called "education catastrophe," similar to the one under discussion in the United States today. There was great anxiety over a declining competitiveness of German industry. The government and industry therefore resolved to spend no less than 3% of GNP on research and development by 1970. In practice, things did not proceed quite so rapidly, but the increase was still remarkably swift once it was underway.

Similar thinking was widespread in practically all industrialized countries. Not long, and the terms "recherche et de´veloppement," "idagine e sviluppo," "Forschung und Entwicklung," or "research and development" were becoming common expressions in day-to-day language. For a country that was eager to be at the forefront of technological progress and depended on the ability to bring high quality, state-of-the-art products to the marketplace, the mastery of advanced technologies was considered an indispensable ticket to the future. The term "future technologies" became a catchphrase. R&D emerged as a topic demanding the attention of corporate boards, politicians and journalists. Jacques Servan Schreiber in France published his stirring book *Le défi américain*(The American Challenge) in which he warned that failing to keep up in technology, Europe would degenerate into an American economic colony. The book was a bestseller in many languages—including Japanese. Even science itself began to take an interest in the subject of science and technology, with "research on research" soon emerging as a field of academic enquiry. In 1972/73, the renowned Massachusetts Institute of Technology introduced the first academic teaching program for the "Management of Research and Development."

In the years that followed, R&D efforts began to exhibit massive increases in almost all industrialized countries. Soon, not only the giant corporations in R&D-intensive industries such as pharmaceuticals and electronics were affected. Also for smaller companies it became clear that to survive, they would have to stay abreast in technology. Whole industrial sectors such as the automobile industry, which had experienced its periods of rapid scientific and technical progress during the early phases of industrialization, and whose products were generally deemed to have reached technical maturity, now discovered improvement potentials undreamed of before. The four-stroke internal combustion engine, for example, was an invention of the late 19th century. Throughout the 20th century it had been manufactured by the millions and had been slowly but steadily improved. Then, partially spurred on by the oil crises of the 1970s, its efficiency improved by orders of magnitude. Limousines suddenly consumed less gasoline than compact cars had previously. Gasoline itself became less toxic. In the metal industries, new alloys and types of steel emerged. Optical goods achieved enhanced brilliance and power. Factories attained levels of efficiency hitherto considered impossible. Textiles became more durable and colorfast, and the detergents with which they were cleaned became both more effective *and* less aggressive at the same time. Simultaneously, in the so-called high-tech industries, new ideas and products were appearing which only a few years previously hardly anybody could have even imagined. Electronic products conquered homes, offices, and factories, and the contraceptive pill promised families and nations new liberties in the shaping of their lives and destinies.

Of course, all of these wonderful things came at a price. Figure 2–10 gives an idea of the orders of magnitude by which total expenditures on R&D had swollen. As early as 1975, the total amount spent by the OECD countries on R&D had reached a staggering $75 bill. a year. It did not remain there. By 1981, it doubled to over $156 bill and then doubled again to $308 bill. by 1989. Enhanced by the German reunification and Mexico's accession to the OECD, total spending reached *over $380 bill.* by 1992 representing an average annual increase of over 10%.

All of the OECD countries, with the partial exception of the United Kingdom, were involved in this growth. At the same time, there was a change in the overall thrust of R&D. During the 1960s and the first half of the 1970s, the non-U.S. industrialized nations regarded it as their first and foremost task to catch up with the enormous volume to which U.S. R&D spending had grown. Matching that volume in absolute terms was, of

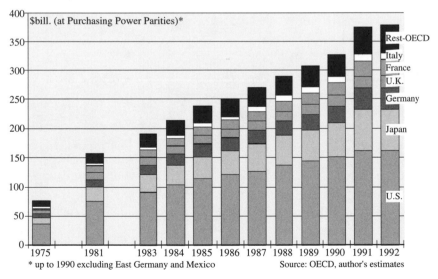

Figure 2–10 R&D Spending in the OECD Countries 1975 to 1992, $bill.

course, out of the question for their far smaller national economies. But at least similar spending volumes relative to their respective GNPs were considered highly desirable.

By the middle of the 1970s, this goal had been largely achieved. Relative expenditures, at least among the larger OECD countries, from then on varied much less. Figure 2–11 shows that a certain equilibrium held sway from the mid-1970s onward. For the next 17 years and in rough accordance with the relative sizes of their national economies, the United States continuously spent almost as much on R&D as the rest of the OECD countries put together with only a very gradual decline to about 44% of the OECD total by 1991. The percentages of the other countries by and large also remained constant. Only Japan's share—again in accordance with the faster growth of its economy and the completion of its catch-up phase—rose from approximately 13% in 1975 to roughly 18% of total R&D spending by the OECD countries by 1990.[31]

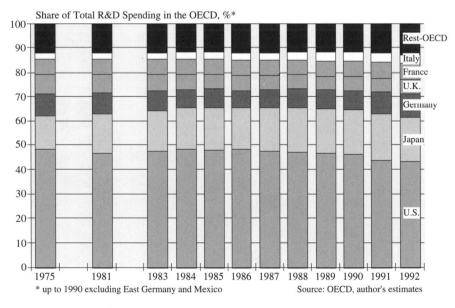

Share of Total R&D Spending in the OECD, %*

* up to 1990 excluding East Germany and Mexico   Source: OECD, author's estimates

Figure 2–11   Share of R&D Spending in the OECD by Countries 1975 to 1992, percent.

31 For an overview over a somewhat longer time frame (1961-1991), albeit with less precision (U.S., Japan, E.U.), see Young, 1993, p. 36, Fig. 2. The message, however, is essentially the same.

...and Turns into a Battle of Attrition

Of course, it is easy to rattle off figures like this. To make them somewhat more meaningful they should be seen in perspective. A comparable frame of reference in Table 2–4 for the total sum of $328 bill. in 1990 quickly makes it clear that research and development in the large industrial countries today has reached orders of magnitude that can easily stand comparison with the national outlays for defence, foreign aid or other major economic indicators. In Italy, for instance, national R&D expenditure in 1990 amounted to 55% of the defense budget. In Germany, it was 76%, while in militarily (relatively) chaste Japan, the figure was an impressive 187%. In 1990, German researchers and developers spent as much money within the country as German tourists did worldwide.

Looking at numbers of people and not dollars, in 1988, there were some two million engineers and scientists employed in research and development in the seven largest western industrial countries, as opposed to 1.6 million in 1983, an increase of 25% in just five years. In no country in the world does the population grow so fast. These two million scientists and engineers are supported by at least a further two million, and perhaps three million, assistants, laboratory workers, students and other scientific and technical support personnel without whom effective R&D work would be unthinkable today. If we consider that on average each of these four to five million employees will have undergone at least 15—and in many cases 20—years of education and training, the huge investments necessary for creating this vast R&D potential become clear.

Table 2–4   R&D Spending in Major Industrialized Countries Compared to Other Spending Indicators 1990, at Purchasing Power Parities

	U.S.	Japan	W.Ger.	France	U.K.	Italy	Canada
R&D Effort, Bill. $	**153**	**58**	**29**	**21**	**19**	**11**	**7**
Foreign Aid, Bill. $	11.4	9.1	6.3	9.4	2.6	3.4	2.5
Tourist Spending, Bill. $	38.7	24.9	29.8	12.4	19.1	13.8	8.4
Military Spending, Bill. $	268	31	38	36	33	20	10
R&D Effort, % of Military	57%	187%	76%	58%	58%	55%	70%

Sources: Military Spending: Sipri Yearbook 1991, otherwise: OECD.

This potential itself is impressive. Just take the Federal Republic of Germany as an example. Today, about 20,000 German companies engage in R&D. In 1992 they spent DM 47.5 bill. (ca. $32 bill.) just for this purpose. They are flanked by 102 industrial research associations, more than 300 universities and colleges that grant over 20,000 Ph.D. degrees annually, and 16 so-called Major Research Centers run by the government which are comparable to the National Laboratories in the U.S. Some of them employ thousands of scientists. There are 67 research institutes and 27 research groups run by the Max-Planck-Society—some of them world famous—doing work across the complete spectrum of the natural and social sciences, plus roughly 50 institutes of the Fraunhofer Society which do application- and industry-related development work and are an object of envy in many other industrial nations. In addition, there is an abundance of committees, boards, authorities, agencies and other standing and non-standing commissions. Among them are many prestigious and well-known organizations, such as the Science Council, the German Research Community, the German Science Foundation, the University Rectors Conference, the Major Research Units Study Group, the Federal Ministry for Science, Technology and Education, and an armada of local and regional offices which in one form or another are conducive to the purposes of R&D (although in practice they do not always work towards a common goal).[32] But even with this vast entourage that encompasses on the order of 700,000 people, Germany ranks only third among the large industrial powers, behind the United States and Japan.

For many years, not only absolute spending on R&D was on the rise in the industrialized countries. Figure 2–12 shows that its *relative* importance also increased considerably. Between 1975 and 1988 the proportion of GDP (gross domestic product) spent on R&D by the five largest western industrialized countries rose by an average of 1%age point, with the steepest rises occurring in Japan and Germany, and the smallest increase taking place in the U.K. Only in the recent past can one observe a levelling off. The reasons for this are manifold. The most important ones are linked to the historic economic and political upheavals which occurred at the turn of this decade and have had important ramifications for R&D spending in the public and private sectors.[33]

At first glance, a growth of 1% in share of GDP over a period of ten to 15 years does not appear to be a particularly fast, but rather a leisurely rate of change. One must bear in mind, however, that R&D spending cannot be

32 Zick, 1993; Hofer, 1994, p. 36.

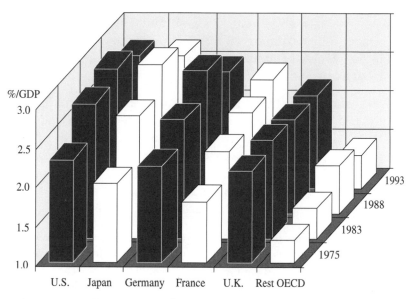

Figure 2–12 R&D Expenditures in Select OECD Countries in 1975, 1983, 1988, 1993 as percent of GDP.

increased from 2% of GDP to 3% of GDP without solving a plethora of more or less closely related other problems. From among these, take the educational dimension as an example: The largest share of R&D costs by far are personnel costs. Only in a very few areas of technology (microelectronics, for example) are salaries and wages outweighed by the loss of capital and equipment. Thus, more R&D, above all else, means more people working in R&D. This in turn places additional demands on the capacities of schools, colleges, universities and industrial training centers. It requires more professors and lecturers, support staff, laboratories, lecture halls, libraries, etc. A higher R&D intensity, therefore, has significant implications for national educational infrastructures. We can see what this means in real life if we stick to the German example above: The number of university students in former West Germany during the winter semester 1991/1992 reached approximately 1.65 million, representing a 75% increase over 1977. In 1991/92, the number of *first year* students alone amounted to 228,000.[34] By com-

33 In the U.S., for example, this included the scrapping, or reconsideration, of various large-scale military weapons programs following the collapse of the Soviet Union. In Japan, it was influenced by the bursting of the "economic bubble" of the 1980s plus the rising exchange rate of the Yen. In Germany, it was the massive cash flows required for the economic, social and technical rehabilitation of Eastern Germany.

parison, in 1930/31, the year with the largest total number of students (not just beginning students) during the interwar period, there were only about a 100,000 in the whole of Germany (then with a larger population).[35] Today, there are that many in the city of Munich alone.

The situation in the U.S. is not much different. As an example, take the annual number of doctoral degrees granted by universities around the country. The national output of PhDs in the natural sciences and engineering in the years 1934 through 1939 averaged about 1,500 per year. By the beginning of the 1990s, this figure had increased to over 30,000! Put differently, over a time in which the U.S. population roughly doubled the national "production" of science and engineering PhDs grew by a factor of more than 20.[36]

Before universities in either country can even hope to cope with such student increases, a whole range of regulatory, financial and coordinative issues have to be addressed (in Germany, for instance, between the federal *Länder* or states). Their resolution is always associated with considerable delays and lead times which can sometimes last many years, especially so if the provision of education is a government monopoly, as it is in many countries. In principle, R&D spending can only rise when all of these questions have been settled and appropriate measures implemented. Only then will there be sufficient researchers and engineers to get any ambitious technology programs going.

It should further be borne in mind that the GDP-base, which R&D expenditures are compared to, did not remain constant during the period under review. Between the mid 1970s and the end of the 1980s, the economy in all of the five large industrialized countries shown in Figure 2–12 grew by a high two-digit percentage value in real terms. In some cases, it even doubled. Keep in mind that even a fairly humble economic growth averaging 2% per year accumulates to some 35% over a period of 15 years. At 5% per year the figure is already over 100%. All this should perhaps give us some idea of the immense displacements and other powerful changes that are associated with a "modest" 1% increase of R&D relative to GDP.

To sum up, national R&D expenditures today are no longer something that can be tucked away under the heading "Miscellaneous" in a country's

34 Altenmüller, 1992.

35 Statistical Yearbooks for the German Reich.

36 Lane, 1995, p. 99.

statistical ledgers. They are often as large as the production volumes of major industrial sectors. According to the World Bank, R&D expenditures in 1990 corresponded to almost 10% of total industrial production in the U.S. In Canada and Japan, it was almost 5%.[37] In Germany, R&D spending in that year amounted to roughly twice the revenues of the textile and clothing industry. In France and Italy, it was, respectively, 80% and 70% of the important national food industries, and in Britain, R&D spending outstripped the total production volume of the chemical industry by more than 10%. One can well and truly say, R&D is big business.

... Among a Small Group of Participants

As a rough estimate, one can probably assume that in the 1980s 85% of the world's research and development took place in the 24 countries of the OECD, including the R&D support expended by the European Union. Up to about 1990, most of the remaining 15% could be ascribed to the Soviet Union and its satellite nations, which placed heavy emphasis on military technologies and aerospace. If we subtract the R&D activities of South Korea, both Chinas, India, Israel, South Africa (and perhaps Mexico and Brazil) from what was left, there was not much to share among the remaining 130-odd countries of the world community. Apart from a few exceptions, (e.g. in the agricultural sciences)[38] practically no independent research and development took place there at all.

The result of all this is no surprise: On December 31, 1993, there was a total of 3.9 million valid patents worldwide. Of these, more than 87% were owned by holders based in one of the OECD countries (38% in North America, 32% in Western Europe and 15% in Japan).[39] Within the OECD club, there is a further concentration on just a handful of countries: In the five year period between 1989 and 1993, for example, various countries applied for a total of 283,000 patents at the European Patent Office. Of these applications, 27.7% came from the U.S., 20% Japan, 19.1% Germany, 8.0% France and 5.7% the United Kingdom. A scant 19.5% was left for the rest of the world.[40]

---

37 The difference between the U.S. and Japanese figures is explained by the higher share of manufacturing GDP in Japan (27.4% in 1990) than in the U.S. (18.3%).

38 On the island of Mauritius, for example, there is a sugar research institute. In Papua-New Guinea there is a coconut research institute. In the Philippines, there is the International Rice Research Institute, probably the world leader in rice breeding methods. This rough estimate does not include the ambitious arms programs of countries like Iraq, Pakistan, and North Korea.

39 Auriol and Pham, 1992/93, p. 16.

Naturally, such rough calculations harbor a certain imprecision. Lower per capita personnel costs, for example, will tend to deflate R&D expenditures in poorer countries, but not necessarily their R&D output. Also, just as in industrial production, one can observe the transfer of labor-intensive R&D-activities to low-wage countries, where there is often an ample supply of qualified engineers and technicians, but insufficient industrial demand to give them jobs. The result is that in many developing countries one can find a so-called "academic proletariat" of substantial proportions. At the same time, in some industrial sectors of the rich countries there is a corresponding lack of trained engineers and experts. Since the beginning of the 1990s and with the collapse of the Soviet Union this lack has become less severe, in some sectors at least. But before the bursting of the "economic bubble" in Japan, for example, there was talk of a shortfall of one million systems analysts and software engineers by the turn of the century. For these reasons, computer companies from Japan, Europe and the U.S. have outsourced some of their labor-intensive software development to China, India, South Korea and Eastern Europe.[41]

Labor market considerations are not the only reasons for transferring R&D-related activities to third countries. Country-specific opportunities, problems and concerns can also offer sufficient grounds to do so. Japanese and Chinese research institutes, for instance, are cooperating in the development of bacterial oxidation processes for breaking down acid buildups in Chinese coal mines. These mines, in turn, supply Japanese industry with raw materials. In Costa Rica, which (still) has a rich diversity of plant life, researchers are investigating the pharmaceutically active agents in plant tissues.[42]

Only gradually do countries outside the hemisphere of Western industrialized nations begin to perform R&D of their own. One widely acclaimed triumph of Third World R&D was the development of a malaria vaccine by Colombian scientist Manuel Patarroyo. Perhaps one of the most ambitious countries in this respect is South Korea where the government has announced a Highly Advanced National (HAN) technology program. HAN (also the Korean word for Korea) was launched in 1992 and will run until 2001. With total funds on the order of Won 37,000 bill. (ca. $46 bill.) it aims to promote increased R&D activities in 14 industrial sectors ranging from semi-

40 European Patent Office, 1991, p. 74.

41 See Masuko, 1991.

42 Merck & Co. in particular has become very active in this endeavor, see Tenenbaum, 1995, p. 49.

conductors and high-definition television to electric cars and communications networks and is seeking to emulate Japan's meteoric rise in many fields of industry. The total of Won 5,000 bill. (ca. $6.2 bill.) spent on R&D in the whole of South Korea in 1992, however, is not much more than the R&D budgets of major U.S. companies like IBM or General Motors.[43]

Different developing countries tend to concentrate on different fields of technology. India is gradually developing an active role in space[44] and is also a hotbed of software development employing on the order of 125,000 developers with revenues growing as fast as 50% per year. As China is emerging as a low-cost manufacturing powerhouse, it is also acquiring the know-how for high-tech production skills. Malaysia is looking at chips and chip packaging and is currently producing semiconductors in 150 plants employing more than 150,000 workers.[45] Taiwan has focused on personal computer technology,[46] Indonesia on aeronautics.[47] Advanced information technology itself is contributing to the advancement of R&D in these countries. Adding to this the lower costs even of highly trained specialists in these countries, plus their long working hours, renders the transferral of R&D activities an extremely attractive proposition. An Indian software specialist earning $10,000 per year is regarded as well-off in his or her home country. High-tech workers in South Korea earn only a quarter of what their Japanese counterparts make, but work 20% more hours annually.

Nevertheless, these Third World R&D activities are still of a largely peripheral nature. As industrialization advances there, this may change, of course.[48] In some cases, technology-intensive international corporations with home bases in the Third World have already sprung up. South Korean *chaebols* (the Korean equivalent of Japanese industry groups) like Daewoo and Samsung, for example, not only export high-tech goods like cars, microchips and consumer electronics, but have also set up transplants in other countries. But for the moment it is still rare for the R&D work performed outside the core of Western industrialized economies also to be managed

43 Burton, 1994.

44 David, 1995.

45 Kandiah, 1995.

46 Gross and Carey, 1994.

47 For an overview of Asian aeronautical efforts, see Davis, 1995.

48 For example, Matsushita maintains a complete development and design team for air-conditioners in Malaysia and is in the process of doing the same for the production of television sets.

there. Therefore, even if the Indian software industry now comprises hundreds of firms whose total revenues reaches into the billions,[49] it still does little to alter the big picture. The bulk of R&D spending still takes place close to the industrial hubs and corporate headquarters in Japan, the U.S. and Western Europe. R&D—so the general view—has become far too important for a company's long-term survival as to risk losing overall control over it by transferring it to other countries. The software development laboratories centered in and around Bangalore, India, to a very large extent are controlled by companies like Apple, IBM, Texas Instruments, Motorola, Siemens-Nixdorf and others. Similarly, Japan's Hitachi has moved much of its VCR production to Malaysia. In the future it will also develop new product generations there, but the "key technologies will continue to be developed in Japan."[50]

Even companies that have made great efforts to internationalize their operations use their foreign-based R&D units primarily for developing and adapting products to local and regional markets. For European technicians, for example, it is difficult to develop printers that can generate Japanese *Kanji, Hiragana* and *Katakana* characters. So this part of the development work is transferred to Japan. National health authorities occasionally insist that clinical testing of pharmaceutical products takes place in their respective countries prior to granting government approval. In such instances, only those phases of development work that are absolutely required for this approval occur in the country concerned. Apart from this, the really essential work is regularly done at home. Sony, for example, is generally regarded as one of the most internationalized corporations in Japan, and perhaps the world. In 1993, 73% of the company's sales were overseas. Nevertheless, 86% of the company's consolidated R&D expenses was borne by the parent company in Tokyo.[51] This is also true of multinational corporations from smaller countries like Nestlé (Switzerland) or Philips (Netherlands), which sometimes achieve more than 90% of their sales volume outside their home base. No doubt, there are exceptions. These include IBM's world-wide R&D arrangements, for example, or the genetic research centers and biotech subsidiaries maintained by European chemical and pharmaceutical companies in the U.S.[52] The Swiss/Swedish electrical engineering group ABB has also

49 Chimelli, 1993.

50 Anon.{18}, 1994.

51 Anon.{22}, 1994.

52 Wintermann, 1993.

decentralized major parts of its R&D in many countries. As a rule, however, transfers of this type do not reflect a general desire of a company to fully internationalize its R&D efforts. More often than not, they are governed instead by the peculiarities affecting individual fields of technology. For example, these could be legal restraints on research in a company's head-quarter country, such as the formerly restrictive German law on genetic research, or the availability of highly specialized experts in artificial intelligence in the U.S. or other areas.

The Role of the State—Training, Sponsoring or Doping?

One question naturally arises in this context: just who is paying the bills? Up to World War I, it was exclusively the private sector that was interested in improving the level of technology. The role of the state was limited to the coordination of these activities, standardization, and the creation of a suitable (physical, economic, and/or regulatory) environment for industrial R&D activities. Among these government sponsored measures was the establishment of the U.S. National Bureau of Standards, for example, or the National Physical Laboratory in England, or the various national patent offices which contributed to the protection of the technical competitiveness of a country and which continue to play a highly significant role in present times. Even today, industry does not fail to emphasize that it regards these types of regulatory functions as the most important tasks of the government in the R&D domain.

However, this has not prevented industry in all of the developed countries from seeking financial assistance or other forms of help in addition to regulatory support from the government whenever it saw the chance of doing so successfully. Nor has the government abstained from straying outside its traditional sphere of sovereign activities and from actively engaging in research and development efforts of its own. Ever since the First World War, the state has taken an highly visible and active role in shaping national R&D, whether as legislator, as financier or as executor of R&D programs. Particularly since World War II, the government's part in R&D has become more and more important, not merely in Germany and the U.S. (see Figures 2–8 and 2–9), but everywhere. A government share of 50% or even more in the financing of individual R&D projects is now the norm in many countries. Only in Japan has this share routinely hovered at lower levels.

The active involvement of, and support by, the government is justified in a variety of ways, depending on which industrial sector happens to benefit. The development costs of weapons systems and space programs, for example, are regularly completely paid for by the government since it is usually the sole customer anyway. Among Western countries, particularly in the U.S., France and Britain, military development work has always constituted a major portion of national R&D efforts. In absolute terms, this has led to huge government payments over the years. But also in smaller countries, such as Sweden, whose policy of neutrality during the Cold War made it feel obliged to develop even its own fighter planes, (relatively) large-scale military R&D work has been undertaken.

Frequently, advanced military and aerospace programs are not carried out exclusively for reasons of defence. They also can, and frequently do, contribute to exports, the implementation of labor market policies, national prestige, and other goals. Even foreign and other policy aims are occasionally pursued under the guise of state-run R&D programs.[53] Under this category, one can sometimes run across exotica: A country's participation in the negotiations on the International Treaty on the Antarctic, for example, requires a permanent research presence on that continent. It was not the least of all reasons to fulfil this requirement and hence gain a voice in determining the future uses of the sixth continent, that the German Antarctica Research Program was launched in the beginning of the 1970s. An example closer to home: Support for the process of European unification is a major motive behind various technology programs such as ESPRIT, RACE, and others, which are financed by the European Union. Their aims are not so much the promotion of specific technologies per se, but rather the promotion of cross-border cooperation among European companies in the development of new technologies.[54]

Apart from political aims, a further reason for the R&D lies in a certain division of tasks among short and long-term technology goals. In the Western industrial countries today, there is a more or less distinct, but implicit

53 Such mixing of goals in governments' activities is nothing unusual. For example, for many years over 50% of the U.S. government's foreign aid went to Egypt and Israel, although neither Egypt, let alone Israel, are among the most needy nations in the world.

54 In absolute terms, however, only very little in the way of R&D funds comes from Brussels. Of the approximately 100 billion ECU (roughly $130 bill.) that are spent annually on R&D in all the EU countries, only about 2.5% is financed by the Union itself. More than twelve times that amount, or about $40 bill., is spent by the EU on agricultural and fishery subsidies.

understanding that private industry should finance the development of new products and processes for the nearer future. There, the outlines, properties, and demand structures for these products are either reasonably well known or can be more readily determined (e.g. the development of a new subcompact car or a new food- and kiss-resistant lipstick). Conversely, the conviction holds that the state should at least partially finance R&D in such areas where potential products and markets still lie in an uncertain and distant future, and where scientific and technical ground work is still necessary (e.g. the development of a thermonuclear fusion reactor or of asteroid mining technologies). The reason for such principles of government technology policy lie with supporting the survival of whole industrial sectors or even the economy in general. Given the normal minimum yield requirements in industry, such extremely long-term and risky projects would stretch the financial capacities of the private sector beyond its limits even under the most favorable circumstances. Lest they not be developed at all, the belief is, therefore, that their costs be at least partially borne by the tax payer.

A final dimension of public financial contributions lies in the application *width* of a prospective technology. The greater the economic impact of so-called "generic" (not to be confused with genetic!) technologies, i.e. the greater the number of industrial sectors that either depend on this technology or might profit from it, the greater the likelihood of the government stepping in to promote it. Until quite recently, for instance, computers and microelectronics were considered to be such key technologies and were correspondingly promoted, not only in the U.S. or Germany. Today, one can read about present and future key technologies such as aerospace, genetic engineering, micromechanics, artificial intelligence, and others almost on a daily basis.

Only rarely can one decide unambiguously on the basis of such qualitative criteria whether a certain item of industrial know-how or an R&D field belongs to the domain of government interest or not. As indicated in Figure 2.13, the boundaries are fluid. As a rule, when the government is involved in an industrial R&D program, a mixed financing package is arranged. Germany's Technology Ministry, for instance, will typically pay for 50% of the R&D costs of a project once it has been accepted. Disregarding direct contracts such as the construction of a new fighter plane for the airforce, 100% financing by the state outside of the realm of pure research and development, which normally takes place at universities, Max-Planck-Institutes and other major research facilities, is rather rare.

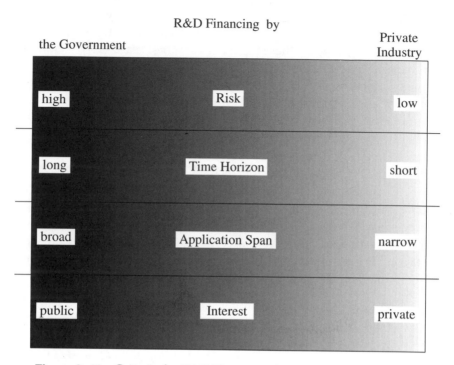

Figure 2–13 Criteria for R&D Financing by the Public and Private Sectors

The *types* of financing by the public sector also vary. A direct contract between the government and one or several companies regarding a specific R&D project, e.g. for the development of a military radar system, always entails a direct flow of funds. Related to this are subsidies aimed at less clearly defined goals, which have to do with individual scientific and technical fields in a more general sense. Typically, these will be industrial technology promotion programs, for example, for data processing, ocean technology, etc. Besides such direct money flows, certain industrial activities are occasionally also supported through favorable arrangements, such as allowances for the depreciation of R&D investments, or of the growth in R&D investment over previous years. A popular practice frequently adopted in Japan is the indirect support of R&D projects through other means. This can involve the loaning of government facilities and personnel to private industry for specific projects. An advantage of this form of R&D subsidy is that there are no direct cash transfers or tax exemptions. Legislative or budget hurdles are therefore considerably easier to clear. The use of such instruments, incidentally, is also much harder to detect than the procedures usually followed in Europe and the U.S. In light of the ongoing arguments among industrialized countries over the alleged or actual subsidization of domestic industries, this effect is perhaps not quite unwelcome in Tokyo. Be that as it may, the instruments and forms of government support for R&D are multifaceted and varied. Their common denominator is that they all either place resources directly at the disposal of industry, or, to a greater or lesser degree, help keep a company from having to commit resources of its own.

Finally, even negative financing, of sorts, can be instrumental in government technology development policies. Taxes on gasoline consumption as witnessed in California and a number of European countries can be highly effective for the development of electric vehicles or other alternative energy sources. On the other hand, taxing (effectively: penalizing) energy consumption in whatever form can be supportive of energy efficiency enhancing technologies.

As indicated above, the various forms of government support for industrial R&D attained considerable levels in all the western industrial countries up to the 1970s. Unfortunately, it is not always possible to make precise comparisons or to assign exact price tags to these support activities. In part, this is due to military secrecy, but partly also to varying definitions of subsidies. The U.S. government and the aerospace industry, for instance, have continuously criticized the considerable support by various European governments for the development of the Airbus family of airliners. The routine response of European governments has been to point out that the technical skills that went into the development of America's successful and market dominating civilian aircraft was in fact based on government-financed military development programs, and was hence equally subsidized.[55] This line of reasoning, in turn, may sound hollow to U.S. aerospace executives ever since the (civil) Airbus Industrie consortium has established a subsidiary for the development of military aircraft.[56]

---

55 Tenbrock, 1990; Butterworth-Hayes, 1993.

56 Coleman, 1994; Betts, 1994. A similar conflict is presently developing over the export of genetically treated soybeans from the U.S. to the European Union, traditionally a large importer of American soy products. A number of European countries require these soybeans to be marked as genetically treated, while the U.S., maintaining that nobody could tell the difference between natural and treated varieties anyway, suspect a European ploy to keep American soy products off the market as long as European biotechnology stills trails U.S. know-how. Source: Oldag, 1996.

Personally, the author would prefer to refrain from taking sides in this matter, but does wish to point out that during the 1970s, sometimes up to two thirds of total national R&D spending was borne by the respective national governments. Undoubtedly, the Cold War and various large defense programs constituted an important share in this. But other factors also played a role. Not the least of these was the economic competition among the western allies, which complemented the political and military rivalry for supremacy with the countries of the Warsaw Pact.

More than anything else, the lingering impact of the "Sputnik Shock" of 1957, and the general effect it had of encouraging governments everywhere to engage in technology development, should not be underestimated. It was, in the final analysis, this "shock" that led President Kennedy to launch the Apollo program and the race to the moon at the beginning of the 1960s.

Indirectly and with some delay, the Apollo program also led to the immense growth of R&D in the European and other Western industrial countries outside the U.S. Non-U.S. companies participated only to a very limited degree in the warm downpour of R&D funds that rained down on American industry in the course of this greatest ever non-military development program.[57] But it was precisely this circumstance and the ensuing technology boom enjoyed by U.S. high-tech companies that caught the attention of the governments and media in the other developed countries. The U.S. technology boom extended from computer technologies to the material sciences (the famous Teflon® frying pan). It ranged from optics and aerospace to miniaturization, sensor technologies and experience in the management of large-scale technology projects involving hundreds of thousands of people in thousands of companies. It also had a mouth-watering appeal to the industrial and political leaders in these other countries. They soon uttered loud calls for massive programs on a national scale, for cooperative ventures with U.S. corporations, or for major pan-European technology initiatives. In a way, even the development of the supersonic Anglo-French Concorde can be seen as a result of this thinking.

In the 1960s and 1970s, one could observe a general technology euphoria not only in the Western world, but also in the countries of Eastern Europe. Travels to the moon and the construction of nuclear power plants were seen as signs of hope and as harbingers of the future. World problems,

---

57 A few readers might recall that the astronauts wore Swiss wrist watches and carried Swedish cameras with German lenses to the moon.

at least technical problems, to the extent that they were noticed at all, could be managed with still more technology. State subsidies for technological development were therefore politically far easier to defend. According to an Allensbach Institute poll in 1966, roughly 60% of all West Germans regarded technology as an unequivocal "boon", only 17% expressed a certain skepticism or ambivalence. In 1986, in the wake of the Vietnam War, the rise of environmental awareness, the study on "The Limits to Growth," flowerpower, the near-east oil embargo, Seveso, Three Mile Island, the Challenger disaster, Chernobyl and other events, the latter figure had risen to 56%.[58]

Given this backdrop, as well as that of changed East-West relations, the days of large-scale government involvement in R&D may not be coming to an end, but have probably passed their peak. Figure 2–14 is an indicator of this. In practice, of course, such declining rates do not necessarily mean that the amounts spent by the public sector for these purposes have declined in absolute values too. For a number of years, the decline in the governments' *contributory shares* were was more than offset by their *absolute increases*. Probably only in Japan, where the government's R&D contribution declined from 27% to 16% between 1971 and 1991, did it lead to a stagnation of government spending also in absolute terms. Gradually, however, the same is also occurring in the other industrialized countries.

Again however, a decline in spending (by the state or industry) has to consider the significant improvements in R&D productivity in recent years. For at least ten years now, very large efforts have gone into the improvement of R&D processes at all levels, either through conscious measures or through experience. Like so many other industrial processes, it has become better managed and partly even automated. As a consequence, "the bang for the buck" now rings substantially louder even though there are less bucks available.[59]

There are several reasons behind the gradual decline in governments' contributions to R&D. In part, it has to do with the diminishing political acceptance of large-scale technology programs. In part, however, it also fol-

---

58 Urban 1993, p. 41.

59 To give an example from the pharmaceutical industry where only one out of 10,000 screened compounds ever makes it to the market as a registered drug, robotization of initial compound screening processes has led to staggering improvements in both efficiency and effectiveness. Zeneca Co. (UK), for one, has reported an increase in the number of compounds tested between 1975 and 1991 from an average rate of 860/month to 18,333/mo in 1992 and to 345,000/mo in the fall of 1995, an improvement of over 40,000%! see Cookson and Green, 1995. In a telephone interview by the author, Bayer AG confirmed similar achievements.

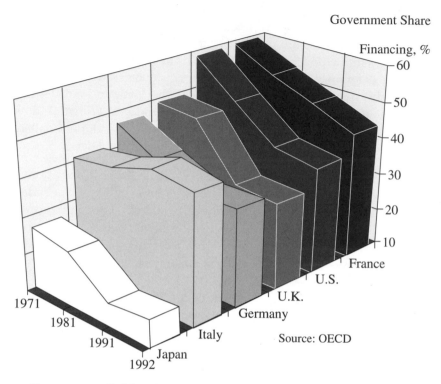

Figure 2–14 Public Sector Share of R&D Spending in Major OECD Countries 1971-1992, percent

lows a growing awareness that industry should best be left to tend to its own long-term future. There is a conviction—more pronounced in the U.S. than elsewhere and shared by this author—that the more the government distorts markets through external intervention, the greater the danger of the emergence of the wrong or harmful products or of overpriced technologies from which nobody will draw any profit.[60] Certain other developments may also have cast further doubts on the wisdom of extensive public interference in the creation of new technologies. On the one hand, it is becoming increasingly clear that the great majority of state-supported technology programs have not exactly been stellar success stories. On the other hand, it did not go unnoticed that U.S. industry, for example, achieved its commanding position in the field of high definition television (HDTV) in recent years, with not just one, but several industrial consortia. None of these had received any

60 Levinson, 1993.

state support whatsoever, despite a distinctly late start. Conversely, the government supported HDTV-programs both in Japan and Europe turned out to be spectacular flops. Additionally, the decline in military spending in recent years which reduced, delayed or cancelled various military aerospace programs in almost all NATO countries, may be a further reason for a growing restraint of governments in supporting industrial R&D. Nor should one forget the simple fact that in economically difficult times, even governments may simply run out of cash. Sometimes, they notice it.

Summary

Historically, one can identify three main periods in the development of industrial R&D. The first began in the second half of the 19th century and lasted until the end of World War I. During this period, the major industrialized countries created the regulatory frame work for the successful establishment of R&D. At the same time—particularly in the U.S. and Germany—the first major industrial laboratories were formed.

The second period lasted from the end of World War I up to World War II (1918-1939). Its development was heavily influenced by the realization gained in the aftermath of World War I that R&D had assumed great importance not only with respect to weapons development but also to the well-being of corporations and whole nations. After World War I, this realization was put into practice, again to a large extent in Germany, but even more so in the U.S. There is only incomplete statistical data for this period, but what there is shows that the number of industrial and governmental R&D facilities, the number of R&D employees and available budgets grew rapidly. In the U.S., this held true even during the crisis years following the Crash of 1929. The first large scale research centers were founded by industry long before World War II, some of them with thousands of employees. In these centers, the first foundations for what was later to become the science of R&D management were laid. Governments discovered R&D as an instrument of national policies, both in times of war and peace.

The third and current period began in 1945. Up to the late 1960s, it was characterized by an overwhelming dominance of American R&D resources and technological capabilities. This eminent technological leadership position was originally founded on the U.S. victory in World War II. It was later further enhanced by the competition with the Soviet Union for world supremacy in the political, military and aerospace arenas. However, beginning with the late 1960s and with the end of the post-war period in Europe as well as the phenomenal economic and technical growth in Japan, the U.S. was faced with a group of increasingly ambitious challengers in many important industries. In due course, R&D budgets in the industrialized nations of the West began to exhibit explosive growth rates. Today, these budgets have assumed immense proportions. Millions of researchers are working in government- and industry-owned laboratories and development facilities. Massive, large-scale projects in aerospace, power generation, data procession, defence systems, microelectronics, biochemistry and other areas have become common place. Some of them are managed as international joint ventures.

Only a very small number of highly-developed countries are participants in this R&D race. For the time being, Third World developing countries are only involved as subcontractors for labor intensive project parts at best. Less and less, national governments are restricting their functions to the legislative regulation of R&D efforts. Instead, they have become active and powerful R&D players themselves, not only as major sources of funding, but also in government-owned labs. Increasingly, R&D and R&D-financing has become a powerful instrument of public policies. Only in recent years can one observe a gradual shift in priorities both away from direct technology support as well as an exhaustion of public financing. Even in industry, R&D budgets are approaching upper limits.

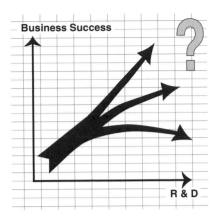

3

Too Much R&D?
—An Exploration

Electronics and Competition

According to various national and OECD statistics, the seven largest Western economies (U.S., Japan, West Germany, United Kingdom, France, Italy, Canada) spent well over $300 bill. on R&D in 1990.[1] This included both private and government-sponsored work as well as military R&D spending. Converting this enormous amount to daily rates, one arrives at about $1 bill. per working day, or roughly the equivalent of the daily costs of the United Nations military campaign following Iraq's invasion of Kuwait in 1991.

If one considers the detailed attention with which the whole world followed a few weeks of war on the oil fields of the Near East, it is remarkable how a process that has been growing[2] and consuming far greater resources than a "real" war draws a much lower degree of public attention. Perhaps it is true that developments which persist for long periods are of little news value. If one considers some of the findings in Chapter 2, there can be little doubt that the spending intensity of R&D is indeed a long lasting condition. On the other hand, one can hardly overlook the fact that, unlike a political/military war, the R&D conflict shows only hesitant signs of abatement even in times of dire economic difficulties and empty coffers.[3] If one is to believe

1   Exchange rates at purchasing power parities, see Fig. 2–10.
2   In 1986, only four years earlier, total R&D efforts in all the 24 OECD countries amounted to about $250 bill.

71

some of the very insightful statements on this subject,[4] perhaps this is so because the stakes are so much higher, and the opponents are of a much more formidable nature than those encountered in the deserts of Iraq and Kuwait. We have seen above that among the participants in the R&D contest one finds the technologically most advanced corporations and nations in the world. Their general aim is no less than a lasting domination of one or several of the decisive industries of the future. The effects of all this reverberate deeply into the political sphere.[5]

The spectrum of technical fields in question ranges from biogenetics and information technologies, through the air and space sectors, all the way to materials sciences, pharmaceuticals, optics and medical diagnostics. In these and other fields, one can observe a growing conviction among corporations and whole industries that competitiveness rests on being a leader in at least one of the underlying technologies. And R&D is regarded as the decisive way to achieve such leadership.

In recent years, an implication of this has been that R&D has given less the impression of an activity that is pursued by a corporation in its *own* interests than of one that is directed *against* the competitor. In pursuit of such considerations, this chapter therefore takes a closer look at one industrial branch that has become notorious for the level of its technology competition.

For well over two decades now, the electrical/electronics industry has repeatedly witnessed headlong technology clashes among companies and industry groups. The American and European industries have reeled under

3   For some examples of industries or corporations maintaining or even increasing R&D in spite of declining profits, see: Hayashi, 1989; Anon. {5}, 1991; Neher, 1991, quote: "Despite the sharp economic downturn in France, the Ministry of Research and Technology said recently that R&D spending by French industry is likely to top 102 billion francs (about $20.7 billion) in 1991, up 6.5 percent over 1990, which itself was up 11 percent over 1989."; Masuko, 1992 II, quote: "...despite an expected 6.4% drop in pretax profits to ¥351 billion in fiscal 1992...the company plans to increase capital spending, including R&D spending, by 5.9% to a record ¥1.96 trillion."; Mizuno, 1991, quote: "But some investments will be made regardless of business conditions. Those aimed at rationalization, research and development, diversification and adding higher value are some examples."

4   For a very lucid investigation of the war metaphor in the information technology context, see Brandlin, D. and Harrison, M., "The Technology Wars," 1987.

5   See, for example, the following statement by Vice President J. D. Quayle: "...the ultimate mission of the space station will exceed the sum of its uses as a life science facility and a microgravity lab. *Its ultimate mission will be to reaffirm America's leadership in space.*" Interview with O'Toole, T. in Aerospace America, May 1991 p. 6-7, emphasis added.

concentrated Japanese onslaughts. In electronic memory chips, European manufacturers therefore only hold a minuscule market share. American companies, on the other hand, have largely resigned in the field of audio and video equipment. Perhaps this will change again with the advent of HDTV (high definition television).

But Japanese companies have also had to pay their price. Sometimes the beleaguered industries rose to defend themselves successfully and caused the Far-Eastern offensives to become horribly expensive ventures. Thus, the Japanese dream of dominating the microprocessor business never came true. At other times, third parties became involved. Korean and Taiwanese suppliers successfully entered the Japanese video and white goods markets, for example. The largest supplier of DRAM chips today is a Korean manufacturer.

On all sides, governments were called in to help, either to secure domestic markets or supply backing for industry initiatives. Sematech, ESPRIT, the 5th Generation Computer Project, VLSI Chips (Very Large Scale Integration) and many others have entered the industry's history books as the names of skirmishes and battles for technology leadership and market shares. Their results will, it is hoped, be measured in billions of sales dollars and many thousands of jobs both today and in the years to come. Rivalries have not ended yet. Individual corporations and industry associations in Asia, America and Europe are presently retrenching and regrouping their strengths. Their preparations are focusing on newly emerging markets and those whose advent can be discerned on a very close time horizon. Among them are multimedia,[6] mobile and wide-band communications, neural networks, local-area networks, optocomputers, HDTV and other products and services.[7]

The R&D intensity of the electrical/electronics industry is perhaps one of its best known features, although in terms of sales, the pharmaceutical industry on average spends even more on R&D. The large electronics corporations complain of enormous development costs and the short development cycles they have to cope with, while at the same time they boast of their willingness to invest the necessary funds. In 1992, for example, the Japanese electronics firm Fujitsu, the second largest computer firm in the world, advertised in large business journals for several months, "This year we'll spend more on R&D than most companies on the London stock exchange will make in sales." More and more, one gains the impression that research

---

6　See Götz, 1993.

7　Matsufuji, 1993, p. 11; Ludsteck, 1993 II.

and development at least in this industry is regarded as the decisive means of achieving sustained success. But is this really the case? Has R&D kept its promises? Or has it become a bottomless pit?

In an attempt to find some answers to these questions, we will use the next few pages to compare the sales, R&D and net profit figures for 30 of the largest electrical/electronics corporations in the world. To ensure an adequate regional representation, ten each of these 30 corporations are headquartered in one of the three pillars of the triad—Japan, North America and Western Europe, respectively. The observed time frame covers a period of intense R&D encounters. It is also relatively long: it begins in 1978 and ends in 1990.

An extension of the time series into a more recent past might have been possible. The author refrained from doing so for the following reasons: When (the German version of) the manuscript was completed, the annual figures for 1992 were only partly available, while the year 1991 was complete. However, both 1991 and the years immediately following it were distinguished by changes of such fundamental nature in the three largest western economies that any development pertaining to R&D would have either been absorbed by other events or would have become so distorted or unrecognizable as to have been meaningless. In Germany, 1991 was the first year in which the consequences of reunification took full effect on the economy, labor markets, government budgets and inflation rates. Essentially, it was no longer the same country. In Japan, the "economic bubble" which had significantly contributed to Japanese economic growth and industrial policies in the 1980s, finally burst. And in the U.S., the readiness to go to war for Kuwait coincided with an election year and a first full awareness, both in industry and public, of epochal budget deficits. Further distorting effects occurred due to declining military budgets in the wake of the collapse of the Soviet Union, especially among NATO countries. The time series up to 1990 shall therefore suffice. Even within this limitation, a number of interesting patterns and relationships have emerged that give food for thought.

Thirty Industrial Giants

Table 3–1 shows the names of the corporations included in our survey. Compiling such a list is not always easy, even if one is led by a seemingly simple criterion like "electrical engineering and electronics." Many companies that are regularly included in this category are also active in other industrial branches. General Electric (U.S.), for example, also manufactures jet engines, Hitachi (Japan) construction equipment. These non-electrical businesses can rarely be filtered out completely. Although they regularly report their revenues separately, they only occasionally do so for their profits and practically never for their R&D efforts. In sum total of all 30 corporations, however, they contribute only marginally to their overall business volume. We will therefore include them in the conviction that they will not distort the total picture to a significant degree.

Table 3–1 Thirty Large Electronics Corporations from Japan, North America and Europe

Japanese Corporations	North American Corporations	European Corporations
Fujitsu	DEC	Alcatel Alsthom
Hitachi	General Electric (USA)	Bosch
Matsushita	Hewlett-Packard	General Electric Co. (UK)
Mitsubishi Electric	IBM	L.M.Ericsson
NEC	Intel	Nixdorf (up to 1989)
Nippondenso (as of 1981)	Motorola	Olivetti (as of 1981)
Oki	Northern Telcom (Can.)	Philips
Sanyo	Texas Instruments	Plessey (up to 1989)
Sony	Unisys	Siemens
Toshiba	Westinghouse	STC (up to 1989)

Apart from this, a precise definition of electrical engineering and electronics is also not quite as simple as it sounds. For example, does it include software? Software is needed for computer operations, and computers are the very symbol of electronics. There is probably no computer company in the world that does not at least also offer the operating system to go with its product. In case of a computer manufacturer, one should therefore include software. A company like Microsoft, however, 80% of whose revenues in 1995 consisted of operating systems and applications software, would not have been included in the category of electronics corporations even if it had already existed in its present size between 1978 and 1990.[8]

In the interest of minimizing selection problems of this kind the author asked several of the major electronics manufacturers which other companies in their opinion constituted "the most important players in the world-wide electrical/electronics industry." The level of agreement in the resulting list of 30 names was remarkably high. Corporations apparently know quite well who their important and largest competitors are.

The author himself employed only two filters: Some companies, which by virtue of their size and market positions should actually have been part of the group, were excluded if the level of their acquisitions or divestments of company divisions or of joint ventures and partnerships over the observed period had virtually changed them into new firms under old names. The French corporation Thomson CSF was an example of this. The same happened if sufficient data could not be obtained without exorbitant efforts. This was true of Sharp in Japan. For all these reasons, the overall picture might contain some instances of blurriness. It is the author's hope that the corporations' size as well as the relatively long observation period of 13 years will let such instances cancel each other out. Perhaps they are not of a significant magnitude anyway.

What can be said about the 30 corporations overall? Among them one finds some of the largest industrial enterprises in the world.[9] They include electro-universalists like GE, Toshiba or Philips which offer a broad range of electrical and electronic products ranging from alarm systems, cassette decks, computer tomographs and dental chairs over flat iron, industrial robots, light bulbs and micro chips to electric motors, nuclear power plants, sensors and telephones. Some of the 30 are specialists focusing on narrowly defined product spectra, for example, Intel on semiconductors, Sony on consumer electronics, Olivetti on office equipment. The majority are somewhere in between. Companies like NEC (company slogan: "Computers and Communications") cover not all, but significant parts of the electrical and electronics market.

Industry, governments and private individuals are among the customers of all 30 corporations. Including their thousands of manufacturing and service centers all over the globe, their sales outlets, agencies and other operations, they represent an industrial potential of overwhelming proportions:

8   Microsoft was only founded in 1975.

9   Sources: Annual reports; interviews; Electronic News of Sept. 2, 1990 and Nov. 12, 1990; author's estimates. All corporate figures at official average exchange rates for 1990.

- Total sales in 1990 amounted to $581 bill., more than the gross domestic product of all oil producing and other countries in the Near East and Northern Africa put together.

- Growth of total sales reflects the dynamics of the electronics industry: Between 1978 and 1990 it averaged over 10% per year.

- Total profits after taxes in 1990 (incidentally, a bad year) amounted to $22.6 bill. This would have been enough to buy one year's total GDP of pre-war Kuwait with sufficient change for a gasoline refill for every private car in the United States.

- And since the electronics industry includes many high-tech areas such as industrial robots, communications, data processing, audio/visual products, microelectronics etc., the 30 corporations also spent a lot on R&D: $46.6 bill. in 1990 alone, corresponding to about 8% of sales, or about 15% of all the R&D performed in the OECD countries,[10] or enough to buy the complete pre-war GDP of Iraq.

R&D and Profits

Impressive figures. Nevertheless, just in looking at the billions of dollars spent in 1990, one cannot help wondering whether the 30 corporations were really well advised to invest more than double their net earnings in that year on R&D. There is, of course, no rule in the law or accounting books that requires corporations to bring the two values in line. Nor is there anything prohibiting one from being greater than the other. Not even the many handbooks on strategic management would suggest such a thing. In many respects, R&D expenditures and net profit cannot really be compared at all. More than anything else, they differ fundamentally in that the former is the result of a managerial decisions and the latter is not. To put it very simply, R&D expenditures are an input, profits are an output. One of them says what ought to be, the other says what actually was.

In actual practice, of course, this is only true to a limited extent. On the one hand, R&D expenditures cannot be re-decided every day. The commitment associated with R&D expenditures is always of a long-term nature and therefore binds the corporation both in good and in bad times. On the other hand, profits cannot be regarded as an inescapable year-end fate. Even without breaking any accounting rules, management has a certain leeway in

10 Source: OECD.

"shaping" year-end profits to a level considered appropriate by the market and shareholders.

Comparisons between profits and R&D make sense, however, if the figures for 1990 should be part of a persistent and increasingly threatening pattern. Figure 3–1 shows that such a pattern does indeed exist. R&D expenditures for all 30 corporations in the more distant past were not always so very much higher than profits. In the second half of the 1970's and even in the first half of the 1980's, both values were usually quite close to one another. By whatever small amount R&D was larger than profits in one year was generally made up and frequently exceeded by profits in the next. In a way, total R&D in the industry gave the appearance of a reasonable investment with an acceptable payback period.

Beginning in 1984/85, however, this connection seems to have torn. R&D continued to rise to unprecedented heights, whereas profit values lagged and never managed to catch up again. By 1990, the total effect of this

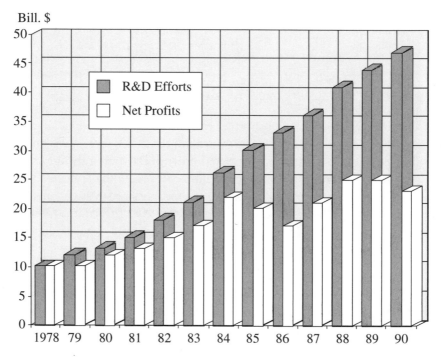

Figure 3–1 Total Net Profits and R&D Expenditures of 30 Major Electronic Corporations in North America, Japan and Europe 1978-1990, $bill

separative drift reached epic proportions: Cumulating both values, one finds that between 1978 and 1990, total R&D expenditures for all 30 corporations exceeded their total profits by a sum of $116.5 bill. And the overall trend was bad. $24.0 bill., or almost 21% of the cumulative total, occurred in the last of the 13 observed years.

The three groups of corporations contributed to this gigantic negative balance to substantially different degrees. Figure 3–2 shows that the differences lay more with profits than with R&D. While all three groups of corporations spent roughly similar amounts on R&D,[11] only in the American group did profits seem to be able to keep up. The result there was, therefore, more or less "in balance." Worst off were the 10 European corporations where profits after taxes were about $73 bill. below R&D expenditures. This means about 61% of the total cumulative "loss", if one were to call it that, occurred in Europe.

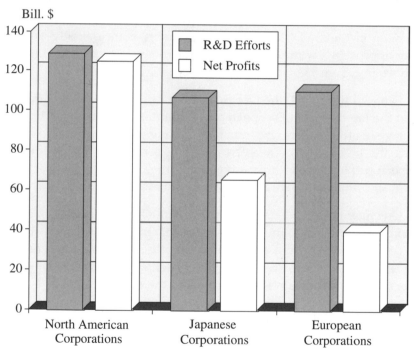

Figure 3–2   Total Profits and R&D Expenditures for 30 Electronics Corporations (1978-1990 by region, $bill.)

11 The problems of differing definitions of R&D will not be addressed here. See Chapter 1 for this question. The assumption was made that at least *company internally*, the definitions of R&D did not change over the period in question, even though substantial differences *between* firms might have existed.

Figure 3–3 shows the same values at the level of individual corporations. It is particularly striking that of the 30 corporations, only two made more profits over the entire period than they spent on R&D. These two were IBM (in 1990 still in admirable health) with a handsome net total of $22.5 bill. which contributed significantly to the overall balance of the North American corporations shown in Figure 3–2, and Matsushita with more modest total net profits of a little under $1.1 bill.

Perhaps one should recall that both companies in this period were also by far the dominant players in their respective markets, IBM in computers and Matsushita in consumer electronics. This is no coincidence. The company with the largest market share can distribute its R&D costs over the largest unit numbers. R&D-induced profit burdens will therefore be correspondingly smaller.

Only a few of the 28 other corporations managed to come out more or less even in their balance of R&D and profits. The majority of companies were deep in the "red." Most of the companies, coincidentally, which the author approached with respect to these numbers, also preferred not to be identified in Figure 3–3.

Even without IBM, the North American balance looks healthier than that of the Japanese and European competition. Among the first 10 companies there are four American companies, among the second 10 also four and among the last 10, two. The corresponding series both for Japanese and European corporations is three, three, four. Among the last seven, or roughly 25%, of all companies there is not a single American one.

One may indeed wonder why the profitability of the ten U.S. corporations in our sample is so much better than that of their European and Japanese counterparts. At first glance, it seems that the American companies have been putting their R&D money to better use. Several considerations, however, reveal that this was not necessarily the case:

- The profitability of American companies was better from the outset. In 1978, the U.S. corporations averaged a net return on sales of 9.3% against 3.4% among Japanese and only 3.1% among European corporations. Maintaining higher profits is far easier than increasing profitability, especially if one also the technology leader as the U.S. was in electronics in virtually every field of the business in 1978.

- U.S. corporations traditionally maintain a far closer watch on profits than those in other major industrialized countries do.

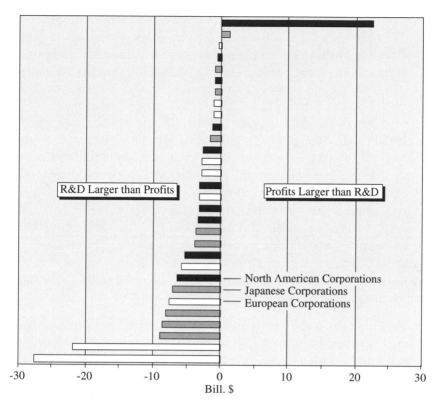

Figure 3–3 Cumulative Profits Minus Cumulative R&D Expenditures for 30 Major Electronics Corporations 1978-1990, $bill.

- The government's share of national R&D spending, on average, is higher in the U.S. than in other countries, notably in Japan. Since this also holds true in the electrical/electronics business, growing R&D ratios would do less damage to the U.S. corporations' bottom lines.

- The specifics of the electronics business might well have contributed to a profit environment that favored U.S. corporations. These include:

  – A larger and homogenous home market over which to spread R&D costs. Other markets, especially those in Europe, are more fragmented and/or dominated by national champions.

  – The predominance of the English language in electronics. Essentially, all modern software languages are based on

English. Or another example: Even the control knobs on Japanese audio or industrial equipment *sold in Japan*, are labelled in English. U.S. electronics companies can therefore sell essentially the same products outside the U.S. as they do domestically, thus improving scale effects further.

What can be deduced from all this? If one agrees with the basic premise that one of the goals of a corporation must be to generate profits, not only in the interest of the corporation itself, but also in the interests of its shareholders, its employees and the public at large, then one may rightfully ask why many of the 30 corporations are pouring more and more money into R&D while at the same time they are achieving smaller and smaller returns. In the long run, R&D as a bottomless pit is not going to work out. Some corporations already felt the effects of this early on. Philips, for example, had to take a net loss of $2.23 bill. in 1990. That does not imply that those losses were exclusively a function of exaggerated R&D spending. But obviously it did not help, either.

The Philips example, moreover, was only part of a general trend. In 1991, the computer giant IBM also experienced an overall net loss for the first time after decades of uninterrupted profits. In the fourth quarter of 1992, even its operating results were in the red. All this was not an isolated phenomenon or the result of a sudden swing in the market,[12] in which for some unfathomable reasons it had become extremely difficult to sell mainframe computers. Figure 3–4 shows that beginning in 1984 (the year in which R&D seriously started to outgrow profits), there was a long-term decline of net return on sales for all company groups. Events at Philips, IBM and others like DEC, Matsushita or Fujitsu that were later all having to cope with serious profitability problems, were part of a larger picture: In 1984, all 30 corporations were making a profit. Their average return on sales was 5.8%. This represented a small improvement over the average return on sales of 5.2% in 1978. By 1990, however, average net return had declined to 3.9% of sales. Three of the 30 corporations had become so weak, that they had been taken over by others. Three more were registering losses.

Whether all this would have turned out differently if the 30 companies had spent less on R&D is hard to say, of course. Profits are determined by many factors, and it is always easy to be wise with hindsight. Considering the increasing speed with which innovations are typically introduced in the

12 See, Zachary et al., 1993.

Return on Sales, %

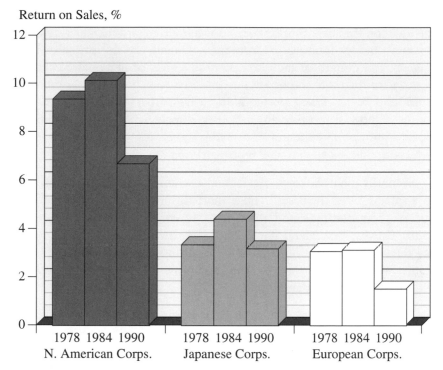

Figure 3–4 Profitability Trends among 30 Major Electronics Corporations (1978, 1984 and 1990, percent of sales)

electronics market, however, there is at least a suspicion that a large part of R&D funds was invested in the wrong products or in mature markets. In the long run, this must do more harm than good to profits. Growing R&D spending, among other effects, will compress product life cycles. The consequences of this for a company or an industry will be addressed in the next two chapters. At this point, we only wish to point out that for every company, there must be some appropriate upper limit for R&D spending and that some companies, to the detriment of their profits, might have already reached this limit or even exceeded it.

R&D and Sales

Now, one might well argue that profits are not the only measure of corporate success. Normally, we also regard an enterprise as successful if it exhibits a large sales volume or—even better—large sales *growth*.[13] It is hard to overlook that nowadays all parties whose lives and fates are in some way dependent on the success of corporations tend to regard increasing sales volumes with tender fondness. Corporate managers are the prime examples. For them, the growth of their company is a sign of personal achievement and is one of the more important success measures. It has a favorable effect on year-end bonuses and portends lucrative careers along with the usual symbols of power and esteem. It boosts respect within the company and general admiration by the public outside. To become "Manager of the Year" or a "Rising Star" is an aim well worth striving for.

Secondly, shareholders, the actual owners of a company, obviously also applaud sales increases. These tend to have a positive effect on the value of their holdings and thus, directly contribute to a shareholder's wealth. Thirdly, financiers, the public, even unions, embrace rising sales since these are a signal of high capacity utilization rates and thus, of job security and credit worthiness. The government, finally, loves both large sales *and* large profits. It taxes both.

In view of this whole chorus of avid supporters, we are probably justified in assuming that sales growth cannot be all bad, all the more so because above average sales growth is an indicator of market share gains which in turn bodes well for future profits. Nevertheless, sales maximization as such can hardly be an (or the) *exclusive* corporate goal, not in the long run at least. After all, it is quite possible to have large sales volumes and still sustain losses. But for the sake of argument, let us, for the moment, assume that this is indeed the case, i.e., that revenue expansion is a corporate goal in its own right. If this is so, then any measure which furthers such sales growth would be a contribution to the attainment of a generally popular goal and would, therefore, justify our most benevolent support. It follows further that if lavish spending on R&D should be such a measure, then it should be duly encouraged. The 46.6-Billion Dollar Question for our 30 corporations in 1990, therefore, must have been: did R&D contribute to sales growth?

13 An interesting contradiction: small start-up companies with high sales growth are the darlings of the business press and the public at large. They are actively supported by governments, shareholders and—sometimes—banks. Once these small companies have grown for a while and have fulfilled the expectations placed in them by becoming large corporations, they are suddenly regarded as bogeymen and frequently held up as symbols of industrial inflexibility or even ethical, monopolistic, ecological or other forms of decay. See, for example, the cases of IBM, Intel, Microsoft, Walmart, Nixdorf and others.

Figure 3–5 shows how R&D expenditures and sales for the same 30 corporations have developed since 1978. To improve comparability, both values were normalized at 100 for 1978. This reveals that sales growth for all three groups of companies lagged far behind R&D growth. On average, sales in all three groups grew by a factor of roughly three, corresponding to an average annual growth rate of 9.6%, in the European group a little lower, in the Japanese group a little higher. R&D in the American and European groups, however, grew by a factor of roughly four, or about 12% per year. In the Japanese group, it even grew by a factor of over six, or about 16% per year. Even if one assumes that the higher average sales growth of 10.6% in the Japanese group (compared to North America's 9.4% and Europe's 8.3%) was caused exclusively by the higher Japanese R&D growth rate (an opinion which does not even find supporters among Japanese researchers) it becomes quite clear that R&D had to grow by disproportionate amounts to gain a relatively small advantage in sales growth.

These differing averages of sales and R&D growth rates, incidentally, were not brought about by a minority of big R&D spenders[14] insufficiently

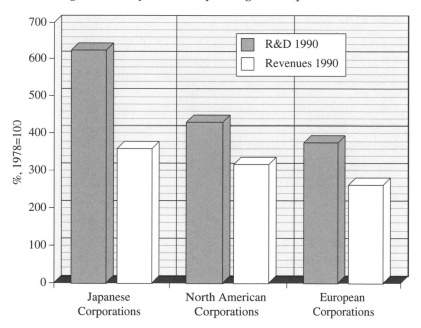

Figure 3–5 Growth in R&D and Revenues for 30 Major Electronics Corporations, 1978=100

balanced by a more thrifty majority. In fact, Figure 3–6 shows that with only two exceptions, sales growth rates in all 30 companies was significantly exceeded by the corresponding R&D growth rates.[15]

One of the two exceptions was Sony (Japan) where R&D and sales growth rates were roughly equal. Interestingly, Sony is generally regarded as a very innovative company. Apparently, it is possible to achieve this reputation without above average R&D growth. The other company was Hewlett-Packard where sales growth was even considerably *higher* than R&D growth. Perhaps it is no coincidence that Hewlett-Packard for a number of years now has been considered one of the best managed and most successful American corporations. Sales and net profits since 1989 have both grown by a factor of three. In addition, it seems to have weathered the most recent crises among many computer companies far better than its competitors.

It should be emphasized that Figure 3–6 is no more than an overall impression. Perhaps it is even an oversimplification because it takes no specific differences between companies into account. No doubt, such differences do exist. For example, not all companies experience similar rates of successful R&D. R&D productivity, i.e., the ratio of R&D results (however one might measure that) to R&D input, varies from company to company and even from project to project.[16] Among other influences, this is determined by the specific characteristics of a technology. Take technology maturity, for example. Achieving a further improvement in a mature, i.e., largely explored, technology that has possibly been known for decades (e.g. extending the useful life of an electricity meter which nowadays can easily survive for decades) is far more difficult than achieving the same degree of improvement in a new technology (e.g. increasing the carrying capacity of high-temperature superconductors) where critical parameters are now only gradually being established.

Other factors can also play important roles in R&D productivity. These include laboratory locations, the growth and size of different market segments, the split of R&D budgets between basic and application oriented

14 R&D spending in terms of sales in our sample of 30 companies ranged widely. They stayed within closest confines in the Japanese group. R&D quotas there ranged from a minimum of 4.7% to 11.1% of sales in 1990. The corresponding values for the European and North American groups were 5.2% to 29.1% and 5.3% to 14.8%, respectively.

15 Shorter observation periods for some corporations were considered in Figure 3–6.

16 For an account of problems regarding the measurement of product development success and failure, see Griffin et al., 1993.

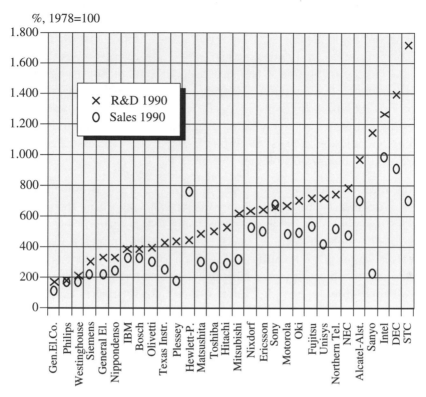

%, 1978=100

× R&D 1990
O Sales 1990

Figure 3–6 R&D and Sales in 1990 for 30 Major Electronics Corporations, 1978=100

research, the quality and duration of researcher education and many other influences which can differ substantially between cultures, between corporations and even within corporations. They all contribute significantly and in varying ways to R&D outcomes. Aggregating these results with respect to total R&D activities loses all these factors and thus fails to explain differences between the more successful corporations and the less successful ones.

Nevertheless, there are some things we do know. One of these is the simple truth that R&D success is not just a matter of money. For instance, one only needs to recall how varied the success rate of Japanese electronics companies was in the 1970s and 1980s. In hardware, they dashed from victory to victory and frequently even manufactured products as subcontractors for their American competitors like Apple and IBM, who then sold these under their own labels. In the world of software, on the other hand, they regularly ended up far behind their American and even European competitors. In spite of often very expensive efforts to the contrary, there is no Japanese Microsoft Corp. in sight. According to a joint U.S./Japanese survey, imports of Japanese non-entertainment software (games etc.) in 1994 were twenty times as large as exports.[17] In the meantime it has also become general knowledge that the much-acclaimed 5th Generation Computer Project, launched amid great fanfare in the first half of the 1980s by MITI and the cream of the Japanese data processing industry, has largely failed. Aggregating all R&D efforts into a single solitary indicator hides such differences between successful and not so successful companies, technologies and projects.

In addition, the nature of R&D is such that there is not only a high degree of uncertainty regarding its results, but also regarding the time when these results will be available. The only thing that *is* certain, is that they do not occur overnight, if at all. As one Japanese R&D manager in the chemical industry once put it to the author, "Research and development is like offering sacrifices to a deity. It would simply be unreasonable to expect results on the way home from the temple." Often enough, R&D projects will take years of work and investment before they even begin to generate revenues. While we are living at a time when product life cycles are continuously getting shorter, the development cycles for new products and processes is not, or at least not as much. In some industries, they are even getting longer, especially if one does not count calendar-years but man-years until projects come to fruition. In the fast-paced electronics industry, development times have occasionally become longer than product life cycles. In the case of semiconductors, for example, the development of a new generation of memory chips on the average takes about four years. Selling this technology as the latest generation is often only possible for two years. This has led to situations in which technologies, whose *preceding* generation has not even been introduced in the market yet, are already in advanced stages of development.

For these reasons, any statements on the revenue effects of R&D efforts should also consider the causal delays involved in this process. It would be best, therefore, to ask if certain R&D outlays of a company at some point in the past have *later* led to certain and identifiable revenues.

---

17   Joint study by the Japan Electronic Industry Assoc., Japan Information Service Industry Assoc., Japan Personal Computer Software Assoc. and American Electronics Industry Assoc. Total exports were ¥13.5 bill. ($131 mill.), total imports ¥259.5 bill. ($2.5 bill). Source: Anon.{31}.

Unfortunately, answering such a question is not very easy, or to put it bluntly, practically out of bounds. Occasionally it might be feasible to associate one specific, or even several, business deals with some specific previous R&D project. Normally, however, this will be quite an exception. For one, corporations regularly take extreme care not to divulge information of this kind. For another, the materialization—or otherwise—of a certain revenue depends not only on the availability of certain technical know-how. Numerous other factors are at least as important, for example, the proper timing of market entry, price structures, competitor reactions, market or company specific cost of capital, liquidity, etc. These and other aspects are only partially subject to company control. But only all of them together determine customer purchasing decisions.

Even if one could determine such a one-to-one causal relationship between previous R&D efforts on the one hand, and later sales results on the other, this would only be of limited use because of the lack of meaningful standards to compare the intensity of such relationships. Unfortunately, the differences between companies, i.e., their varying sizes, structures, operational environments, cultures etc., render such comparisons largely worthless. This would even be true if two companies were to engage in identical markets, aim for the same applications and work on the development of identical technologies. For example, not even comparing the total R&D budget or even the specific project costs of, say, General Electric and Siemens would tell us which of the two has developed a certain computer tomograph with greater "success." We also would not know if this was a (or the) decisive factor in the later fortunes of either company. As indicated previously, success is measured along many dimensions, not only R&D.

In spite of these difficulties in determining the revenue effects of R&D efforts, it can be revealing to compare earlier R&D spending patterns of a company with its revenue patterns at some later time to determine if there is any relationship between the two. At the center of interest would be relative changes, not absolute values. Furthermore, one would have to look at a longer time frame and not just one-year changes. The latter will only rarely be meaningful because short-term erratic movements in budgets and sales will create random noise that hides any gradual, but more basic changes. Over a longer time frame, one would therefore have to determine if an above average increase in R&D expenditures of a company in some earlier period has led to an above average increase in sales volume in the same company over later years.

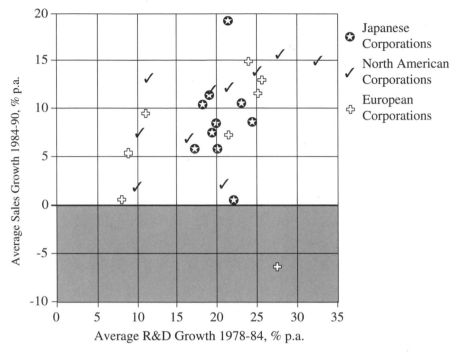

Figure 3–7   R&D growth 1978-84 compared to Sales Growth 1984-90 for 28 Major Electronics Corporations, percent per year

Following this notion, Figure 3–7 seeks to determine if such a relationship exists. The average annual R&D growth of each of our corporations between 1978 and 1984 in the horizontal axis is plotted against its average annual sales growth in the following six years between 1984 to 1990 in the vertical axis. If it were found that a high growth of the former should coincide with a high growth of the latter more often than can be explained by pure chance, then we would have found at least one argument to justify increasing R&D budgets.[18]

Unfortunately, this is not the case. In a simple regression model[19] relating R&D growth to sales growth, only 11% of the variation in sales growth could be explained by R&D investment growth. Other factors must therefore explain the remaining 89%. The model provides empirical support for

18   To be on the safe side, partially incomplete data sets for General Electric Co. (UK) and STC were excluded from Figure 3.7. Their inclusion, however, would have served to emphasize the figure's main message even more.

what is intuitively suggested by the distribution of points in the graph. For one, R&D grew at a very much faster rate than sales. For another, the highest sales growth rates did not concur with the highest R&D growth rates. On average, all corporations increased their R&D budgets in the first six years from 1978 to 1984 by 17.1% per annum and achieved a sales increase of 7.3% per annum in the second six years from 1984 to 1990. In contrast, sales increases over the *total* twelve year period averaged 10.1% per annum, in the first six year period therefore very much faster than in the second. This is almost the opposite of what one might have expected given the enormous rise in R&D outlays between 1978 and 1984. At the same time, it confirms other studies which have generally shown little correlation between the level of R&D spending and [revenues] success.[20] A more recent three-year study of several hundred corporations (90% U.S.) across a dozen industries in fact showed no relationship whatsoever between R&D spending levels and sales, operating income and net income,[21] which seems to contradict the conventional wisdom that spending more on R&D must surely have positive financial impacts.

As a precaution, and since a cause and effect delay of six years in Figure 3–7 was assumed somewhat arbitrarily because the available data happened to cover a time span of 13 years, further regressions with shorter delays were also run. But even under the assumptions that increasing R&D efforts would be reflected in growing revenues after a delay of two, three, four or five years, the predictive values did not improve.

Of course one cannot completely rule out the possibility that the delays between R&D input growth and revenue output growth in the electronics industry are even longer than six years. This could not be tested with the available data on our 30 corporations. However, if this should indeed be the case, then a further question immediately arises: How can substantial R&D budgets be financed in the first place? Even if chief financial officers in industrial corporations were characterized by uncommonly long time horizons (not a property for which managers in this field are—or should be—

---

19 Regression analysis is a statistical technique for investigating the relationship between a response variable (the dependent variable) and one or more explanatory, or independent, variables. It is used to predict the behavior of the dependent variable from given values of the independent variables. Predictive values can lie between 0% and 100%.

20 McGrath and Romeri, 1994, p. 214.

21 Curtis, 1993, unpublished results of the third yearly (1994) contained in a private communication with the author.

generally renowned) and in addition, were willing to accept uncommonly low rates of minimum returns on R&D investments, it is highly unlikely that they will joyfully concur with any further budget increases. One can hardly blame them for this. Even with very low interest rates the expected yield from any R&D project with lead times of seven, ten or even more years adds up to very high amounts.[22]

A simple calculation may serve to illustrate this. Let us assume an R&D project to develop some new product needs $1 mill. annually for ten years with a return requirement of 10% per year before taxes. This means the project has an expected yield of at least $17 mill. ($10 mill. principal plus $7 mill. compound interest) at the end of the tenth year. At the end of this period, the manufacturing and distribution costs of the new product are not covered yet. In an average industrial corporation these can easily run up to 85% of sales. Assuming further, a (relatively modest) return on sales of 5% before taxes, the $17 mill. R&D investment can, therefore, represent only 10% of the total life-time sales of the product. As a result, the new product has to generate sales on the order of $170 mill. before it is withdrawn from the market. Of course, these $170 mill. in revenues will not all occur immediately at the end of the tenth year, but, in turn, will be spread out over time. If this period (the product life cycle) again lasts ten years, then given an equal distribution of annual sales and a 10% interest rate, the required sales volume goes up to $277 mill. Finally, as we have heard above, R&D deities are not always in a mild or generous mood. Sometimes they are not even listening. One successful product development, therefore, can easily be joined by several complete or partial failures. The lone winner then also has to recover their costs, in addition to its own. This can easily double or even triple the required sales yield again.

That such calculations are not completely unrealistic can also be seen in industrial branches other than electronics. According to the Swiss pharmaceutical firm Hoffmann-La Roche,[23] the average costs of developing a new medicine have risen sharply in recent decades. Whereas in the 1950s and 1960s they were on the order of $20 mill. per product, they already reached $40 mill. by the middle of the 1970s and $125 mill. by the middle of

---

22　Given this delay, even Sougiannis', 1994, finding that a one-dollar increase in R&D expenditure leads to a two-dollar increase in profit *over a seven-year period*, does not look very attractive.

23　Drews, 1993.

the 1980s. In the first half of the 1990s, costs averaged $231 mill. per product, corresponding to a growth of about 1,000% over 30 years.[24] These costs include a share in the costs of other (failed or cancelled) projects as well as the costs of non-product-oriented basic and applied research expenditures. Since only about one pharmaceutical product in ten entering clinical trials ever makes it to the market, this cost allocation is relatively high. Compounding $231 mill. for an average product life cycle of ten years at 10% already amounts to $600 mill. Adding the average 75% share of sales for manufacturing and distribution typical in the pharmaceutical industry means that, on average, every approved product has to generate $2.4 bill. in sales to be profitable.

The value of such extrapolations lies not so much in their numbers as in their ability to show that interest rates as well as R&D lead times and product life times are critical parameters. The former is predominantly determined by the capital market. It is largely an exogenous factor. The latter two are far more easily influenced. A company would be well advised to think about them and use them as levers in the shaping of its R&D policies. Very long R&D lead times can have rather unpleasant consequences, both financially for the company, as well as career-wise for the responsible division or R&D managers. It is little wonder, therefore, that the acceleration of development times has found such intense interest in management literature in recent years.

Evaluation

Although the foregoing remarks and figures cover a fairly long period and a relatively large number of companies in a single roughly defined industry, the conclusions which can be drawn from them are limited in one respect: They rest on only three variables which describe the investment in, and the results of, industrial research and development. It would certainly have been interesting, for example, to break down R&D costs further into product and process development costs, or into personnel and material costs. Equally informative would have been a differentiation between mature and emerging markets. Unfortunately, the available data did not allow this.

---

24 Zell, 1994, p. 43, also gives $250 mill. per product as the development cost of one conventional (chemically based) pharmaceutical, as opposed to $125 mill. for a genetically based one.

For these reasons, it would be a mistake to arrive at any final verdicts regarding the role of R&D in a corporation based only on the above observations. In any case, they do not apply to "the industrial firm" in general. If at all, they could only refer to large industrial corporations. The smallest of our 30 companies had revenues of $2 bill. in the last year of our survey. As such, it is already a giant among industry in general. The largest company had revenues of close to $70 bill. The situation in small and medium-sized companies and especially in technology-driven start-up ventures differs dramatically from that in large corporations. In smaller and highly specialized companies, the R&D function or the attention to technology is often the very mainspring of the organization's functioning. Frequently, it is not even located in a central or divisional department, but is the essential core of the entrepreneurial activity as such.

While the foregoing analysis should, therefore, not be employed as, say, a guideline for appropriate R&D budgets in the electronics industry, it does lead to some serious questions and considerations. Some of these considerations might very well contain objections to the foregoing analysis. One could argue, for example, that only the volumes of R&D, sales and profits were used, with no consideration for any other indicators of corporate performance. Any doubts regarding the sense of enormous and growing R&D spending would only be appropriate if one:

a)   looked at the complete value-added chain, not just R&D, sales and profits. Only then, would it be possible to conclude that R&D had indeed grown disproportionately and not just at the expense of some other item.

b)   supplied unambiguous proof that the increase in R&D and the decrease in profitability of the 30 companies between 1978 and 1990 was not merely coincidental or specific only to the electronics industry.

c)   measured the utility, or disutility, of R&D not through aggregate values but only on the basis of specific R&D projects or activities.

Essentially, all three objections are valid. In reply, however, one should point out the following:

a)   It is quite possible that one or even several elements of the value-added chain in our 30 corporations has been partly or completely substituted by R&D. One could imagine, for example, that as a result of a major R&D project, it has become possible to replace product parts made of expensive gold with cheaper aluminum. Increased technology costs might then have been offset by lower raw material costs. If that were the case, however, judicious planning and management of the substitution process under no circumstances should have allowed the simultaneous decline in profits as we have observed above. Otherwise, it would have been cheaper to stick to gold. The same is true of process technologies: Improving the efficiency of the production process at great expense without due consideration of the excess capacities created thereby, is not without risks. The problems of the highly productive Japanese automobile industry which is now in frantic search of a corresponding domestic demand is ample evidence of this.

b)   If profitability in the years prior to 1990 had declined anyway, irrespective of increased R&D spending (for example, due to market saturation, declining rates of investment by customers etc.) then our 30 corporations would have had all the more reason to adapt their R&D spending to a changing situation. In the long run, it is very difficult to sustain growth in a stagnating market just by increasing R&D. Moreover, it is very dangerous to place all one's bets on R&D or on new technology when the overall health of a company has already declined. Due to the rising costs of innovation, this often does more harm than good. In addition, there are always delays to be considered: R&D spends money today to earn benefits at some point in the future. A corporation that is fighting liquidity problems now needs this money in the present, not at some later time. In spite of many technology promises, one should not forget that the decision to invest in R&D is hedged with greater risks than any other management measure. This investment typically also has the longest payback and can therefore be a very dangerous gamble. The prospect of sitting at a rich table tomorrow or the day after is no good if one is starving today. All too often, the grand new R&D initiatives of companies that are fighting for survival with their backs to the wall[25] are reminiscent of betting against the bank: double or nothing. Even with double, there is the danger that they will end up with nothing.

c)   It should be stated clearly that it is not argued that all and every piece of R&D in our 30 corporations is superfluous and should therefore be given up. In electronics, possibly even more than in other areas, there are, and will to continue to be, a virtually unlimited number of important R&D projects. These make eminent sense, both for the corporations pursuing them, as well as the markets and consumers they serve. Basically, the world does not wish to forego the benefits of technological progress in electronics. In the view of this author at least, there is also little doubt that, to a certain extent, the world really needs this progress too. More or less the same is true for all areas of industry, perhaps with the exception of the arms industry. But this very point also underlines the essential message of this chapter: The conflict between justified R&D, on the one hand, and a hard to justify cost explosion on the other, emphasizes the need for a far more judicious and careful selection of R&D projects.

Overall, the foregoing analysis of our 30 corporations and the ensuing questions highlight the usefulness of *continuously* reassessing the role of R&D for the realization of corporate success. There is little doubt that over the last few decades the contribution of technology to corporate success has grown significantly. Technology has also received the attention it deserves from management, markets and the world of finance. Like all good things, however, it can be overdone. One is left with the distinct impression that this is exactly what happened among of the corporations studied here. Judging from some other cases the author has had the opportunity to see, they are not the first and certainly not the last were this has occurred. The R&D function was assigned a far greater role for the attainment, or defense, of compet-

---

25 Both Yamaha (during its "motorcycle war" with Honda, see Stalk and Hout, 1990, p. 58 et seq.) and AEG in times of crisis did this.

itive advantage than was really justified. That can turn out to have been a costly delusion.

The conviction that is at the heart of this type of delusion runs somewhat like this: If a company is not technologically ahead of its competitors (frequently equated with spending more on R&D) it does not stand a chance of winning the contest for market shares.[26] Technology, so the belief often goes, will sell itself[27] and will even offset higher costs and prices.[28] The truth is that there are numerous examples where it was not the best technology or the pioneering firm which achieved lasting success. Some of these examples are listed in Table 3–2.

Probably one of the better known examples of this was Matsushita subsidiary Victor's triumph in setting the world video recorder standard in the 1970s. The two competing systems at the time—one, Sony's Betamax system, the other, Philips' Video 2000—were both technically superior to Victor's VHS System. In addition, Betamax also had time on its side, since it was introduced a year earlier than the subsequent market leader. The Matsushita engineers decided to leave the pioneering efforts to Sony. Until a significant market had been built, they used the time that passed to develop a sufficiently competitive product and additionally to establish a mass distribution system instead. Based on a larger distribution network, better licensing arrangements and greater software availability, Matsushita was then able to achieve its dominant market position.[29] As it turned out,

26 This can sometimes lead to remarkable statements. In an advertisement in the magazine Der Spiegel of 12 December, 1994, p. 6-7, in which Japan's Fujitsu emphasized some of its many technological achievements, the company made the following profound observation (translated from German): "Just like you, we have learned that today's competition leaves only two possibilities: Take the lead or stay behind."

27 A similar conviction seems to hold true for whole countries: "By in effect carving out entirely new industries that turn out intriguing new products never before seen by consumers, manufacturers will be able to tap untouched veins of consumption in Japan. And this will eventually lead to the expansion of world markets in the long term." Source: Yoshikawa, 1994.

28 For example, this was the typical strategy followed by the European motorcycle, automobile and camera industries when first faced with the successful import of Japanese low-end products that were competing on price.

29 Cusumano, 1986, p. 161; Cusumano et al., 1991.

Matsushita's decisive competitive advantages did not have much to do with technology.

Table 3–2 Market Pioneers and Later Market Leaders

Product Innovation	Pioneer	Later Market Leader
Home video recorder	Philips/Sony	Matsushita
Laptop computer	Epson	Toshiba
Electronic typesetting	Intertype	AM International
Permanent four wheel drive	Audi	Subaru
Computer tomograph	EMI	G. E. / Siemens
Kidney lithotripter	Dornier Medizin	Siemens
Computer numerical control	Bendix	Fanuc
Industrial robot	Unimation/Puma	GMF

Source: UBM

In spite of this and other examples, many firms still prefer to stick to an unspoken rule that seems to strongly influence innovation thinking: If in doubt, put more money into technology development. It is this thinking that lies at the heart of today's R&D escalation. To return to the war metaphor, it is also reminiscent of a widespread battle tactic in World War I, i.e., to dig into trenches and lob as many grenades as possible at the other side in the hope that the enemy will run out of grenades first. On the battlefields of France, tens of thousands of soldiers on both sides were sacrificed in this manner for a mere stretch of road or even a ditch.

In spite of many R&D managers' conviction to the opposite, it has yet to be shown that throwing more and more R&D resources at technological problems will always lead to decisive competitive advantages. In microelectronics, for example, millions of R&D dollars are sacrificed with every new generation of chips for a market entry headstart of sometimes only a few weeks. Frequently enough, these dollars are gone for good. The high initial prices that the market pioneer supposedly can charge do not survive anywhere close to long enough and occasionally even evaporate before they have really begun.[30] The large Korean technology-intensive industry groups like Samsung, Gold Star and Hyundai that are presently doing their utmost to break into Japanese technology domains and even enter the market with new generations of products before their Japanese competitors can do so, are just learning this the hard way.[31] Precisely *because* a clever imitator or technology follower is not faced with many of the uncertainties and market opening costs with which a pioneer has to struggle, the number two on the starting blocks again and again can be number one across the finishing line.[32] But having achieved that position, number two will also have to cope with number one's problems.

To repeat, however, the reader should beware of hasty conclusions. The intention of this simple analysis is only to cast some doubts on whether investing more in R&D will invariably result in more profits or larger sales volumes. It does not mean to imply that R&D has become superfluous, but only that some rethinking would be in order. Think of R&D as supplying an arsenal. Similar to World War I, having cannons and grenades alone was not enough to win the war. Of course, *not* having them would have quickly led to severe problems. In other words, having them and using them was important, but not decisive. Since everybody had them, they offered no strategic advantages. They only allowed each side to hold its ground as long as it had the means to do so. Even for the later victor, this is a very wasteful way of waging a war.

Applying this thought to R&D, changes its character in a subtle, but immensely important way: R&D is not a *sufficient*, but only a *necessary*, condition of success. Access to the right technologies at the right time is only the entry ticket to participate in the fight for market shares. It is not the (only) means to win the fight.

30 A typical example: the case of the 4MBit DRAMs.

31 Arai and Ando, 1993.

32 In the pharmaceutical business, where manufacturers of generic drugs have managed to gain significant market shares by taking advantage of other companies' previous R&D efforts, this has become very visible in recent years. See Clifford, 1992, p. 60 et seq.

What then are the means? More about this point later. For the time being, one can safely state that in many areas, technology is still important, particularly where totally new and emerging capabilities drastically improve the productivity of the manufacturing process or basically change the acceptability of products in the marketplace. But this does not remain true for all times. Whether a car can be manufactured in 16 or 32 man-hours may be a crucial competitive aspect today. But if the most efficient producer should one day only need two man-hours and the most inefficient four, then any R&D for further improvement of labor productivity by either one will not count for much. Other things will then be far more important. Increasingly, corporate success will not only hinge on the technical features of a new product or on introducing a new generation of microchips on the market a few weeks ahead of competitors.[33] More and more, customers will consider other criteria in their purchasing decisions. These will include service, durability, utility, price, design, maintenance, long-term supplier viability and a number of other factors, only part of which are determined by technology.

From the point of view of corporate management, changing the character of the R&D function in this way transforms it into one of the necessary costs of doing business. It becomes comparable to the costs of the personnel department, office materials, raw materials, capital or even periodic window cleaning. It also means that R&D can become an area of rich potential cost savings. This is not only true of the improvement of R&D efficiency where much has already been achieved in recent years. Also, the careful identification of those R&D projects which are really essential for the well-being of the corporation, or vice-versa, the determined cancellation of those that are not, becomes a crucial activity. In World War I terms: what one needs are not piles of cannons and grenades to devastate the enemy, but just enough to prevent being overrun. Given the enormous business volume associated with our 30 corporations and their average R&D expenditures of 8% of sales, approaching R&D budgets not with the thought to what is maximally possible, but to what is minimally necessary can translate into enormous savings.

---

33 Excellent on this point with many examples: Crawford, 1992.

Summary

For an improved understanding of the role of R&D in relation to other corporate activities, the R&D expenditures, net profits and revenues of 30 very large electrical and electronics manufacturers were compared over a period of 13 years lasting from 1978 through 1990. A third of the corporations were based in the US, in Japan and in Western Europe, respectively. Total revenues of all 30 corporations in 1990 amounted to $581 bill., their net profits to $22.6 bill., and their R&D efforts to $46.6 bill.

The comparison of R&D and profits revealed that both values were roughly balanced in the first half of the observed period. However, while the former exhibited exponential growth over the complete 13-year period, the latter began to stagnate in 1984. In later years, the difference between both values grew by significant amounts annually. Cumulatively, this difference reached a total value of $116.5 bill. in 1990. The greater part of the negative balance occurred among European corporations. Only in two of all 30 corporations, however, did total profits achieve a higher value than total R&D expenditures between 1978 and 1990. Interestingly, both of these corporations were also world leaders in their respective market segments.

The comparison of R&D and revenues conveyed a similarly problematic impression. While R&D efforts among U.S. and European corporations grew roughly by a factor of four, Japanese corporations increased their R&D by a factor of six. For this significantly higher R&D growth rate, however, Japanese corporations were only rewarded with a marginally higher sales growth rate of 1% per year over U.S. corporations and 2.1% per year over European corporations. Total sales of all 30 corporations grew by an average of about 10% per year over the 13 year period.

Again, with only two (different) exceptions, the growth of R&D budgets was far higher than that of sales for all 30 companies. In the interest of avoiding overhasty conclusions from this result, the possibility of a delayed influence of R&D investments on sales was also considered. However, only 11% of the variation in sales growth between 1984 and 1990 could be explained by R&D investment growth between 1978 and 1984.

Overall, the observations lead to the conclusion that the contribution of R&D to corporate well-being should be subjected to serious and continuous scrutiny. It is argued that R&D on its own is a necessary, but not a sufficient, condition for the attainment of decisive competitive advantage. Technology leadership alone is not enough; technology followership is not deadly. In formulating R&D budgets, it is therefore advisable to follow the principle of investing only what is minimally necessary rather than what is maximally possible.

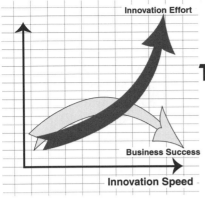

4

The Growth of R&D and the Acceleration Trap[1]

In Chapters 1 and 2 it was shown how the R&D function emerged in the second half of the last century as a systematic and structured industrial discipline in its own right. This happened first in the wealthy nations of North America and Europe, joined later by Japan. One section in Chapter 2 showed the orders of magnitude to which R&D has grown after World War II and especially over the last twenty years. Today, roughly 50% of the R&D effort is financed by industry. An even greater share is carried out there. For this reason, in Chapter 3, the R&D efforts, net profits and revenues of 30 major corporations in North America, Europe and Japan were analyzed in greater detail over a period of 13 years. The most important finding there was that while expenditures for R&D had witnessed explosive growth in all 30 corporations, the results of this spending boom justified some severe doubts.

Technology and the Product Life Cycle

An outsider's reaction to these findings could be to just lean back and wait. At some point, or at the very latest when one or more of the participating companies could no longer afford it, one might reason, the R&D race must come to an end.

---

1   See von Braun, 1990 and 1991 I, II and III.

Apart from the fact that ending it in this way would have disastrous effects for the corporations involved and their work forces, such an attitude also fails to take the feedback mechanisms in such escalation processes into account: An increase in A's R&D leads to an increase in B's R&D which directly or indirectly leads to an increase in A's R&D again. Breaking out of such vicious circles is not always easy. More will be said about this in Chapter 6. For the moment, we will take a closer look what effects growing R&D budgets and their resultant technologies have on a company's product spectrum.

We will begin with what everybody knows: Ever since mankind has produced goods it has depended on the availability of certain underlying technologies. These can either be essential requirements for manufacturing, for components, for the functionality of the end-product, or for all three. For example, anybody who wants to make and sell computers nowadays needs microchip technology; food storage requires preservation technologies; a camera will not work without optical technologies; and without printing technologies, the reader would be spared the effort of reading this book. One leads to the other. As new technologies are developed, new products become feasible. Piano concertos, for example, were therefore only "produced" after "piano technology," the pianoforte, had been developed, a stringed keyboard instrument that could be played both softly (*piano*) as well as loudly (*forte*).

Keep in mind, though, that a new technology does not *always* lead to products that hitherto did not exist. Not infrequently, and perhaps in the majority of cases, there is already a previous product which can fulfill the same functions, even though at a higher cost, or not as fast, or with more noise or in some other "worse" way. Before Gutenberg's printing press, books were written with pens. Before detergents, laundry was washed with curd soap. Before jumbo-jets, the oceans were crossed in clippers (first the sailing, later the flying kind). And although it may be difficult to imagine, before computers, one could even do calculations: with fingers, an abacus, a slide rule or log tables. That was often quite tedious, but using the latter, which in Kepler's (1571–1630) days were a brand new innovation, he did manage to shatter our concept of the world.

To the extent that new products and the technologies which they incorporate are cheaper, faster, stronger, smaller, bigger, cleaner or in some other way "better," they will replace products that incorporate, or were manufactured with, older technology.[2] This is not only true for epochal technology changes such as the switch from piston-driven propeller aeroplanes to jets, from sailing ships to steamers or from stone tools to metal tools. Inconspicuous, evolutionary technology changes, such as a slightly easier-to-use or cheaper can-opener or cork screw, the improved version of a software package, the more appealing design of a ball-point pen can also shift market shares and sales figures.

Shorter Product Life Cycles

New technology thus leads to new products, leastways sometimes. The reason is simple: If a new technology allows better products than an old one, it will limit, or even end, the saleability of products based on the old technology. In other words, one product life cycle ends, a new one begins. But the opposite effect is also true: The speed with which an industry introduces new products in the market forces a company to take on corresponding R&D efforts in order to keep up. It follows, that the introduction of a new product on the market, i.e., the beginning of a new product life cycle, will lead to R&D efforts by competitors, which in turn will lead to new technology. And from this new technology, new products are created. We have come full circle.

Time plays an important role in this. Typically, the substitution of old for new products does not occur instantaneously. For example, even when a new and improved car model is introduced, some customers prefer the old one for a while, perhaps because it can now be had at a lower price, or even because they need some time to come to terms with the new model. The duration of such substitution processes can vary widely between goods and markets and last anywhere from a few weeks or months to decades or centuries. It addition, it can also involve two or more generations of a technology at the same time.[3] For example, there are some remote regions on this planet

2   For a definition of "better" as "value to the customer," see Forbis and Mehta, 1981; see also Abernathy et al., 1982

3   Fisher and Pry, 1971; Saito, 1990, quotes Tsuyoshi Kawanishi, senior managing director at Toshiba, with a nice example: "At Toshiba, 4M DRAMs are in the mass production stage, 16M DRAMs are under technological improvement, and 64M DRAMs are in the research and development stage. We make it a policy to handle three generations of our products simultaneously."; Anon. {9}, 1993, has another example: "In a lesson learned from Japan, Gilette has waves of new products moving continuously through its laboratories—with a replacement nearing completion even as each new product is being launched. The firm now has as many as 20 new prototypes under development at any one time."

where muscle power has not yet been replaced by the steam engine while in other regions its successor technology Diesel power generation has already been replaced by solar cells. On the other hand, when spray cans containing non-CFC propellants appeared on the market, it quickly became difficult to sell spray cans containing CFC, even before there were laws condemning it.

In industry, the length of time that a technology was superior to a previous one, without itself being replaced by an even more recent one, used to be quite long. Occasionally, it lasted many years. To give an extreme example, even after the introduction of the automobile, horse and cart still remained in use for decades. In some of the rural areas of the industrialized countries, one can sometimes still see them today. Also within the automobile industry itself, a lot of time passed before innovative changes were accepted everywhere. The automatic shift, for example, was in widespread use in the United States for many years before European manufacturers even bothered to seriously think about it as a standard option. Management would always rest in the comfortable confidence that there was enough time to worry about it, "when the need should arise." Technology-induced substitution processes in the past, therefore, were something which occasionally demanded the attention of corporate management, but did not rob anybody of their sleep either.

All this is changing. Today's telescoping of events over time is a generally recognized phenomenon affecting many walks of life. The explosive growth of science and technology in recent decades described in Chapter 2 has accelerated the speed of change in industry, government and society enormously. More things now happen in five years than previously did in 50.[4] These changes have also taken hold in industry. In many markets, one can observe how products based on old technologies are being replaced increasingly faster by products based on newer technologies. One consequence of this has been that the period between the introduction of a new product on the market and its withdrawal because of technological obsolescence[5] is getting shorter and shorter.[6]

There are numerous examples of this. Some are included in Figure 4–1 which also shows that decreasing product life cycles are by no means

---

4   See Singh, 1993.

5   The emphasis here is on saleability, not on the technical functionality of a good. The latter period can be much longer than the length of time a product is successfully marketed. Many products (e.g. home freezers) have, in fact, exhibited lengthening useful lives, see Bayus, 1988, Tab. 2, p. 217.

6   Very instructive in this context: Ricca, 1988, p. 35.

restricted to technology-intensive branches of industry such as aerospace or pharmaceuticals.[7] In the field of detergents, for example, there were no important innovations between the middle of the 1960s when low-foam machine suds were introduced and 1985. Then phosphate-free detergents entered the market. This set off a whole avalanche of innovations. Non-phosphate detergents were followed by liquid detergents, compact detergents, super compact detergents and color friendly detergents. These were only the changes relating to the detergents themselves. Ecological pressures and raw materials economics began to target detergent packaging too. This has recently led to all sorts of innovative refill systems, emulsifiers, material and volume reductions and other product modernizations, most of which have required extensive R&D and investment efforts.[8]

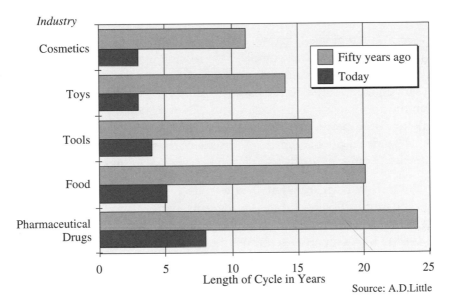

Figure 4–1 Decreasing Product Life Cycles

7   According to Zell, 1994, p. 43, development times for biotech pharmaceuticals are only five to nine years as opposed to conventional medicines with an average of about twelve. Development costs are also 50% lower. Since an increasing share of pharmaceutical development money is being spent on biotech this will contribute to a faster obsolescence rate for conventional drugs. Prerequisite for this, of course, will be a success rate among biotech firms that is somewhat better than that observed in recent years.

8   Interview with Henkel KGaA, Düsseldorf.

In the food and household goods industries, which are also normally not associated with a high degree of technology content or technology change, the picture is much the same. In 1994, a total of 20,076 new consumer goods appeared on the shelves of America's supermarkets, a 14.3% increase over 1993. This compares with only 1,365 new products launched in 1970. Since by now over 90% of all product innovations in supermarkets are taken off the shelves again within two years of introduction,[9] product life cycles must, on average, have become very short indeed. Similar trends can be observed in other industrialized countries and in other industries, too. For example, with about 1.5 million units per year, the largest selling automobile during the mid 1960s in the U.S. was the Chevrolet Impala. In 1991, the largest seller was the Honda Accord with only 400,000 units although the total market was far larger.[10]

On a different level, Figure 4–2 shows the average age of the product spectrum of one individual company decreasing over time. In 1975, 40% of this company's sales represented products that had been introduced less than six years ago, 33% of sales represented products that had been introduced within the previous six to ten years, and 27% represented products that had been introduced more than ten years earlier. By 1986, or only 11 years later, sales of products introduced less than six years ago had increased to 56%, while sales of older products had decreased correspondingly.

Such overviews are often used to reflect the innovativeness of a company. The implication is that the younger its average product spectrum, the more up to date and state-of-the-art its products, and thus, the more nimble and flexible the company itself must be. Numerous corporations do in fact include such figures in their advertisements, company brochures or annual reports, although they usually fail to state how they define the age of product or what "a" product is and what makes it into a "new" product.[11]

---

9   Anon. {28}, 1995.

10   Wheelwright and Clark, 1992, p. 3.

11   For example, Clorox Company in its 1995 annual report states: "As you can see from the graph below, we introduced a record 38 new products worldwide in fiscal '95, up from 28 a year ago and only six in fiscal '91." 3M Corp. used to insist that 25% of each division's annual sales come from products developed in the preceding five years, see Smith, 1990, p. 25. Today this value has been increased to 30% from products developed within less than the last four years. Additionally, 10% of revenues must come from last year's innovation, all this apparently with some mixed results, see Anon. {29}, 1995, Anon.{32}, 1995.

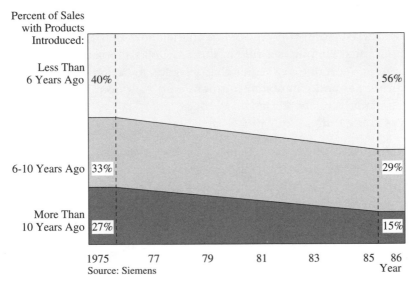

Figure 4–2 Declining Average Age of Products

There is, incidentally, also the opposite case where a firm wishes to emphasize the continuity of a product line, even though such a continuity only exists in outward appearance. For example, Persil has been one of the best selling washing detergent brands in a number of European countries since the beginning of the century. According to industry sources, typical product life cycle lengths in this business today are on the order of five years. "Persil stays Persil" ("Persil bleibt Persil") was therefore an extremely effective advertising slogan in Germany a few years ago for a product that seemed to defy this rule and that generations of families were therefore familiar with. Although its marketing emphasizes unbroken presence, Persil's formulation has actually been changed many times since its introduction. The Volkswagen Beetle, another example, was claimed to be the same car for decades, yet the last one probably did not have a single bolt in common with the first one. At best, its outward appearance and its basic concept (two doors, air-cooled rear engine) showed a certain resemblance.

There are no standard or generally accepted rules to determine the newness of a product unambiguously. In the author's experience, however, two basic criteria seem to be emerging which can help in judging a product's newness: The first follows a value-added approach. According to this, a product is new if a certain *minimum share of the value-added con-*

tained in the product is based on functions, features or components which were not there before. There is nothing in the books that says how high this minimum must be, but as a rule of thumb, 20-30% looks about right. The 30%-limit is a soft one. A smaller change tends to be in a realm where the same processes and components as before are still dominant; any change could equally well be termed an adaption. A larger one increasingly involves doing things really differently.

The second criterion is inspired by the teachings of the marketing enthusiasts and follows customer perception. According to this, a product is new *if the customer thinks* it is new, irrespective of any actual technical, physical or other changes it might have undergone. The product's newness, in this case, is judged purely along subjective lines and can, but does not have to, be based on new performance characteristics or a new design. Even a new selling price can fulfill this criterion.

Applying both rules can obviously lead to different results. Changing the color of a camera body from black to red, for instance, or introducing a new taste for an established brand of chewing gum hardly constitutes a "new" product in the sense of the first criterion. But in the sense of the second, it might. Typically, innovations in areas which are subject to changing fashions or taste preferences will be judged by aspects of this kind. Replacing a rotary phone with a push-button phone, on the other hand, will probably fulfill the first, but possibly not the second criterion. While the telephone's functions and outward appearance from the point of view of the user are not very much different from the old product, its technical insides have undergone a complete overhaul.

On the Emergence of Shorter Product Life Cycles

Company attitudes regarding the phenomenon of shorter product life cycles differ. On the one hand, a faster pace of new product introductions promises new business opportunities in livelier markets.[12] On the other hand, this causes competition in the overall business environment to become fiercer. R&D budgets will therefore have to grow because new technologies have to be developed at increasingly faster rates or because the greater variety of products on the market forces them to follow more technology paths at the same time.[13]

12 See, for example, McCreadie, 1989.

A good question would be why product life cycles have to continue to get shorter in the first place.[14] After all, technology does not become obsolete all on its own. It does so because somebody wants it to. As a rule, that "somebody" is a corporation or a research lab which develops something new because it has happened to stumble across some new discovery, or—more frequently—because it is convinced that the market will take a fancy to a new idea, or because it feels that it has to keep up with competitors. At the same time, however, the development of new technologies is getting more and more expensive.[15] Normally, any rational corporate decision maker would seek to reduce such costs if they do not contribute to corporate well-being, either through the expansion of sales or through the reduction of costs. One would expect that this should be enough to balance any tendencies toward a further shortening of product life cycles.

As we have seen in the example of our 30 companies in Chapter 3, many companies today assign R&D, technology and technology leadership a crucial role in attaining competitive advantage, both in principle and in specific instances. This conviction is certainly not completely wrong. In the rich and frequently saturated markets of the West, where huge production capacities are available at almost a moment's notice and where manufacturers are wooing increasingly choosy customers, technology and technology-related aspects like quality and delivery times count more and more heavily in shaping customer purchasing decisions. This is true both in the industrial markets, where purchasing decisions are usually (or at least, should be) based on more rational criteria, as well as in the consumer or fashion markets, where the sheer drive of novelty or "change for the sake of change" may be decisive.[16]

If exaggerated, however, the conviction of technology's role in shaping business success can lead both markets and competition significantly astray. A little story may serve to illustrate this: In May 1984, Asahi Shinbun, one of the leading Japanese dailies, carried an insufficiently confirmed story that Bravice International Inc., Japan, had developed a personal computer for the automatic translation of Japanese texts into English.[17] The claim was that the

13 Wheelwright and Clark, 1992, p. 4.

14 For an excellent discussion of whether product life cycles are really getting shorter or whether empirical findings just make it seem that way, see Bayus, 1994.

15 Petroni, 1985, p. 109.

16 See Buskirk, 1986.

17 See Nishioka, 1991.

computer system's recognition rate was 85-90% accurate and that it could distinguish up to 240 different idioms and meanings of Japanese written characters from the context of their use. To top it off, it would also be fairly cheap. This performance went far beyond anything that was possible then (and maybe still is today), even with mainframes. At the time, it led to what was to be called the "Bravice Shock" among firms working on automatic translation systems. The Shock triggered a whole torrent of new product announcements. In a very short period the market was flooded with translation systems, which only equalled Bravice in that they could not keep the promises with which they were marketed. A single premature technology announcement had set off a competitive blaze and caused enormous unrest in the market. Many suppliers, research establishments and gullible customers lost a lot of money. A few years passed before calm was restored in the automatic translation business. Bravice International filed for bankruptcy in January 1991. The responsible editor of Asahi Shinbun is said to have had very red ears.[18]

In day-to-day business, the "newness" of a product or the high-tech image of a company is often equated with the level of its technological development. In this way it contributes to a company's or a product's market success. A firm's technical image can also be nourished from other sources, however. In the pharmaceutical industry, for example, the average age of a company's patent portfolio plays an important role in the valuation of the company's share by the stock market.[19] If the patents contributing significantly to present sales are about to run out, pressure builds to develop successor patents. Since this will soon be the case for a number of its presently profitable products, it is not surprising that in 1991, Hoffmann-La Roche spent 14.9% of sales on R&D. This is quite high already, but isolating just its pharmaceutical business, Hoffman's R&D efforts reached a staggering 23.1% of revenues. Other firms followed suit, Pfizer with 10% overall and 20.1% for pharmaceuticals, Ciba-Geigy with 10.4% and 16.7%, Glaxo

18 A similar case is reported to have occurred in June 1992 when TSD Corp., a small Japanese computer software company, managed to persuade investors that it had the rights to a miracle vaccine for AIDS that was due for clinical trials in Thailand and Russia. Share prices immediately shot up to ¥3,650 from a previous ¥1,000. This allowed TSD to save some ¥1.5 bill. through the exchange of shares for maturing convertible bonds. When it was later revealed that there were no clinical trials in the offing, share prices nose-dived again. TSD went bankrupt in November 1993. As of this writing, the case is under investigation by the Tokyo Securities and Exchange Commission, see Morishita, 1995.

19 Sullivan, 1993.

with 14.0% and 14.1%, and Merck with 11.1% and 13.7%. By 1994, the five firms increased their overall R&D expenditures again to 15.8%, 13.8%, 9.8%, 15.0% and 9.6%, respectively, implying even higher increases in their pharmaceutical R&D spending.[20]

A company offering a new product with improved or radically new technology will do so because it hopes to profit from the quasi-monopoly position it holds as long as competitors for technical, financial or legal reasons cannot offer the same or better features. Similarly, a company whose market share is eroding because its products are no longer state-of-the-art will attempt to strengthen its competitive position by improving the technology incorporated in its present products or by designing new products based on completely new technologies.

Thus, as companies rely more and more on technology as a means of differentiating their products in the market, the instruments to achieve such differentiation naturally attain a greater prominence in the company's thinking and actions. In other words, R&D budgets will rise.[21] And as companies spend more money on R&D they will also develop new technologies faster. The products based on these technologies will thereupon enter the market more rapidly and thus lead to a faster and faster substitution of old products.

Strategies of Technology Leaders and Followers

A technology leader, i.e., the company that is most advanced in a given technology, but not necessarily the leader in the market where that technology is employed, typically has two options in a technology-flavored competitive situation: Either it can take advantage of its quasi-monopoly position and seek early and high profits as long as there is no competitor in sight that might endanger this monopoly position. Or it can establish entry barriers to competitors which render attempts to challenge its leadership position either too risky, too expensive or otherwise unattractive. There are a number of ways to go about building such barriers, including the following:[22]

20　Sources: Annual Reports, interviews; R&D budgets for the pharmaceutical businesses of the five companies in 1994 were not available at the time of writing.

21　See IMEDE, 1989, p. 164.

22　For the general case, see Porter, 1979.

- secure a patent, thus protecting the company's R&D investment;

- lower sales prices, thus extending or even preventing adequate pay-back periods for competitors;

- occupy exclusive distribution channels, thus hindering market access for competitors;

- constantly improve the underlying technology, thus securing the present lead.

In practice, technology leaders usually try to follow both options. They attempt to maximize profits from a strong, leading position *and* aggressively extend the period during which this is possible. This can be a delicate balancing act. Reaping too many profits attracts predators. Maintaining a two-lap-lead indefinitely costs a lot of money. The emphasis will therefore sometimes lie more on the former, sometimes on the latter considerations.

The strategic deployment of patents was first perfected by Japanese corporations. In some instances, new products have been fortified literally with hundreds of related or similar patents, surrounding a core invention. The intention is not only the prevention of direct product imitation, but also the obstruction of similar or even technologically different competitor products which might endanger the core product. This is in accordance with the now classic strategy of Japanese corporations to exploit innovations through the establishment of a dominant long-term market position. In contrast, Western—and in particular U.S.—corporations with their often shorter time horizons during the 1970s and 1980s tended to cash in on leadership positions early on.[23]

In recent years, however, Western firms have begun to assimilate Japanese tactics. Hewlett-Packard, for example, managed to defend its lead in PC laser printers over Japanese dot-matrix printers through a thicket of patents. A telling tale is also that of Procter & Gamble's Fairy Ultra, a glucamide-based dishwashing liquid advertised as particularly agreeable to the skin. In April 1992, it was introduced in the European market. Also in April 1992, Procter & Gamble published 18 international patent applications in connection with Fairy Ultra. Ten of these concerned the use of glucamides in washing and cleaning detergents. A further six revolved around combinations of tensides with glucamides. The last two involved the otherwise

23 Abernathy et al., 1982.

unpatented manufacturing process. In the course of the next 18 months, five further patent applications were added. All of them protect Fairy Ultra, by preventing either identical or similar imitations by other manufacturers.

Such preemptive measures are typically applied with an eye to the options of the technology *follower*, for whom shortened product life cycles take on a completely different outlook. This outlook is by no means always dismal. In fact, relative to the technology leader, the follower even has certain advantages, both with respect to time and money. For one, it is always easier to duplicate somebody else's solution to a problem rather than finding that solution oneself. Secondly, one can avoid various R&D dead-ends, and thirdly, at least one knows that there *is* a technical solution to a given problem, even though it may be fenced in by patents. Development times for the technology follower are therefore regularly shorter and often cheaper than for the leader.

On the other hand, the existence of shorter product life cycles means that a follower has less time to catch up and compete with the leader. If the follower is smart enough, he will catch up before the end of the life cycle. But there may not be enough cycle time left to recover any investments and earn a profit before an even newer technology rings the bell for the next round. For the technology follower, therefore, the most pressing requirement is to decide whether to compete at all and—if so—how to master the necessary technology fast enough to catch up with, or even leapfrog, the leader.

Thus, although the market perspectives for leader and follower are different, their resulting actions can be the same: Both types of market participants have a powerful motivation to push their level of technological know-how toward further improvements. Both are equally under pressure to ensure a viable position as early as possible in the lifetime of the product so as to guarantee maximum return on their R&D investments. It follows, that as product life cycles get shorter and shorter this pressure will increase.[24]

At first glance, all this seems like a good thing, both for suppliers as well as customers: As product life cycles get shorter, the former will learn to be more agile and technologically on their feet. On the other hand, they profit from a concentration of revenues on a shorter and earlier period. The

---

24 For excellent overviews of this subject, see Yip, 1982; and Teece, 1986.

latter, conversely, are better off to the extent that better technology leads to new and better product features and/or lower prices.

A game with no losers, therefore? We will come to that in a moment.

On the Significance of Shorter Product Life Cycles

In the press, the scientific literature, and in business practice, much is talked and written about the shortening of product life cycles that can be observed in almost all branches of industry. Unfortunately, the discussions of this phenomenon are usually confined to the question of how corporations can adapt to the changes that follow from it or how they can meet its challenges. This includes, for example, measures to speed up product development times by changing from sequential to parallel steps in the product development process.[25] Whole industry associations are studying and discussing measures to optimize one of the more recent indicators of managerial success, TTM (Time-to-Market).[26] The decline in product development times resulting from such measures in the petrochemical industry, for instance, can be seen in Table 4–1. In addition to such changes in management procedures, strategy planners have come up with technology portfolios to help managers compare alternative investment opportunities, identify promising R&D avenues and make faster technology decisions.[27] Competitive and market researchers are increasingly concerned with keeping track of competitors' R&D activities and how these relate to customer needs. Both laboratory and business managers everywhere are worrying about the improvement of know-how transfer from laboratories to shop floors and distribution outlets.[28] No wonder, that in recent years R&D- and technology management has become a promising growth area for business consultants[29] and academic publications.[30]

25 See, for example, Schmelzer, 1990.

26 EIRMA, 1994.

27 Pfeiffer et al., 1983.

28 For example, in software development, see Phelps, 1987.

29 See Anon.{7}, 1991.

30 See, for example, Roussel et al.; 1991, Wheelwright and Clark, 1992; Smith and Reinertsen, 1991 and many others.

Table 4–1 Typical Development Cycles for a New Polymer or Monomer Factory

Development Steps	1960s	1980s and 1990s
Laboratory Work	2 Years	1 Year
Prototype-Constr./Market Development	5 Years	4 Years
Plant Construction	2 Years	1 Year
Total Development Cycle	9 Years	6 Years

Source: Mitsubishi Petrochemical

In the midst of all this activism, however, only scant attention is paid to the actual implications of shorter product life cycles for corporations or industries. This is rather surprising. It would seem that before one can come to grips with certain changes and their consequences, one would first need to determine what these consequences are. The first question should therefore be, what happens in a company or an industry where the average time between the introduction of new products in the market and their substitution by even newer products gets shorter and shorter? Furthermore, do such changes only imply that schedules will be a little more hectic, and that cost and sales curves will fluctuate a little more wildly, but that otherwise everything else will be "business as usual"? Or do such developments signal the need for qualitative changes in the way a business must and will be run? Is there a danger if product life cycles continue to get shorter? Is there a lower limit to the length of product life cycles? Where might this limit lie and what happens when one approaches it?

An examination of these questions is not only a matter of idle curiosity. It also serves a practical purpose. It was stated earlier that industrial corporations do not spend millions or even billions of dollars on the development of new technologies just for the fun of it. Rather, they picture themselves as participants in a technology race that leaves them no choice but to maintain a serious R&D effort if they do not want to fall behind and lose their competitiveness. Simply put: *R&D secures new business*. On the other side of the coin, we have also seen that the widespread shortening of product life cycles can be traced to the rapid increase in the share of technology- and development-intensive products and manufacturing processes in industry which ages products faster than would otherwise be the case. Simply put: *R&D reduces existing business.* Putting both together leads to a startling conclusion: The problem's solution is also its cause.

The Acceleration Trap

At first glance, this is neither good nor bad. One could ask, however, whether the beneficial effects of the paradox are greater than its detrimental ones. In other words, does R&D secure more new revenues than it endangers old revenues? Only if we discover whether shorter product life cycles are associated with more positive consequences than dangerous ones will we be able judge the expediency of R&D budget increases. The following sections of this chapter are devoted to an attempt to do just that. We will outline some of the basic mechanisms involved in the process of shorter product life cycles and show their implications for a company or an industry. We shall do so by building a mental model that simulates shorter product life cycles and their consequences. In the interest of clarity, we will first make some simplifying assumptions which one does not encounter in real life. Step by step, we will then drop these assumptions and approach a more complex model that is closer to reality. At the end, we hope to arrive at some significant conclusions regarding the implications and consequences of technology-driven product life cycle decline.

Static Model

As shown in Figure 4–3, the life cycle sales of a product can be shown in the form of a curve over time. Sales start at a sluggish rate, then pick up rapidly and grow at an exponential rate until reaching an inflection point, after which growth rates decline and turn negative, reducing sales to zero again after a certain period of time.[31]

The sales curve depicted in Figure 4–3 is symmetrical. In practice of course, this is not necessarily the case. As shown in Figure 4–4, sales curves may lean to the right or the left, for example, indicating a sales peak either in the early or later phases of the product life cycle. A sales curve might also have several peaks over time, reflecting ups and downs in the demand for a product or service. For all practical purposes, it can even be endless. This is not only the case for raw materials such as iron ore or timber, but also for

---

31 For a general discussion of product life cycle curves, see Easingwood, 1988.

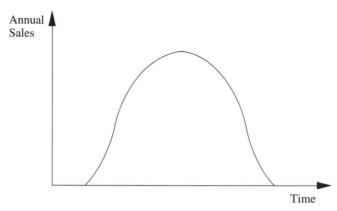

Figure 4–3   Idealized Product Life Cycle

manufactured goods. For example, the car has replaced horse and cart. But there is still a market for harnesses and buggy whips, just as there are still manufacturers of conventional phonograph records (for nostalgic natures) or of vacuum tubes (for replacements in old radios). As far as this discussion is concerned, the behavior of these other curves is not fundamentally different from that in Fig. 4–3. They will therefore not be considered separately.

Business corporations typically rely on introducing a continuous stream of new products, which replace older and more mature products, either their own or somebody else's. After a certain time, these new products are, in turn,

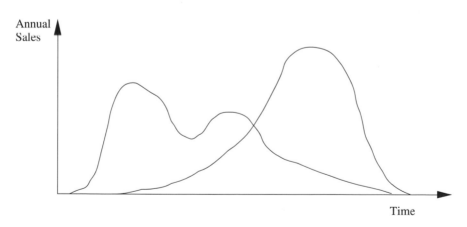

Figure 4–4   Assymetric Product Life Cycles

replaced by even newer ones. In this way, a corporation (or an industry) provides a continually changing spectrum of new, mature and declining products in the market. This state of affairs is illustrated in Figure 4–5.

In the interest of simplicity, we will assume in our model of an imagined corporation or industry that every year a product is introduced in the market. It stays there for twelve years and is then retired. We will further assume that each new product will follow the same development pattern: total sales and sales distribution over time of each product will be identical. These are not realistic assumptions, of course. Every corporation with a spectrum of more than two or three products will typically have some profitable money spinners or cash cows that will sometimes endure for decades. At the same time, it will also offer products that never really take off, just manage to cover their costs or possibly not even that. The two simplifying assumptions of a continuous stream of identical products are introduced here not to reflect real life, but to reveal the effects of changes in life cycles more clearly. In this way, it is possible to exclude the influences of different markets and production volumes as well as external factors such as inflation rates, business climates, currency exchange rates and so on. Some of these will be added back in later to allow for greater realism.

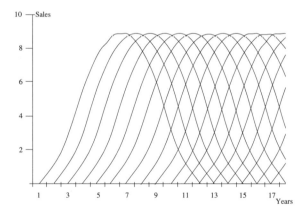

Figure 4–5   Continuous Product Life Cycles

Given these assumptions, the total annual sales of our company or industry will be derived from a spectrum of products in various stages of maturity. Obviously, it will be the sum of all products in the market at any given time. Since all products in our model exhibit identical growth and

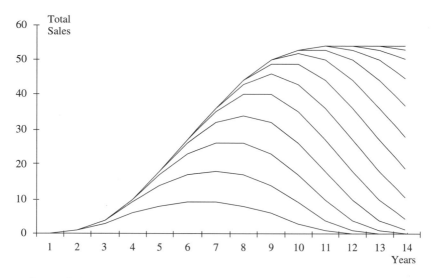

Figure 4–6   Cumulation of Continuous Product Life Cycles

decline patterns at regular intervals, total annual sales volume will settle at a value that remains constant as long as the underlying sales behavior of the individual products does not change. The cumulation of individual product sales volume is shown in Figure 4–6. After the end of the initial build-up phase, it describes a world of permanence.

One-Time Reduction of Life Cycle Lengths

For this reason, we will now introduce some change in our model. Specifically, we will assume that the life cycle for a given product changes in the manner shown in Figure 4–7: Instead of twelve, increased R&D budgets have led to the obsolescence of products after a period of only ten years. To keep matters simple, only this time spread has changed. The basic symmetrical *shape* of each individual product curve continues unaltered, as well as the total area *under* the curve, indicating that it will be possible to achieve the same total revenues over the life of a product in a shorter period than before.

This, of course, brings one question to mind immediately: Does the total (lifetime) sales income of a product really stay the same if it is sold for a shorter period of time? To put it in numbers, if we assume that a single product in our model will accumulate a total sales volume of, say, $1 bill. over a period of twelve years, then average annual sales of that product will be $83.3 mill. Can we infer that just reducing the product's life cycle length to

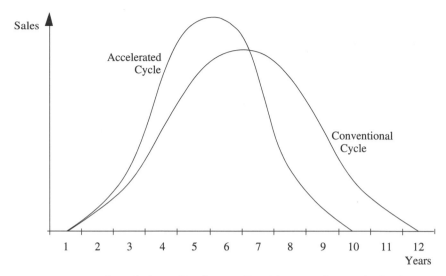

Figure 4–7   Switch from Twelve- to Ten-Year Product Life Cycles

ten years will automatically lead to average annual sales of $100 mill.? If that were the case, why not reduce the product life cycle to one year, better still, to one week and make the $1 bill. right away? Obviously, this is not possible. To name only two reasons, why should present sales rates be influenced by whatever happens ten years down the road, and where would the extra purchasing power come from?

The truth is, of course, that we cannot know if the total sales income of a product will stay the same over a shorter period of time because an individual company's sales cannot be analyzed outside of the total market for a product, i.e., the combined sales of all competing suppliers of the product. To answer this question one would have to take into account the sales of all competing suppliers, the features of all competing products, and the prevailing economic conditions in each of the markets involved. Finally, one would also have to know how they interact with each other.

Even under static conditions and only for the present this would be a daunting task. Adding in any future developments renders it practically impossible. Just looking at the technology dimension, for example, one would have to take into account that in a free market economy a technology leader will at best have exclusive dominance in a specific technology only for a limited period of time. In today's technology- and substitution-intensive markets, like those for audio and video consumer products, such a period will rarely exceed one year. Sony, for example, invented and introduced the famous Walkman and for a certain period was therefore the only supplier of this outstanding innovation. Effectively, the company had a monopoly. But not for long. Within six months, at least a dozen other suppliers in the fiercely competitive Japanese market had caught on and offered similar devices.

As long as they are operating in anything even remotely resembling a free market economy, other companies will inevitably try to catch up and compete with the current technology leader. This is in everybody's best interest, including that of the regulatory hand of the government. Moreover, no firm operates in splendid isolation on a planet of its own, but is instead tied into a complex network of technical and financial information flows. It woos the same customers, uses the same distribution channels, employs the same kind of workforce, and can therefore never be so far ahead of all other companies that none of them will even begin to compete. At least this author has never heard of a situation in which a certain technology was nurtured entirely from invention to obsolescence by a single company. Besides, this would not even make sense. As long as a technology monopolist has secure and unendangered access to a successful technology, replacing it with a newer one to serve the same market would lead to nothing but extra costs.

As every business manager knows, the revenues of all competing suppliers dynamically interact with one another. None of them can change their conduct without influencing the conduct of all the others. Since their reactions will in doubt be more competition-minded than otherwise, the expectation of unchanged total sales over shorter product life cycles is therefore very optimistic, to say the least. Nevertheless, in the following sections we will assume that such optimism is indeed justified and that life cycle sales will not change with life cycle lengths. More than anything else, this is of didactic convenience: By restricting ourselves to only one model change at a time, we can see the effects of this change all the more clearly. Building on this, we will later go on to examine the effects of smaller life time sales.

Figure 4–8 shows the consequences of our company continuing to introduce a new product annually under the given assumptions. Just as in Figure 4–6, total revenues first climb to a steady level. In year sixteen, the company switches to ten-year cycles and overall sales begin to increase. This happens for two reasons:

- Beginning sales growth for ten-year products is steeper than for twelve-year products.
- Vice-versa, old products' sales volumes at the end of the product life cycle do not decline as fast as those of new products.

The combined effect of this is a situation where for an interim period the company is adding "new" volume faster than it is retiring "old" volume. In our example, this leads to a sales peak of about 20% within the five years following the switch in cycle lengths. Increased innovativeness, or, indirectly, R&D, has thus yielded extra sales. But only for a limited time. Later, and as the ten-year cycle develops into a steady state and introduction and retirement rates approach each other again, total revenues start to decline and finally settle *on exactly the same value* as before the change (in our example, a value of 54).

This result is no coincidence. Nor were the figures manipulated by the author in such a way as to arrive at this result. The explanation is quite simple: As long as neither the lifetime sales volumes of products nor the rate at which products are introduced and retired changes, total annual company revenues in a steady state must always add up to the life time sales volume

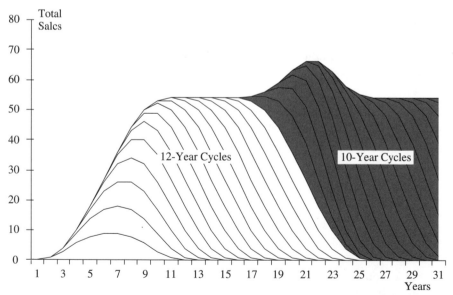

Figure 4–8 Switch from Twelve- to Ten-Year Product Life Cycles (Constant Life Cycle Revenues)

of a single product (in mathematical terms: its integral), irrespective of the prevailing length of product life cycles. Only during the switch from longer to shorter cycles will total revenues surge.

Continued Reductions of Life Cycle Lengths

Now, one might argue that a product life cycle reduction is not a one-time event that can never reoccur. Particularly because of its positive growth effect, any ambitious and creative business manager would not rest with ten-year cycles. Instead, having seen the positive effects of shortening cycle lengths once, she or he would try to do so again in order to achieve further growth. Figure 4–9 is based on the assumption of such a continuous acceleration process. As with the previous model run, we start with twelve-year cycles from year one to year fifteen. Beginning in year sixteen, cycle lengths begin to shrink. Every two years the cycle length of the newly introduced products is reduced by one year, first to eleven, then to ten, nine, eight, and finally seven years. All other assumptions are the same as those underlying Figure 4–8. Again, products are introduced annually, and the sales volume for each product remains the same over the course of its life. This implies that at the end of the scenario (in year thirty-two) the company can generate the same sales volume with a single product in seven years as it previously did in twelve. As before, the sales of all products are added annually to arrive at total revenues over time.

The result is that the transitional increase in Figure 4–9 is somewhat more pronounced than it was in Figure 4–8. The maximum value reaches about 35% over steady-state conditions. The general appearance of both curves, however, is quite similar. In particular, the decline back to steady-state conditions reappears, once the acceleration phase has ended. This leads to an important realization: *Even under the optimistic assumption that shorter and more dynamic product life cycles will generate the same volume of sales over the life of a product, total revenues of a company will not increase on a sustained basis.*

Limits to Life Cycle Reductions

Naturally, if one were to continue to reduce life cycle lengths, one would also continue to enjoy increased revenues, even though with a gradually declining effectiveness. However, a few words of caution must be added here.

First, life cycles cannot continue to get shorter endlessly. Not only systems analysts, but also newspaper readers, managers and politicians have learned by now that growth and decline processes do not go on forever. In

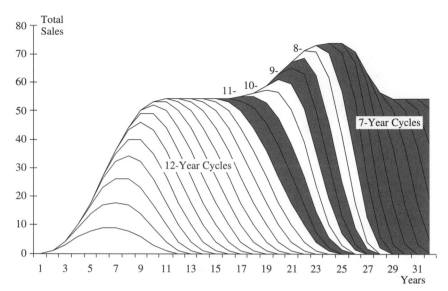

Figure 4–9   Acceleration from Twelve- to Seven-Year Product Life Cycles, (Constant Life Cycle Revenues)

any self-regulating system—physical, economic, biological, social, or other—there are limits to how much change can be accommodated. The world's energy consumption cannot increase endlessly. The efficiency of factories or automobile engines cannot be improved indefinitely. Aeroplanes cannot cope with infinite speed increases. Populations or organizational memberships under conditions of less than infinite resources cannot grow forever, and so on.

The same is true for a product life cycle. Its length has at least one theoretical lower limit: It cannot be equal to, or less than, zero. *Some* time, however short, must always remain for the production and marketing of a product. Once the ultimate goal of the "demassed society," i.e., 100% customization and one-of-a-kind products, has been reached, product life cycles can no longer shrink. A product and its product life cycle are then the same thing.

Secondly, the length of any product life cycle also has a *practical* lower limit, which is considerably larger than zero and which will be of varying length for different products and industries. To name just one reason, a continuous decline of product life cycle lengths will be increasingly difficult to maintain if customers and markets demand a certain minimal period during which the goods they have purchased are not substituted by innovations.

For an airline, for instance, such a minimum period can result from training and depreciation requirements for new aircraft. A Boeing 747 costs on the order of $150 mill. It can easily stay in service for 15 years, with proper maintenance, even 25. The premature introduction of a more efficient successor model by the manufacturer would not exactly be welcome if competitor airlines should purchase the new model while the first airline is still stuck with the old one.

In the same vein, some hospitals are having trouble accommodating all the novelties the developers of medical technologies are coming up with, even if they are free. A world-famous research and teaching hospital like Massachusetts General, for example, now has 45 different types of operating theatres where these new devices are installed and used not only for research purposes.[32] The rate of equipment turnover is said to be quite high and certainly much higher than the average regional or urban hospital could ever afford. The buyer of a new car would also (even if for emotional reasons) like it to remain state-of-the-art at least for a while. Millions of customers have probably been annoyed when the "latest" piece of stereo equipment or the single lens reflex camera they have just bought is replaced by a successor model in the shop window only minutes after they have left the store. This type of miscalculation was one of several causes of Sony's failure with Betamax video recorders. "A person who bought a $1,000 machine didn't want to find it obsolete ... a year or two later."[33] In this way, increasing the speed of new product introductions can easily backfire. Faced with a flood of new product generations, potential customers might even postpone the purchase of a device indefinitely. "If I wait just another six months it will be even better, even faster, even cheaper, even smaller ..."

Essential requirements for manufacturing and distribution times, minimum lot sizes in production, retooling periods, inventory and transportation processes and others all contribute to the limitation of product life cycle reductions. In some branches of industry, this lower limit has apparently already been breached. One of these is the fashion business. Traditionally, this industry's cycles follow the yearly seasons. But the winds of change are blowing here too. For major apparel chains like Armani and Benetton, for example, it has frequently become impossible to identify any product cycles at all. Many designs show up in the chains' store outlets only once, but then worldwide. There is no repetition. The next delivery consists of new models.

32 Anon.{19}, 1994.

33 Krasoll and Mandel, 1989, p.21.

Smaller European fashion designers are steadfastly resisting pressures by retailers to switch from the customary winter and summer or quarterly seasons to a bimonthly fashion rhythm. Supply and manufacturing delays, smaller unit volumes, and an increasing dependence on the vagaries of the weather would make their business simply unprofitable. Anyone who has ever tried to buy a summer suit in August and finds only a few leftover sale items or not even that, will have noticed that clothing is typically sold months in advance of the season it is intended for. "In season" itself it is practically not available.

It would seem that a product life cycle that has already overtaken the natural rhythms it is supposed to serve must encounter increasing resistance to further acceleration. Moreover, one can expect that this resistance will begin to intensify a long time before a critical cycle length has actually been reached. For all these reasons one can infer that sooner or later, any acceleration of product life cycles will come to an end.

In addition, there is one more critical concern: *The longer one waits to discontinue the shrinking of product life cycles, the more painful the awakening*: The shorter the cycles are when the shrinking process ends, the more dramatic the drop in sales. A comparison of Figures 4–8 and 4–9 reveals this. Not only does sales volume drop off far more in the latter case than in the former, it also does so much faster. The interim peak in Figure 4–10 (a partial magnification of Figure 4–9) is not symmetric, i.e., the revenue decline at its end is much faster than the revenue buildup at its beginning. The reason for this is that at the end of the peak, the company has arrived at seven-year product life cycles and will therefore settle into the steady-state sales volume much faster than with the longer cycles at the beginning.

The implications of all this are not surprising, but traumatic: A company that experiences "healthy" growth for ten years and whose revenues then decline by 26% in four years, as in our example, is, without doubt and measured by any standard of corporate well-being, in deep trouble. This is the kind of business development that dismays shareholders and creditors and swiftly terminates management careers.

Shorter Product Life Cycle and Lower Life Cycle Revenues

Let us now question a further assumption underlying our analysis so far, namely that the total sales volume over the life of a product is independent of the length of time during which it is available in the market. The

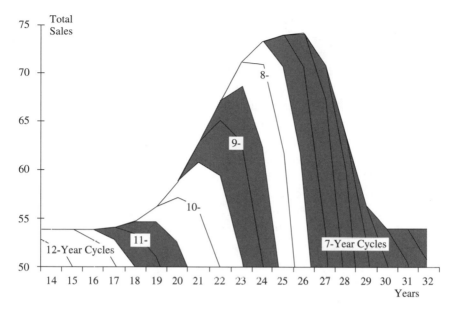

Figure 4–10 Twelve- to Seven-Year Acceleration (Detail)

assumption also implies that with shorter product life cycles, the average annual sales of a product will rise.

There is, of course, little doubt, that a new product can contribute to a significant increase in revenues.[34] Customers who were previously unwilling to buy a product might do so now if any added or new features appeal to them. For example, Yamaha Corp. claims that one third of the buyers of its new "silent piano" (equipped with earphones) would not have purchased a piano at all if it did not have a silencing switch; Diet Coca-Cola with less sugar might be more attractive to weight-conscious soft drink consumers than the classic Coke; the new minty fragrance of a skin cream might exert a greater appeal to the young-at-heart than the sweet-smelling old one did. Similarly, new process technologies might reduce costs and prices of conventional products sufficiently to stimulate a more than proportional increase in demand.[35]

On the other hand, an innovation can also fail to stimulate any additional demand and simply satisfy the existing demand for a product. For

34 Petroni, 1985, p. 110.

35 Bayus, 1988.

example, the added convenience of electronic typewriters might just lead to the substitution of conventional typewriters without attracting any additional customers who would not buy a typewriter in the first place. In these cases, a new product life cycle will not lead to business expansion. It follows, that the stimulation, or non-stimulation, of additional revenues by a new product depends on its characteristics and features[36] and not on the length of time during which it is available. This would only be the case if this period of availability could be regarded as a product feature, suggesting some sort of rarity attractiveness. Such products do exist. Certain commemorative postage stamps, or time-limited editions of art prints, books, or even—recently—fashion cars which are produced only for a brief duration or with a view to certain events can create purchasing temptations. Later, their markets evaporate. In 1977, for example, memorabilia of the U.S. Bicentennial were no longer sold with great success. However, such products tend to be exceptions. Everything else being equal, there is generally little reason to assume that shorter life cycles as such will induce larger average annual sales for a product and, thus, guarantee constant lifetime sales.

In view of this more likely interdependence, Figure 4–11 assumes a decline in total sales over the life of a product as life cycles get shorter. Some growth elements will still be retained in our model, however. These might be justified by an increase in customer purchasing power, for example, or by the stimulation of additional demand by an improved technology, or even some degree of a general attractiveness of "the new." Our model therefore assumes that the decline in total life time *sales* of new products is not as high as their decline in total life time *lengths*. In Figure 4–11, this was achieved by reducing cycle sales only half as much as cycle lengths. Thus, if a cycle was shortened by, say, 10% from ten to nine years, then life cycle sales were reduced by only 5%. Otherwise, all assumptions are the same as in Figure 4–9.

As expected, when product life cycle lengths finally settle down to seven years, steady-state sales are significantly lower than they were with twelve-year cycles, *although average annual sales per product have actually increased*. Also, the acceleration-induced sales peak is not nearly as pronounced as before (about 12% over beginning values, instead of 35%). To show this more clearly, Figure 4–12 contrasts only the company sales totals in Figure 4–9 (no decline in product lifetime sales) and in Figure 4–11 (some decline in product lifetime sales) with average annual growth curves of 3% and 4% as of year fourteen. Year fourteen was selected as a base year because at this point, the initial

36 Forbis and Mehta, 1981.

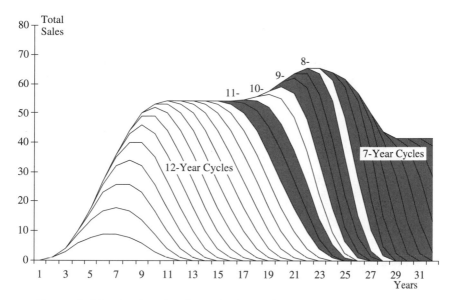

Figure 4–11 Acceleration from Twelve- to Seven-Year Product Life Cycles, (Declining Life Cycle Revenues)

twelve-year cycle has reached a steady state. Acceleration begins as of year fifteen. The two growth rate values were chosen because of their agreement with the business growth experienced in the beginning phases of both acceleration scenarios. Following usual practice, the annual reports of our company in year twenty-one or twenty-two would have given these two values as "average annual growth of the last seven years," implying that the company is enjoying stable and reasonable growth.

The increasing gap between constant growth rates and acceleration-induced changes only becomes visible in later years. Figure 4–12 reveals the trap that a business manager might run into if he mistakes acceleration for "real" growth. He or she might easily assume that business growth goals can be fulfilled by speeding up the turnover of the company's product spectrum. The manager might even *define* these goals based on past business growth, without realizing that this growth was nothing but the beginning of an acceleration phase.

One might indeed wonder whether some of the sparkling "growth businesses" one hears so much about, are not in fact rather lackluster "acceleration businesses." In the computer and automobile industries, this confu-

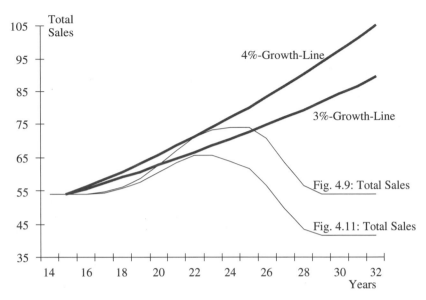

Figure 4–12   Deviations from Business Growth Goals

sion probably contributed at least in part to the problems with which both are presently beset. In any case, once a company—or an industry—has begun to seek its fortunes in the acceleration of product life cycles it will be increasingly difficult to turn back, without forced sacrifices both of business volume and business growth.[37] On the one hand, maintaining the acceleration becomes increasingly painful. On the other hand, bailing out does too. Acceleration has elements of addiction.

What is true of reducing life cycles is also true of lengthening them, only with the inverse effect: It will initially lead to a sales decline. Among competing companies it is therefore not very popular to suggest such a thing. And for a single company it is difficult to do so on its own. Some time ago, the second largest Japanese automobile producer Nissan, which had been suffering under severe profitability problems for a number of years, ventilated the idea of extending new model cycles from four to five years among its Japanese competitors. Not surprisingly, it did not find much sympathy. Figure 4–13

37 An interesting question, in this context, will be to see whether Chrysler Corp. can uphold the success it enjoyed during the 1994/5 period in the future. In the four years between 1990 and 1994, the company introduced a total of 20 new models, more than in the previous 20 years, and at the same time reduced its dependence on minivans.

shows that in 1993, product life cycles in the Japanese automobile industry were still hovering around 48 months, undercutting those in the American and especially German automobile industries. As a general observation, one should be aware that not only do shorter development cycles allow shorter product life cycles, but, after a while, shorter product life cycles will also create pressures to shorten development times and to increase R&D efforts. No wonder, therefore, that in 1995 when automobile sales were low the three major Japanese automobile manufacturers Toyota, Nissan and Honda decided to slash development periods for new automobiles by a further ten months. Such vicious circles can easily become habit forming.

Dynamic Model

The analysis so far has been exclusively concerned with shorter product life cycles in a static environment. Conditions, opportunities and constraints for a company or an industry were considered constant. The idea was not to show the historic development of the real world or any part thereof, but to demonstrate the effects of accelerating product life cycles in a

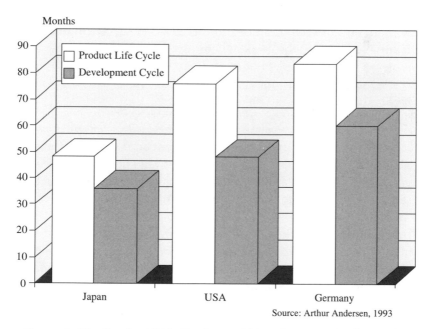

Source: Arthur Andersen, 1993

Figure 4–13 Product Life Cycles and Development Cycles in the Automobile Industry, Months

general and unchanging context. Excluding external changes allowed these effects to be traced all the more clearly.

Shorter Life Cycles and Economic Growth

Of course, one might argue that such assumptions are of little relevance in an outside world that does *not* stand still. Markets, disposable incomes, and economies tend to grow, if only on a nominal basis. This growth—one might point out—will more than offset any volume losses a company or an industry might incur if the acceleration process comes to halt, which it inevitably must for the reasons given above.

Figure 4–14 portrays a scenario in which this line of argument is taken into account. It uses the same assumptions as Figure 4–11, but it factors in a constant 5% per year market or economic growth rate, which seems like a reasonable value. In addition, life cycles lengths are in steady-state conditions from the outset.

Total sales in Figure 4–14 differ from the static model in that they exhibit continuous growth, even while there is no change in product life cycle length. As long as the company stays with twelve year cycles it grows with the market. With the onset of product life cycle acceleration, business growth initially outpaces the market. Later it stagnates and with the onset of seven-year cycles, it severely plummets. Only very much later does the permanent 5% market growth rate take over again. But it takes at least eight years before the previous sales peak is reached.

Figure 4–14 clearly reveals that *market growth does not grant immunity from the consequences of the Acceleration Trap*. It is not hard to imagine what goes on in a company that experiences a slump of the kind and extent shown here between the years fourteen and eighteen. Company management will be hard put to explain to shareholders, creditors, customers and other interested parties why sales are declining while the market is growing at a healthy 5% per year. This explanation and the assignment of responsibility for the decline is particularly difficult if the original reason, i.e. the decision to reduce product life cycle lengths, was taken many business periods ago. More than likely, the original "sinners" will not be the ones to suffer the penalty.

Shorter Life Cycles and Additional Innovation

We will finally add one last consideration and examine an objection which is occasionally forwarded against the concept of the Acceleration

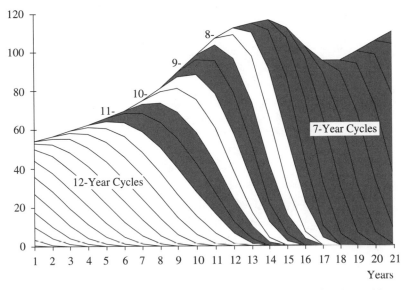

Figure 4–14 Acceleration of Product Life Cycles with 5% per Year Underlying Growth

Trap. The objection runs roughly as follows: Even if the length of product life cycles cannot decline indefinitely, it is possible to offset any of the difficulties and sales downturns associated with ending the acceleration simply by extending the range of the product spectrum. This implies the introduction of *more new products or avoiding the detrimental consequences of faster innovation with more innovation.*

Basically, of course, there is no reason why a company should be restricted to one new product introduction per year. Indeed, it can—and should—innovate as often as an opportunity to do so arises. Particularly in a competition-based free market economy, it is only justified if a company that does not take advantage of such opportunities goes under or at least ends up trailing its competitors.

Since this is a perfectly valid argument, we will consider it in Figure 4–15, which contrasts the total sales curve from Figure 4–14 with a continuous 5% and a 7% growth-line. The 5%-line would have been the company's development if it had *not* accelerated its product life cycles and had simply grown with the market. The 7%-line corresponds well with the actual development of the company *including* product life cycle accelera-

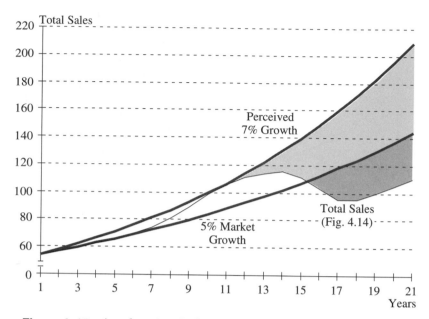

Figure 4–15   Acceleration-Induced Gaps in Sales Volume

tion between years one and eleven. In year twelve, 7% would therefore probably have been reported as the company's "historic growth rate."

Figure 4–15 shows that during the acceleration phase, the company initially performs better than if it had grown with the market. But as seven-year cycles take hold, it slips back and from then on *permanently* lags about 30% (dark shade) behind what its development could have been if it had stuck with twelve-year cycles. Another way of putting it: The company has lost market share. If the company had continued to grow at 7% per year—which might be what unsuspecting shareholders have come to expect by year eleven or twelve—its sales volume would have been almost double the value actually achieved in year twenty-one (dark plus light shade).

To close the smaller or the larger gap to the 5% or the 7% growth-line again, the company can pursue one or both of the following strategies:

- It can try to reduce product life cycle lengths even further and generate another transitional sales peak as it has done before.

and/or:

- It can introduce additional products and from then on have a product spectrum of more than seven products at any one time.

The first strategy: Assuming a further acceleration of product life cycles is actually feasible, the company would sooner or later find itself back in the Acceleration Trap it was originally trying to escape from. Only this time, the situation would be worse. After a further halving, average product life cycle lengths would have arrived at four or even three years. All the ensuing problems would be the same as described above, but magnified. In addition, the company can expect stiff resistance against any further acceleration from markets, suppliers and other quarters.

The second strategy looks more promising. The introduction of *additional* products would imply that the company would increase the average rate of new product introductions *without* reducing the average length of product life cycles. In our model so far we have assumed one innovation every twelve months. If the company aims to stay on the 5% market growth curve with product life cycles of seven years, that is to increase its total sales volume by 30% over the value in Figure 4–14, then it would have to increase its new product introduction rate from 1 to 1.3 per year. This works out to a new product every nine months and one week, on average. Correspondingly, if it wished to double its sales volume (so as to return to the 7% growth curve it enjoyed at the beginning of the period we have been observing—not a very likely prospect in year twenty-one) it would have to halve its new product introduction period to an average of one new product every six months.

Before getting carried away with this solution, however, one must remember one thing: Even apart from R&D, new products do not come about for nothing. Whatever the industry and irrespective of all managerial efforts to reduce the costs of innovation, there is always some extra cost involved in the introduction of a new product. This holds particularly true for our present considerations. Additional innovations will only generate additional sales if they do not cannibalize the company's existing products. Otherwise, the company is only back where it was before: in the Acceleration Trap with new products substituting old ones. Hewlett-Packard experienced this when it introduced its Laserjet III printer only twelve months after its highly successful Laserjet IIP had entered the market. Since the Laserjet III was only a few hundred dollars more expensive, but provided double the printing speed of the Laserjet IIP, sales of the latter plummeted overnight.[38] This does not imply that Hewlett-Packard did something stupid. The company may have had no choice for competitive reasons. But applied to our considerations, this experience shows that any additional innovations have to be sufficiently distinct from existing products. They have to be targeted at different market segments, may not compete with them, or replace them.

Figure 4–16 shows a change process in the computer industry, where precisely this was not the case. Between 1991 and 1992, technical progress did not lead to additional products, but only to substitution effects which essentially turned the whole industry on its head. Particularly the rapid advance in the performance characteristics of electronic components did not lead to growth of all suppliers, but rather to a sales decline for the suppliers of mainframes and mini computers and to sales growth by the suppliers of software, personal computers and work stations. Unfortunately for the former, these were different companies.[39]

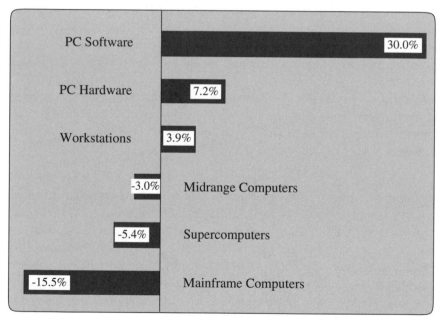

Figure 4–16   Change in Computer Manufacturers' Revenues 1991 to 1992, percent

38 EIRMA, 1994, p. 12.

39 Zachary and Yoder, 1993; see also Lewis, 1989.

The computer industry is not an isolated case. Japanese machine tool makers are presently only partially successful in their attempts to stimulate a stagnating market by intensifying their R&D and innovation efforts.[40] Examples are manifold and not restricted to whole industries. The same thing can happen to individual companies. The Japanese electronics manufacturer Sharp, for example, is presently trying to counter the falling demand for its products through more innovations.[41] Whether this will actually work, remains to be seen.

In principle, therefore, new or additional products can offer a way out of the Acceleration Trap. But this path is only promising if it involves different technologies, approaches new customer segments, uses other manufacturing facilities and distribution channels, or a combination of these factors. Past experience shows, however, that this form of corporate expansion, where new customer groups are approached with new technologies through new channels and in unfamiliar markets, is among the riskiest and most difficult of all corporate undertakings. All too often, companies that attempt to be good at many different things end up losing their core expertise. Witness the example of Kanebo Ltd., founded in 1887 as one of the first Japanese industrial textile manufacturers. Faced with low-cost competition from other Asian countries, the firm expanded into a whole array of new businesses in recent years, among them cosmetics (one of its few profitable ventures), designer clothing, waterproof construction materials, pharmaceuticals, and instant noodles. In none of these new businesses did the company manage to achieve a dominant market position. Sales in 3/1991 declined from ¥510 bill. (ca. $5.2 bill) to ¥382 bill. (ca. $3.3 bill.) in 3/1995. Operating profits went from ¥17 bill. ($112 mill.) to a loss of ¥13 bill. ($133 mill.). At present it is trying to spin off its traditional textile business.[42] Komatsu, the world's second largest maker of construction machinery, is another example. Faced with a maturing construction market at home and in many other industrialized countries, the company is diversifying into manufacturing equipment for liquid crystal displays, engines, personal computers, and factory automation. Analysts regard this with some scepticism.[43]

---

40 Mitsusada, 1993.

41 See Rack and Schwarzer, 1992, p. 77.

42 At constant exchange rates. Lashinsky, 1995; Tsukagoshi, 1995; Japan Company Handbook, Winter 1995.

43 Matsuo, 1995.

There are only a very few companies that have successfully moved out of their traditional domains or have complemented these with completely different businesses where the decisive parameters of success were different. Perhaps the best known example of this is Finland's Nokia. But even there, the expansion did not come about without instances of extreme pain and effort—and some luck. In the beginning of the 1980s, Nokia was a small conglomerate with sales of about $3.5 bill. It made toilet paper, rubber boots and power cables, mostly for the domestic Finnish market of about 5 million inhabitants. To brighten the company's prospects, it acquired four European color television manufacturers and a Swedish computer company. By 1988, this pushed Nokia's revenues up to $5.4 bill. and made it a fairly big European player. Profits plunged, however, the chief executive committed suicide and in due course a number of businesses like paper, rubber, chemicals, and computers were sold off again. But one business in particular was suddenly doing very well: telecommunications equipment and cellular telephones. At the time, the Scandinavian countries had just established the world's first international cellular system. U.S. commercial service followed shortly thereafter. The market had materialized and Nokia had something to offer. Today, Nokia is number two worldwide in the mobile phone business after Motorola.[44]

Even entering into fairly closely related areas can pose significant difficulties. IBM, for example, not exactly a newcomer to the field of data processing, lost a lot of money in its failed attempt to get into supercomputers. How much more difficult must it then be to turn, say, an automobile tire manufacturer into an aluminum foundry or a machine tool firm, or even to expand into these areas? A few years ago, the German giant Daimler-Benz, more renowned for its cars, trucks and busses than anything else, strove to change its character into that of a "technology concern" that also included electronics, aerospace, and information technology services. In business year 1995, this adventure resulted in the largest one-year loss in German corporate history of over DM6 bill. (over $4 bill.). A number of Japanese steel producers have developed similar ambitions and are expanding into new areas such as ceramics or into biotechnology. How does one—to name only one hurdle—get managers, or sales representatives, or quality control engineers into a mindset where they will contemplate micrograms, or molecules, or parts per billion, when they are used to thinking in terms of hundreds of thousands tons of annual production volumes? In any case, the success of

---

44 For more details, see Meeks, 1994, and Edmondson, 1994.

many these ventures has yet to be seen. The only thing one can be sure of so far is that they cost money.

To gain an impression of *how much* money the closing of the "innovation gap" shown in Figure 4–15 could cost, consider the following: Every new product is associated with certain innovation costs. These consist of R&D costs plus any other investments like market research, tooling-up etc. which are required to develop a product to the point of market readiness and market introduction. They do not include on-going production costs like raw materials, depreciation on plant and equipment etc. Such innovation and introduction costs vary widely among industries. In the software industry, for example, the largest cost factors typically lie in product development and market launch. Actual production costs, in contrast, i.e., the duplication of diskettes or magnetic tapes, printing of handbooks etc., are almost negligible. On-going marketing costs also stay within limits (although apparently they have been increasing recently, as witnessed by Microsoft's Windows 95® campaign), so that the innovation costs of applications software might not be too far from 100% of total costs. In other sectors, for example, in certain mature segments of the machinery or chemical industries, where a new product entering a familiar market requires only a minor degree of retooling or process change, innovation costs can be quite low and manufacturing costs high. Further, a high level of R&D does not have to coincide with high levels of total innovation costs. In the pharmaceutical industry, for example, which boasts the highest average ratio of R&D to sales of all major industrial branches, later market introduction and production costs can be surprisingly low once the enormously cost-intensive laboratory and clinical test phases for a new drug have been completed.[45]

Thus, depending on the specific innovation costs of the business in which our company is engaged, any change in the rate at which new products are introduced in the market will also change the company's cost structure. To take an average case, an industrial concern like a machine tool manufacturer offering a broad range of both conventional and technically advanced products, might typically experience a share of about 25% of sales in innovation costs. Assuming this value to hold for our company, then any sales increase that is based on a 30% increase in the average number of products introduced annually will raise total innovation costs by $30 \times 0.25 = 7.5\%$ of sales and thus, to a total of 32.5% of sales. To the extent that the company

---

45　Interview with Hoechst AG, Frankfurt.

cannot pass on these increased costs to its customers, this will have serious repercussions for its profitability.

Furthermore, this will not only happen once. Since the higher rate of new product introductions has to be maintained *continuously*, its negative cost effects will also last. Compare this to the identical but far more profitable sales volume based on the conventional product introduction rate of one product per year and twelve-year cycles. The same result can affect whole industries if they insist on increasing their innovation rate. This may well be the reason why some industries that boast high degrees of innovation, such as computers, are suffering from significant profit declines.[46] They are literally innovating themselves out of business.

Concluding Remarks

Time Horizon of the Acceleration Trap

In closing this chapter, one should bear in mind that the long time spells considered in Figures 4–5 through 4–15 offer only little or no protection against the painful effects of the Acceleration Trap. For purposes of the above model, we have chosen periods of 21 and 31 years, respectively. Such time frames are regularly far beyond the decision horizons of most managers and may even exceed the length of their whole professional lives. But this should not lead us to conclude that the message of the model is irrelevant for actual business practice. Instead of years, we could also have redefined the time axis to quarters. Product life cycles in our model would then have shrunk not from twelve to seven years, but from twelve to seven quarters or from 36 to 21 *months*. Such short product life cycles are by no means

---

46 See Lewis, 1989. An interesting example in this context is the famous H-Y War between the motor cycle manufacturers Honda and Yamaha in the years 1981 to 1983. In the years leading up to this period, Yamaha had managed to slowly close the gap to the market leader and in a blaze of public announcements, was set to overtake Honda. At this point, Honda decided to strike back. Both companies had a product range of about 60 different motorcycle models. In the author's estimate, the average product life cycle for motorbikes at the time was two to three years. In the course of 18 months, Honda introduced a firework of *113 new models*, practically renewing its product range twice. Yamaha could only counter with 37 new models and was quickly stuck with an inventory of one year's production of technically obsolete motor cycles. The conflict ended with a public apology by the Yamaha chairman and the recognition of Honda's leadership. Honda itself had won the war, but needed some time to recover from the financial consequences of its innovation offensive. A more detailed report is contained in Stalk and Hout, 1990, p. 58 et seq.

unknown in industry. In electronics, a vast range of products today features cycle lengths of less than 18 months, some even less than one year. Video cassette recorders, for example, are obsolete within eight months, lap top computers in six, camcorders even in four.[47] Under such shorter frames of reference, changes can come about quite rapidly and painfully.

More importantly, however, even under long time frames, primary threats to the survival of organizations frequently come not from sudden events. Every so often, it is the slow and gradual processes[48] which for all their ponderous speed relentlessly and inexorably take their toll. Because of their inconspicuous beginnings, one tends to take them lightly or to consider them less urgent. Only late, perhaps too late, one realizes that one is utterly at their mercy. In other words, once the acceleration process has started, it is very difficult to return to the *status quo ante*. At some point, the Acceleration Trap is triggered. The later this happens, the more painful its consequences.

Empirical Evidence

No doubt, it would be interesting to investigate some further variations of our model and its parameters. But theory shall end here. Interested readers should not have too many difficulties in devising their own models which could include some of the specifics of their own industries or firms. A simple spread sheet program—preferably with a graphics package—or even a pencil and a pad of paper would suffice. Perhaps it would be particularly instructive to track historic product data and then try to determine the extent to which any past business expansion was in fact founded on acceleration effects rather than on "real" growth.

There are so many indicators and clues for the workings of the Acceleration Trap and its symptoms[49] that its existence can hardly be cast in doubt. Nevertheless, hard statistical, empirical evidence is hard to come by. For one, the concept is new, so nobody has looked for any traces it might have left in real life, although some researchers are beginning to investigate the matter at least from a theoretical point of view.[50] For another, it is difficult to isolate acceleration-induced data from other factors. In practice, the overall development of a company or an industry is subject to a whole host of different and varying influences. These include sales and profit contributions of various products, product innovation rates, life cycle lengths, growth and

47 See McCreadie, 1989.

48 See Senge, 1990. p. 22.

maturity levels of technologies and others. In addition, any number of external factors, such as currency exchange rates, interest and inflation rates or even political developments can mask any acceleration-induced changes almost beyond recognition.

Even where changes can be isolated unambiguously from acceleration-effects, uncertainties for other reasons still remain. Longitudinal studies of product ages within corporations, for example, reflect only little consistency with respect to the definition of "a" product. Investigations by the author in three different companies as to how they had arrived at published statements regarding the age of their product spectra revealed considerable discrepancies.

In one company, certain employees at divisional levels made rough definitions of products and estimated their ages. Company totals were then calculated simply by adding across divisions. In another company, a product catalogue number served as a product definition substitute. Changing the catalogue system would thus create a completely new product range. Further ambiguities also arose because estimates were made at varying intervals, not always supplied by the same person and without any generally applicable rules of product definition.

Sometimes companies are also somewhat generous with their definition of a product for publicity reasons. In 1993, for example, sports car

49 That Japanese manufacturers and distributors of automobiles, for example, are
    implicitly aware at least of the positive initial consequences of faster product life
    cycles can be deduced from the following two quotes:

    1) "'Unless automaker *conduct model changes of small cars more frequently to stimulate
    the compact car market*,' another dealer warns, "we will not be able to maintain the
    sales boom.' Shorter model changeover periods are believed to encourage buyers to
    trade in their vehicles more often." Source: Anon. {8}, 1990, p. 1, 13.

    2) "'If you make attractive cars, *it is possible to keep expanding the market*,' said Toyota
    President Shoichiro Toyoda." Source: Mitsusada, 1989.

    For a very good example with data for the PBX (private branch exchange) telephone
    market that follows the pattern of the theoretical model described in Figure 4–13
    remarkably well, see Rica, 1988.

    It is also revealing that an innovation-hungry market like that for consumer electronics in Japan is stagnating at a time when the growth engines of the past like CD players and VCRs are approaching market saturation levels with apparently no major
    breakthrough innovations in sight. See Lanus, 1990. The same seems to be true of the
    computer industry, See Schäfer, 1990. (Emphasis added).

50 Eisele, 1993, particularly Chapter 4; Bayus, 1994, p. 305; Gruner et al., 1994; Backhaus
    and Gruner, 1994, particularly p. 30-46.

maker Porsche, not exactly known for the enormous breadth of its product spectrum, celebrated the 30th birthday of its by now classic model 911. Between 1963 and December 1992 the company built a total of 350,000 units. A number of brochures and books about "the" 911 have been published. They show that over the years, the 911's engine had 12 different displacements and 27 different power ratings. The 911's weight ranged from 900 to 1,470 kg (2,000 to 3,240 lbs). Top speeds were between 178 and 317 kph. (111 and 197 mph.)[51] —All *one* product?

All this leaves us with the question, does the Acceleration Trap really exist? Fortunately and in spite of the difficulties mentioned above, evidence is materializing.[52] 592 companies (90% headquartered in the U.S.) from various technology-intensive branches of industry participated in an in-depth survey of the influence of product development cycle lengths on profitability.[53] The study's original intent was to find empirical support for the widely-held belief that being faster will always lead to financial advantages. Instead, it found that accelerating product life cycles through shorter development times would have favorable financial effects only once, at best. If a company insisted on the repeated and permanent use of this tool, it would rather rapidly encounter serious negative effects.

These results are being confirmed in ongoing work. Companies participating in the survey to whom the results were presented in follow-up interviews reacted to the notion of an Acceleration Trap in unequivocal agreement: "Of course, it's common sense... The acceleration trap exists."[54] All of them—including major corporations such as Alcoa, Allied Signal, Celestial Seasonings, Corning Glass, and Grumman—were highly receptive to the idea. The same reactions could also repeatedly be found among managers in Germany where first results from ongoing identical surveys are pointing in the same direction as the U.S. studies. Finally, some avid time-to-market enthusiasts who in the past have strongly embraced the concept of innovation acceleration as a strategic lever,[55] are now having second

51 Kaufmann, 1993, Table on p. 241.

52 Curtis, 1993, particularly p. 190 et seq.; Curtis, 1994, particularly p. 23-25 and footnote 11; Ellis et al., 1995.

53 Product *development* cycles and product *life* cycles are obviously not the same thing. Nevertheless, they do interact: Reducing the time it takes to develop a new product only makes sense if it means shorter reaction times and thus earlier market introduction. This will then also cause an earlier ending of existing product life cycle(s). See also Fig. 4–13 above.

54 See Ellis et al., 1995, Tables 2 (p. 45) and 3 (p. 46).

thoughts and tending to the view that a fair degree of restraint in this respect might be wise, particularly among Japanese industry.[56]

Independently of such views, one should bear in mind that the findings of this chapter on the Acceleration Trap are not intended as numerical forecasts of what is bound to happen. Its aim is not to describe a certain company's or industry's future, but only to show the forces a company is exposed to if it seeks its fortunes in exaggerated innovation strategies. Obviously, changing the model's parameters will also change its behavior. For example, if we were to halve product life cycle lengths over a period of twenty years instead of roughly ten years, as we have done here, we would also observe smaller revenue fluctuations, and vice versa. The changes in life cycle revenues as a function of cycle lengths also play a role. But these *details* are not the decisive point. If one accepts the underlying assumptions of the model, namely

- that increasing R&D efforts accelerates the development of new technologies,

- that new technologies shorten product life cycles based on old technologies,

- that there is a lower limit for the length of any product life cycle, and

- that average life time sales of products will decline with average life time lengths

then one also accepts the *basic behavior* of the curves and their consequences, readily visible or not. Some of these consequences for corporations and their competitive environment will be investigated in the next chapter.

Summary

New technology can lead to new or better products. These reduce the competitiveness of conventional products which, in turn, reduces the lengths of the product life cycles of conventional goods. For this reason, competitors strive to establish leading technology positions or at least catch up with the technology leader as rapidly as possible. In recent years, corpo-

---

55 Stalk and Hout, 1990.

56 Stalk and Webber, 1993. Bayus, 1995, gives a number of examples of the harmful effects of excessively speeding products to market.

rations and markets can observe a technology-induced acceleration of product life cycles in many branches of industry. In a model, it is shown that a shortening of life cycles seems attractive at first as it is initially accompanied by a significant growth in sales. However, since cycles cannot continue to shrink forever and since it can be justifiably assumed that life cycle sales volumes of products will decline with shorter cycles, the initial period of sales growth is later followed by a period of even larger and drastic sales declines. This holds true even in periods of macroeconomic expansion. Increasing the innovation rate by diversifying into other businesses so as to offset this decline in revenues seems like a solution to this problem. In practice, however, it is also a very costly solution and is consistently associated with extremely high risk levels.

The instrument of accelerating product life cycles in many respects is similar to a trap. It has therefore been termed the Acceleration Trap. Once embarking on the route of shortening life cycles, it becomes increasingly painful to stop and increasingly costly to continue. Recent empirical findings in the U. S. confirm these theoretical results and suggest that many so-called "growth businesses" are in actual fact only "acceleration businesses" whose decline can be expected in due course or has already commenced.

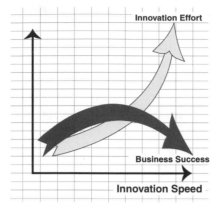

Implications of the Acceleration Trap

Let us briefly recall what was established in Chapter 4: Companies walk into the Acceleration Trap if they succumb to the temptation of increasing their innovation rates through shorter product life cycles. Initially, they enjoy substantial sales increases. But as the length of product life cycles settles down to shorter periods, this sales increase is followed by an even faster sales decline. The later this happens, the worse the decline. This interdependence was demonstrated with the aid of a theoretical model that showed the causal relationships between the length of product life cycles and sales development.

In this chapter, we will now try to add some color to theory's pallor. In particular, we will determine if the above analysis is of more than just academic interest and what the consequences of the Acceleration Trap can be in practice. In following such intentions, it is easy to get lost in details, especially if one has the ambition to identify *every* possible consequence, including all of the indirect effects of a secondary or even higher order. Many books have been written about the pressure to accelerate and improve product development, or about the concentration of business processes into shorter time frames and how these can be successfully managed.[1] The author's aspirations, however, go less far and point in a different direction. His aim is only to identify some examples of the Acceleration Trap's symp-

1 See, for example, Smith and Reinertsen, 1991; Wheelwright and Clark, 1992; Stalk and Hout, 1990; Rosenau, 1990; Saad et al., 1993.

toms. These symptoms may serve as warning. For the reader who wishes to involve himself more deeply, others will readily spring to mind. Dealing with them is tempting, although it does not remove their underlying causes.

The Acceleration Trap and Business Risk

In this section, we will examine some of the processes and shifts occurring *within* a company that has strayed into the Acceleration Trap. For easier understanding, we will start out from the familiar set of conditions described in Chapter 4. Figure 5–1 thus shows a phase in our company's history in the accustomed form. We have left out the start-up phase so that from the outset, it is already in the steady state where it introduces one product per year, sells it for twelve years and then retires it. Acceleration begins in year four and follows the assumptions described in Figure 4–11. The changes and consequences described in the following subsection are based on these assumptions. In their *quantitative* manifestation, they therefore only hold for this one case. As *qualitative* phenomena, however, they also reveal general principles.

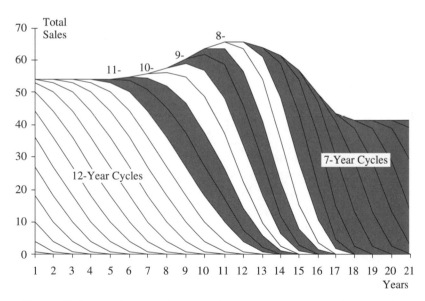

Figure 5–1 Acceleration from Twelve- to Seven-Year Product Life Cycles

The top part of Figure 5–2 shows total revenues of our company as already depicted in the summation curve of Figure 5–1. This total first climbs from an initial value of 54 units to a peak of 65.4 units. Then, as older and longer-lived products are retired and replaced by products with seven-year life cycles, total sales decline to 41.6 units. In parallel with this development, the center part of Figure 5–2 shows that the company's product spectrum declines in a straight line from 12 products up to year fourteen to 7 products by year nineteen. One should note that the decline in product spectrum width only *begins* long after total sales have begun to increase and even three years after sales peak. The reason for this is that the company does not retire the last of its twelve-year products before year fourteen. Up to this point in time, twelve-year products still contribute to total revenues. For an interim period, therefore, there is a net gain, while short-lived new products add more sales volume than volume from long-lived old products is being retired. Seen in context, the top and center parts of Figure 5–2 together reveal that the acceleration-induced sales increase reflects, not actual business growth, but rather additional present sales volume at the expense of later sales volume.

The lower part of Figure 5–2 reveals a further effect of these changes. It shows the average sales per product, calculated by dividing the top part of Figure 5–2 by its center part. Since at first total sales rise without any change in product spectrum width, average sales per product initially also increase. A first peak in average sales per product is reached simultaneously with the total sales peak in year eleven. After this, things become unpleasant for our company. Total sales begin to decline before the number of products in the market do. Basically, this is a consequence of the original decision to replace long-lived products with short-lived ones. It inevitably implies that, after a certain delay, some short- and long-lived products will be phased out *simultaneously*, instead of a constant retirement rate of one product per year. For a while, there will now be years when more than one product leaves the product spectrum. Only when product introduction and product retirement rates fall in step again do average sales per product rise to reflect the reduced width of the product spectrum. Before this happens, however, company management faces an unpleasant situation lasting for several years:

- Total sales decline by a substantial degree.

- The number of products in the company's spectrum falls.

- The average sales volume of each of the remaining products gets smaller.

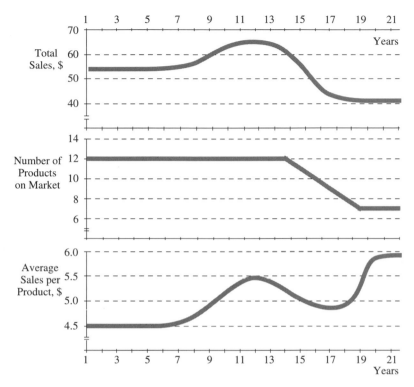

Figure 5–2   Total Sales, Product Spectrum and Average Sales per Product

Younger Products

Let us now turn to the question of how the average *age* of our company's products changes as product life cycles become shorter. In its top part, Figure 5–3 reflects the sales contribution of the three youngest, i.e., latest, products to total sales in absolute terms. The lower part shows the same values as percent of total sales. As product life cycles are accelerated, both values rise rapidly. At the end of the scenario, the sales volume of these three products is more than double the average sales per product (see Figure 5–2) and represents almost 32% of total sales.

Such changes are neccessarily associated with a significant increase in risk exposure for the company. Just visualize the implications: If one third of total sales depends on products that are three years old or less,

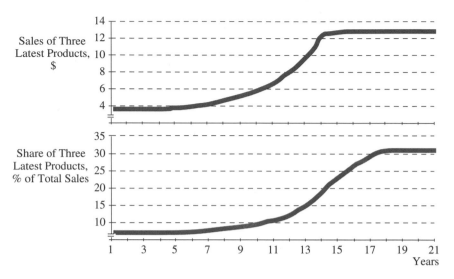

Figure 5–3   Sales and Share of Sales of Three Latest Products

then the penalties for not "getting it right the first time," or of missing the market window altogether, are going to be extremely severe. Under such circumstances there will also not be much time for correcting any mistakes. In fast-cycled businesses, such as cellular phones, margins are often so low that fixing anything is essentially unaffordable, even if there were the time. Quality control, not only in production, but also in the premarketing phase, especially in R&D and tooling, both attains prime importance and becomes extremely difficult. This can become very painful, wherever faults and their corrections represent an important part of total costs. Debugging in the short-cycled software industry, for example, by its very nature has always been very time consuming.[2] In these cases, orderly product development can either become a nightmare or is not done properly in the first place.[3] With neglect, this can lead to an *industry-wide decline of product quality*. It may well be that these are the effects that lie at the heart of the many complaints heard all over the world regarding the deficiency, lack of comprehensibility and poor user friendliness of application software, handbooks and instruction manuals.

2   Littlewood and Strigini, 1992.

3   For an excellent analysis of the problems associated with accelerated product development, see Crawford, 1992.

Shorter Time Horizon

This last consideration is also part of the message of Figure 5–4. It shows the weighted average age of the products sold on the market at any point in time. As the share of younger products increases, the share of older products obviously declines as does the average age of all products. The time pressures involved in new product development increase correspondingly.

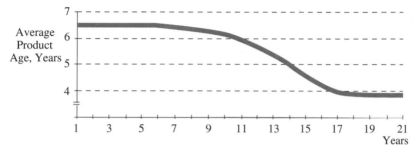

Figure 5–4 Weighted Average Ave of Product Spectrum

Figure 5–4 also shows something else. It reveals how much longer, on average, the present product spectrum will contribute to company revenues. One can not only use it to read the average age of a product, but also how much time remains before it will be withdrawn from the market. In a way, Figure 5–4 can therefore also be seen as a statement of the relevant time horizons and the length of the strategic concepts under which our model company will be managed. In our example, this time horizon sinks from an initial 6.5 years to 4 years, or by almost 40%.

In most industrial firms, the attention of middle and upper management traditionally focuses on manufacturing and selling the present product spectrum. The concern for "tomorrow or the day after" is the responsibility of top management, of strategic and long-term planners and of the R&D department. As the time horizons and the planning periods for future products in a company shrink, they will also have less time to develop new ideas, solutions and breakthroughs. Correspondingly, there will also be less opportunity to bring to proper fruition the far smaller number of new concepts that remain in spite of this time pressure.

This is not just a theoretical speculation. In today's corporate reality, shorter time horizons are an everyday phenomenon. They inevitably accompany the general decline in product life cycles. A vivid example was shown in Figure 4–2. In the 1970s, many of the large European industrial corporations still based their long-term planning on five-year time horizons including an outlook over a ten year period. In U.S. corporations, time horizons were probably somewhat shorter, while in Japanese corporations, they were longer. In *all three* regions, they have since declined significantly. This is not only reflected in the day-to-day work of planners, but has also become part of a general mind-set. A market study, for example, that aims to look more than three years into the future is hardly taken seriously anymore except in industries with particularly long cycles, such as timber or power generation.

The usual justification for this is the declining predictability of future development and events. The speed of change, it is claimed, has become so fast, one has to be content just to keep up. "For us, long term planning is deciding where we are going to have lunch tomorrow," an American sales manager once quipped to the author. That is not surprising. Whatever happens after the demise of the present product spectrum is automatically unknown because it is beyond the range of current interest. Shortening this range by means of short-lived products even further, will automatically lead to a less discernible future. It seems that, in many respects, the lack of knowledge of the future is homemade.

All this is no secret. Since the future seems to loom larger and more threatening everywhere, the business press regularly and critically follows the attempts of corporations and industries to meet its demands.[4] Unfortunately, what frequently escapes attention is that many of the processes by which corporations are seen to be adapting to the future are determined by time horizons which do not go far beyond next year's closing. No doubt, company interest in the future is intensifying. The problem is that, because of shorter product life cycles, it is concentrating on a closer and closer future. Even in an unchanging world, such an attitude would be dangerous enough. It becomes shortsighted in more than one sense, however, if the world at large increasingly begins to think in longer time frames and worries about questions such as climate changes, the north-south conflict, raw materials issues, population pressures, ethnic conflicts and other problems. The crucial parameters in these matters are often measured not in months or years, but in decades, sometimes centuries. At some point, perhaps sooner than expected, they will become relevant concerns for industry too. Industry

4   See, for example, Krubasik and Stein, 1989.

might be well advised to think about that day now. Otherwise, today's or tomorrow's lunch might be the last one a company will ever have.

Increasing Risk Consequences

As product lives get shorter, not only do business processes become more risky. In many respects, the *actual onset of risk events* also becomes more painful. The following consideration will show why:

The behavior of markets, technologies and customers can never be predicted perfectly. At best, it can be reasonably well surmised. For this reason, a company cannot expect to be successful with every one of its innovations. Time and again, a product will fail completely or will not fully live up to expectations. This is one of the rules of a free market economy. The rule's existence is also independent of the length of product life cycles, so no more needs to be said about it here. What does change with product life cycles of varying lengths, however, are the *consequences* of a product failure.

Figures 5–5 and 5–6 compare these consequences under twelve- and eight-year steady-state life cycle conditions. In both figures it was assumed that the company experiences a one-time failure in its normal rhythm of annual product introduction. The next year's innovation is successful again and business resumes as before the failure.

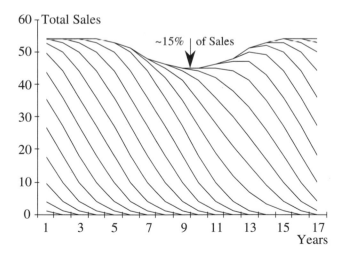

Figure 5–5　Twelve-Year Cycles, Effect of One Product Failure

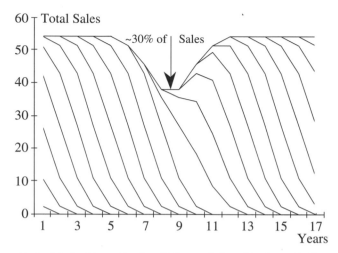

Figure 5–6   Eight-Year Cycles, Effect of One Product Failure

Even though the total volume of lost business is the same in both cases, the effects on sales development of the total company are remarkably different. In Figure 5–5, total revenues decline over an extended period of time, but at its peak not more than about 15% of steady-state revenues. Figure 5–6, on the other hand, reveals a maximum of about 30% of total revenue loss concentrated on a much shorter period. Observe also that peak losses are not in proportion. A shortening of product life cycles by one third *doubles* maximum sales losses. It is hardly necessary to emphasize that a company will have much less difficulty adapting its financial, personnel, and other policies to the situation depicted in Figure 5–5 than to that in Figure 5–6.

The Acceleration Trap and Value Added

Corporations generally choose between two opposing ways to overcome the difficulties associated with tighter innovation schedules and increasing development costs. One choice is to intensify vertical integration, that is, to maintain an increasing share of total value-added in-house. The idea is to assume tighter organizational and financial control and to permit a better focus of company resources. The other choice argues exactly the other way around: The company contracts out to partners, subcontractors or subsidiaries as many parts of the innovation process as it possibly can and maintains control only of those elements which it regards as crucial.[5]

Depending on the situation, each strategy has its merits and disadvantages.[6] Unfortunately, it seems that as product life cycles get shorter, the disadvantages of *both* methods begin to grow.

The most important drawbacks of the integrative approach are its costs. If suppliers of new products want to maintain exclusive control, then they also have to bear the large amount of time and funds necessary to build or acquire the marketing, production, and distribution assets for successful product introduction. This is already true for constant product life cycles. But as innovation schedules get tighter, it is obviously going to become more difficult, if only because producers will have to concentrate manpower and funds into a shorter period of time.[7] In the long run, this will lead to increases in the costs of these resources or to a decline in the efficiency or effectiveness of their deployment.

Frequently, essential ingredients of the innovation process such as land, specialized equipment, or technical experts will simply not be available on the market at short notice, at an acceptable price, or even at any price. For example, some software companies are having a hard time finding programmers familiar with modern software languages like C and C++ which are needed to write applications for Windows or UNIX platforms. They have therefore begun to offer substantial "bounties" to their own employees for successfully luring job candidates.[8] In a similar vein, there is

5   A procedure mixing elements from both approaches is one followed by large pharmaceutical companies like Merck and others in recent years. It involves the acquisition of small or mid-sized companies that own certain genetic engineering technologies. In extreme cases, the complete development cycle—sometimes all the way from the cloning of a gene to clinical testing—is essentially outsourced before the acquisition. This reduces the acquirer's risk of, course, but comes at a price: For example, a 63% share in Genentech, cost Hoffmann-La Roche over $2 bill. Ciba-Geigy bought a 49.9% stake in Chiron for $2.1 bill. See Zell, 1994, p. 45; Anon.{30}, 1995. Naturally, it is also possible to see this the other way around: In recent years, poor business results have made it an attractive proposition for biotech firms to be acquired by large chemical firms.

6   For a good discussion of this choice, see Teece, 1986.

7   Wheelwright and Clark, 1992, p. 5 point out: "Because the number of products and new process technologies has increased while model lives and life cycles have shrunk, firms must mount more development projects than has traditionally been the case ...In the U.S. automobile market, for example, the growth of models and market segments over the last twenty-five years has meant that *an auto firm must mount close to four times as many development projects simply to maintain its market share position*" [emphasis added].

8   Boslet, 1995.

little point in setting up a major genetic engineering technology program, as was done in Germany a few years ago, if the supply of technical specialists has essentially dried up and the best ones have left due to restrictive legislation on genetic research, leaving just a few second-class researchers at best. In R&D, just like everywhere else, the best people are employed first. The next best researchers only find a job in the second or even third round of hirings, if there is one. With increasing R&D expenditures, the marginal productivity of every additional R&D dollar therefore declines because it will buy only the less productive researchers and other resources. If estimates are correct that only about 1% of the working population is suited and willing to work in R&D,[9] then this effect will be felt sooner there than in other sectors of the labor market. As the competition for thinly spread first-class talents intensifies,[10] one can therefore assume that not even corporate giants like General Motors, IBM, Philips or Shell will still have the full range of know-how and instruments at their disposal to introduce an advanced product into the market quickly and efficiently.[11]

Maintaining a policy of integration thus becomes both more important *and* more difficult. In industries with rapid rates of technological change, such as electronics, having access to the complete spectrum of technologies and areas of knowledge relevant to a core technology (so-called complementary technologies) is often crucial. For example, offering the best or most powerful videogame machines, as companies like Nintendo, Sega, Sony, Matsushita and a number of others are presently trying to do, is really not much good if there is not enough videogame software available to keep the game machines busy.

Today, scientific and technical information flows literally at lightning speed around the world. Laboratories of global corporations are applying similar methods to the solution of identical or similar problems. Because no important national or regional market is isolated any more, this has the effect of pushing up the prices of complementary resources. Instead of only one, there will now be the demand of several corporations for the same— and possibly rare—specialists or goods.

9 Interview by the author on May 30, 1991 with Prof. Ken-Ichi Imai, Economist at Hitotsubashi University, Japan, who also pointed out that the number of R&D employees in Japan which at that time totalled in excess of 500,000 was already approaching the 1%-limit.

10 That this happens even in difficult economic times is confirmed by Boslet, 1995.

11 See, for example, the famous case of the IBM Proprinter development, Gomory, 1989.

It also means that a company can no longer be technologically years ahead of its major competitors. The typical lags between technology leaders and technology followers today are no longer measured in terms of years, but in terms of months, sometimes weeks. Occasionally, a technology leader will even contribute to such short lags by granting licenses to its major competitors only shortly after achieving a breakthrough. This can make sense, for example, if the leader's technology becomes a de-facto industry standard in this way. The same can be true if the leader knows that the competition is working on the same problem anyway and is therefore likely to come up with a solution of its own in the near future. Selling a license will then at least allow the recovery of some of the previous R&D-expenditures. The German chemicals concern Henkel, for example, sold licenses to its major rivals only weeks after having developed a phosphate substitute for detergents. On the one hand, the company knew that its competitors were subject to the same pressures (both by legislation and the public at large) to replace phosphate by some other substance less damaging to the environment and would therefore come up with a solution of their own at some point. On the other hand, the company managed to generate some very attractive licensing income from this deal for a number of years.

As an aside, one might add that for these and similar reasons, it is very unlikely that a company will ever again manage to achieve a dominant position such as that enjoyed by Xerox in copier technology for many years or by Apple in personal computer technology for most of the 1980s. This would only be possible if a technology leader could protect its know-how with impenetrable legal fortifications. In all but the rarest of cases, this has become very difficult indeed. It becomes even more difficult if the delays in the patenting process become longer than the product life cycle that is based on the technology in question. A technological head start will therefore represent a barrier to entry for competitors only for a very limited period at best. Profits that are solely based on being able to do something that nobody else can do become correspondingly short-lived. In February 1995, for example, NEC (Japan) announced the development of an experimental 1-gigabit DRAM chip. *Only two days later* competitor Hitachi announced its own version. South Korean manufacturers are hot on their heels. Industry analysts submit that, "The technological difference between Japanese and South Koreans is very narrow."[12] It is unlikely, therefore, that on the day of market introduction of the 1-gigabit chip expected around the turn of the century

12 Ishizawa III, 1995.

even the leading company will be able to enjoy innovator profits for very long, if at all.

In the high-tech branches of industry, other sources of competitive strength than the R&D ratio of a company increasingly tend to determine the outcome of market battles. These include design, price, service, responsiveness, etc. As growing R&D spending shrinks product life cycles to shorter durations, these market battles occur more and more often. In the long run, this can become prohibitively expensive. In seeking to spread these costs either over time or over a larger number of participants, integrated companies tend to give up on the attempt to keep everything under control. Instead, they come to depend more on external organizations and partnerships. In many instances, this will even include the performance of major segments of R&D activities.[13] In this way, however, the companies also become more exposed to the frictions, cultural differences and coordination difficulties typically associated with cooperative ventures.

Most companies are well aware of these drawbacks, of course, both theoretically or from their own experience. Nevertheless and in view of exploding R&D costs, the current boom in joint ventures and international cooperative agreements such as that between IBM, Siemens, and Toshiba for the joint development of a 256M Chip, between aerospace firms for the development of new generations of airliners, fighter planes and space craft, or even between car makers is not surprising. Even the Japanese computer and communications specialist NEC, for many decades perhaps the most insistent of all lone wolves in the electronics industry, is gradually softening up.[14] Unfortunately, it is also well known that a depressingly large share of such external partnerships do not live up to expectations. Managing partnerships successfully is fraught with many difficulties, to say the least.[15] With experience, companies can probably learn to be better at it. But so far at least, only very few companies like Corning in the U.S. or the members of

---

13 "In the 1980s ... companies believed that 80 percent of their technology competitiveness came from internal R&D. They invested heavily in developing core competencies and turning those competencies into products. Today, however, companies believe that internal R&D determines less than 50 percent of technology competitiveness.", source: Jonash et al., 1994, p. 28. This has become particularly evident in the personal computer business where contract manufacturers are involved in practically every stage of the value-added chain, beginning with design and lasting all the way to after-sales service.

14 Ishizawa I, 1994.

15 For an analysis of the forms and tools of technology alliances, see Tucci et al., 1994.

the European Airbus consortium, both of which now look back on many business years of cooperative ventures, gradually seem to be accumulating a good track record in this area.

Turning now to the opposite strategy, the main advantages of subcontracting the noncritical parts of the innovation process result from reduced capital expenditures and thus, a smaller risk exposure for the innovator. As a general rule, contracting is likely to be a better strategy than integration if the innovator has exclusive and tight control over the critical elements of the new product, *and* if all other elements are available from a competitive choice of sources.[16] Frequently, the advantages associated with the external procurement of goods and services can be quite substantial, if only for the reason that an outside vendor faced with competitive threats will listen to a customer's wishes and schedules far more carefully than the manager of a fellow division.[17]

In spite of these advantages, one must ask how far this can go. It has frequently been pointed out that component suppliers have borne the brunt of advanced technology development costs.[18] On the other hand, they have almost no influence on the business success of the products incorporating these components. The development of a sensor that activates an airbag in a car, for instance, can be quite expensive. How many of them are sold, though, depends far more on the manufacturer of the car, than on the supplier of the airbag and even less on that of the sensor. It is also undeniable that profits on the whole are much higher for the makers and sellers of end products than for the makers and sellers of components. As a rule, big profits tend to come from selling telephone exchanges and tv-dinners, not from selling microchips and plastic trays.[19] With shorter product life cycles and increasing risks, this preprogrammed conflict with suppliers will become more pronounced. Car makers and their suppliers in Europe, Asia and North America have become very painfully aware of this in recent years.[20] In addition, short cycles leave less time to sort out the problems involved in

---

16 Teece, 1986.

17 Ohmae, 1985.

18 See, for example, Kumpe and Bolwijn, 1988: "(The) trend among component factories is from high-precision mechanics to ultra-high-precision mechanics, from micron technology to submicron technology, from plastic or metal parts to integrated plastic/metal parts. Tolerances in these factories have become very exacting. Costs in R&D are unprecedented."

19 ibid.

these conflicts. If a company has infinite time on its hands, it does not have to worry about coordination. But as time frames get tighter, coordination becomes critical. In these cases, vertical integration might offer a solution. But as we have seen earlier, that solution has its own inherent limits.

The Acceleration Trap and Market Dynamics

Time-to-Market and Customer Acceptance

The greater part of the business managers, scientists and corporate officers with whom the author has had the opportunity to discuss the dangers associated with the Acceleration Trap, were in agreement with the concept. In an interview with the author, one of them expressed it drastically: "I am convinced that if we keep increasing this rate (of new product introductions) we are cutting our own throats."[21] The literature has also seen this subject critically already quite some time ago.[22] Others, though, even if in agreement, occasionally viewed the matter as a moot point. The realities of a free market, they generally claimed, left no choice but to keep up with the competition.[23] A typical quote: "Manufacturing corporations that do not work to shorten product life cycles in this way will almost certainly be leapfrogged by the competition." A competitor could choose to enter the market with a new or better product at any time. Insisting on maintaining the original retirement schedule for one's own, now uncompetitive, product would not make much sense under such circumstances. Customers would see to this. Essentially, so the argument went, one was at war, not only in terms of price but also of time.[24] All parties in this war wanted the same thing: to beat the competitor to the market with new products and follow up with further innovations before the competition had the opportunity to catch up or recoup its investment.

20   It seems that Japanese suppliers of automobile components, faced with massive and profit-consuming cost cutting demands from automobile manufacturers such as Honda and Toyota have recently agreed to follow these demands only if they can relax some of the excessively strict quality standards imposed on them in the past, see Okino, 1995.

21   Prof. Jay Forrester of MIT, November 1992.

22   For example, see Lund et al., 1977.

23   Kumpe and Bolwijn, 1988.

24   At Siemens AG, for instance, this attitude has led to the pursuit of shorter product life cycles as an explicit strategy, see Pierer, 1993; Holzwarth, 1993.

Apart from the fact that by blaming everybody else one is effectively also blaming oneself, in many respects this argument is very similar to the standard price war argument: "We don't want to, but we have to because all the others are doing it." Except during certain market development phases, price wars are usually a bad idea for everybody, including the customer. The same is true of an unrestrained time-to-market war. While it may frequently (not always!) be beneficial to be the first in a new market and garner the innovator's profits, this does not imply that a constant barrage of new products makes sense. In such races, where every innovator tries to be faster than every other innovator, only to be overtaken by a third, not much room is left for innovator profits.

The capacity of customers to absorb innovations is limited. On the one hand, their purchasing power is less than infinite. On the other hand, they cannot be expected to switch prematurely to some new technology or product before having had the opportunity to put a *previous* product to use for some reasonable period. After all, they have already paid for it. It is now sitting on their desks or in their factories or homes and is waiting to be utilized. Customers are quite justified in demanding some minimum period of residence on their premises before it becomes obsolete. Otherwise they need not have bought it in the first place. If suppliers attempt to reduce this minimum period they can, therefore, expect to encounter innovation fatigue and buying resistance. Such resistance can occur, for example, whenever potential customers repeatedly delay a purchase or even abstain all together precisely *because* there is a rapid succession of new product generations. Why buy now if a new generation is due in a few months anyway? Sometimes, of course, customers will even refrain indefinitely from buying anything new because they are quite comfortable with what they already own and do not want to make the effort to switch, even if a new product is better.

It is perhaps for this reason that the software language COBOL—declared dead by software developers some 20 years ago—is still alive and doing well. Users have become familiar with it, know what they can expect, are aware of its limitations, and may therefore be less enthusiastic about technological "progress" than their suppliers would like them to be. The same has happened in the chemical industry. In the 1970s, many new high-tech polymers were developed in the conviction that they would substitute conventional mass products like polyethylene, polystyrene and polypropylene. In practice, they had only very limited market success. Engineers in the automobile and machine tool industries preferred to use materials with known characteristics that could be applied for a multitude of purposes rather than experiment with exotic and sometimes more expensive polymers even if they did exhibit superior performance.[25] Even the military has a prime example of preferring to stick to the old, but useful: The B-52 Stratofortress was first flown in 1952 and placed in U.S. Airforce services in 1955. It is the longest serving military aircraft in aviation history and is still going strong. At present, there is a strong movement to keep the versatile B-52s in service until well into the next century instead of replacing them with far more expensive B-1B Lancers or B-2 Spirit stealth bombers.[26]

Such minimum periods of residence will differ widely for different products and businesses, just as customer resistance to innovations will vary. One can be quite certain, however, that the resistance will increase if the supplier of the old product is also that of the new and will therefore either charge higher prices for the support, service and maintenance of the old product or refuse to do so at all.

An interesting innovation story is presently developing in the field of photography. Five major film and camera manufacturers (Eastman Kodak, Canon, Fuji Photo, Nikon, and Minolta) have agreed to introduce a new film standard APS (for Advanced Photo System) that would be somewhat smaller than the standard 35mm film currently in use world wide. It uses a simplified development process and also magnetically records photo-taking information such as shutter speeds on the film itself. Unfortunately, it is incompatible with existing camera equipment. Also, development laboratories have to acquire new equipment to process films. No wonder that critics fail to see the benefit of the new standard and are beginning to regard the whole venture just as a means to put some spark into a sluggish photo market by getting consumers and developers to buy new equipment.[27] At the same time, Ricoh, Olympus Optical, Casio and other companies are developing digital still cameras which do away with film altogether. To be on the safe side, Eastman Kodak, Canon, Fuji Photo and Nikon are jumping onto this bandwagon, too. No doubt, both projects are aimed at different market segments and applications. It is hard to believe, however, that there is not a significant overlap between them.

25 Schröder, 1994.

26 See Dorr, 1995.

27 Ikegami, 1994. Among the various amateur photography magazines the author occasionally likes to leaf through, he has yet to find a single letter to the editor that welcomes the new film standard.

It would be an interesting and worthwhile exercise to attempt to find optimum innovation intervals for varying industries and market segments from the point of view of the buyer instead of the developer/supplier. That is, how long would it "normally" take before a car owner becomes tired of his present model? When would he or she want a new deodorant fragrance? Considering all maintenance, repair, and other life cycle costs, when does it really make economic sense to replace a machine tool with a new one? How long before a user has mastered the potential of a software package to a degree that he or she will regard it as a limitation? More than likely, such an analysis would not be easy,[28] all the more since it would have to compare technical, financial and many non-quantifiable factors. If followed, however, its results would be an extremely useful guideline for the orientation of manufacturers' R&D budgets more closely along the *real* needs of the market. Furthermore, while revealing the discrepancy between customers' preferences for tried and true solutions and suppliers' interests in selling new products, it would also be a sign of genuine customer orientation.

Innovation and Productivity

A more measured innovation policy would also benefit suppliers. A head-over-heels sequence of new products often forces older products off the market before they fully profit from learning curve effects. The products never achieve a cost and price level that might otherwise have been possible.[29] It is interesting to note, for example, that in the memory chip business the delayed substitution of 4-megabit chips by the next generation of 16-megabit chips boosted the profits of 4-megabit manufacturers in 1995 through the roof. Similarly in the field of consumer electronics, one can safely assume that the unit costs and prices of television sets in the last few decades would have been far lower if the time between model replacements had been longer to start with. This would have allowed the same technical improvements, but concentrated them at longer time intervals and would therefore have allowed larger production runs. Technology enthusiasts beware: there is a trade-off between innovation and productivity.[30] Shorter cycles lead to higher prices, notwithstanding the effects of improved technology. Rural educational programs in India, for example, do not use videotape recorders and other standard consumer electronics products on a

28 See Takaki et al., 1993,

29 See, for example, the case of application specific integrated circuits, Cole, 1989.

30 For a very clear elaboration of this point, see Goldhar, 1986.

sufficiently wide scale for just this reason. The frequent introduction of new models has never let unit prices decline far enough to allow their massive utilization in an environment that is chronically short of cash.[31]

In addition, the pressure to keep up with competitors under all circumstances can, and has, led companies to focus on product "improvements" along only one or two dimensions of the whole range of product characteristics. The race for the lightest video camera is symptomatic of this and, by no means, an exception: "When Matsushita unveiled its 750g NV-S1 in June [1990], the company proudly announced it as the world's lightest camcorder. The title was quickly taken back by Sony later the same month, when it launched the TR45, weighing only 690g. However, Matsushita sources last week said the company has developed a ... machine, weighing 680g."[32] In such cases of camcorder diets or similar obsessions with the enhancement(?) of just one of many product features, there is typically a lack of concern for the improvement of the overall product. In the desperate attempt to seem innovative, a product is occasionally even equipped with additional features which are only apparent, or pseudo-, improvements and sometimes do nothing at all to increase its usefulness. In 1994, for example, Oral Logic, Inc. introduced a three-sided tooth brush, claiming that it would clean teeth faster (top, front, and back simultaneously). Has tooth brushing speed really been a problem in the past? In 1995, car manufacturer BMW announced that its newest models would offer a heatable steering wheel as an option. The claim was that this would enhance driving safety by warming fingers stiff with cold. Do BMWs not have heaters or can BMW drivers not afford gloves?

Conversely, the development of complementary technologies and assets which *are* urgently needed is sometimes simply forgotten.[33] No sane person would drive a car whose engine and chassis are capable of 150 m.p.h. but whose tires disintegrate at 75 m.p.h. But in other areas of technology, users are expected to do just that. There is, for example, little doubt that the rapid development of data processing hardware has left corresponding operating systems and applications software generations far behind.[34] Fast PC software development, on the other hand, has, on occasion, promised

---

31 Shane, 1989.

32 Isaka, 1990.

33 For an excellent discussion of this point, see Teece, 1986.

34 Tepper, 1990.

features far beyond operating systems' capability to handle them, causing them to crash or leaving the programs' effective usage rate at only 20% of capacity.[35] Many innovations, in fact, might only come into their own, when complementary technologies have finally been developed for them. The Internet, "the mother of all networks," for example, or commercial systems like Compuserve and America On-Line are likely to experience a significant boost, once a fast, flexible, safe and global form of digital monetary transactions has become available.[36]

All in all, it seems that in the rush to push a product, *any* product, into the market on very short notice, a lot of the required homework in proper innovation management is simply not possible and therefore not done.[37] More and more money is then spent on the faster and faster development of the wrong products. No wonder that many manufacturers are complaining about the declining productivity of their R&D departments.[38] In truth, the real problem lies with the *aggregate* of all the measures belonging to successful innovation, not only with the technical work in the R&D lab. Thus, managers do not obtain an adequate understanding of possible market developments or market adaption processes,[39] nor do they conduct sufficient product planning several years before actual product introduction.[40] Typically, this can result in increasing project failures, bad timing, locking into wrong technologies, and other severe and costly mistakes, which cost both customers and suppliers a lot of money. No wonder that among the users of high-tech products a new rule of thumb is making the rounds: "Never buy an innovation that is less than a year old".

Examples of such poorly introduced product developments abound. They include bubble memories (narrowing of opportunity windows by other newer or better technologies), the Japanese high-resolution TV stan-

---

35 Bökers, 1989, offers an illuminating and amusing tale of this (author's liberal translation): "A never-ending spiral: A-Soft, supplier of spreadsheet programs, offers a new macro. B-Soft and C-Soft follow half a year later. B-Soft's spreadsheets can now be the size of football fields. Of course, this is purely theoretical. No PC hardware could manage it. A-Soft and C-Soft retaliate. C-Soft comes up with 3-D sheets. A-Soft plans to go directly to 4-D and to allow sheets the size of Denmark. B-Soft and C-Soft have heard of this: 'We can do that too—and better.'"

36 Anon.{15}, 1994.

37 See Raelin and Balachandra, 1985.

38 Anon.{7}, 1991.

39 See McIntyre, 1988.

40 Krasnoff and Mandel, 1989.

dard (outdated analog technology base maintained for too long), and digital audio tape recorders (legal problems, increased attractiveness of compact discs as computer peripheral devices). Whether the Integrated Digital Services Networks (ISDN or data highways) will be another example remains to be seen.[41] In any case, even industry experts have begun to regard it as "utter madness only to accelerate product development and production cycles without ascertaining that products meet the needs of the market and of production."[42]

The Acceleration Trap and Manufacturer Responsibility

Customer Relations

The useful life of many technical products, that is, the period during which they technically function and have not worn out or before maintenance costs become excessive, is significantly longer than its salability period. To put it simply, today's products tend to be out of date before they break. These lines, for example, were written with a personal computer that is in perfect working order but can no longer be bought. In a different sphere, there are still sailing ships ploughing the seven seas, although no significant numbers have been produced for a century. It is also interesting to note that while product life cycles have generally become shorter, many industrial products themselves (e.g. kitchen appliances) have exhibited a lengthening of their useful lives.[43] This implies that the commercial value of a product at the end of its product life cycle can still be significantly above zero. Economically, therefore, if a new product generation is introduced before the usefulness of the old one has expired, two things happen:

- The market value of the old product declines.
- Assuming that the new product is in some way better or cheaper than the old one, the holder of the old product becomes less efficient, less competitive, less fashionable, or in some other way less "good" than the holder of the new product.

41 Davis, 1988; Koyanagi, 1989; Botskor, 1994.

42 Sommerlatte, 1990.

43 See Bayus, 1988, p. 217, Table 2. Theoretically, of course, some products, e.g. any software application or even a poem, for that matter, have endless useful lives in that they never wear out. It is only the changing specifications and requirements of their operating environments that (can) effectively limit their useful lives.

Suppliers of new products replacing previous ones should therefore bear in mind that they are also reducing, or even destroying, the assets of customers, either their own or some other supplier's. This "creative destruction" is perhaps not exactly what Schumpeter had in mind when he was extolling the virtues of innovation at the beginning of this century.[44] The fact that there is a secondhand market for many kinds of products does not contradict this, but rather serves to emphasize the point: Many users will simultaneously switch their orders from one generation to the next as soon as it becomes available. At the same time, they are hoping to unload their old equipment. Supplies of the old generation will increase while demand falls off. Typically, therefore, used product prices tend to decline faster once the next generation of products has been introduced in the market.[45]

Since there are practical and legal limits for offsetting such value losses (by accelerated depreciation, for instance) there is also a limit to what holders of old products will accept. For a supplier, previous customers are generally also among his most important future customers. Resistance against new products from these customers can therefore be quite effective. They will be even less likely to accept a new product generation if the costs of switching (e.g. training requirements, reformatting of data files, adapting production processes, reconstruction of buildings) are added to the costs of a premature purchase.[46]

Suppliers might try to meet this rapid value attrition by reducing not only product life cycles but also the useful lives of their products. This, however, is a very dangerous strategy. Customers often equate shorter useful lives with lower quality. Terms like "planned obsolescence" and "throwaway society" have attained a very negative ring. Even in quality-conscious and quality-proud Japan, where consumers are said to be more openminded regarding innovations than in Europe, excessively short product life cycles have been blamed for an increasing occurrence of faulty products, recalls, and accidents. "In order to stay competitive, companies [in Japan] have developed new products within six months, produced them in the next three and then sold them in the next three. The complete life cycle only lasts one year. This speed allows no time for testing product endurance."[47]

44 See above Chapter 1.

45 This is very well documented for the computer mainframe business by Wiener, 1986.

46 See, for example, Beam and Mitchell, 1986.

47 Shimura, 1990, translation by author.

Nothing, it would seem, could hurt the cause of innovation more than a reputation for shoddiness, and there is little that can contribute more to shoddiness than an overhasty product development. Because it does not have the time to allow for new or unexpected results during development or to conscientiously design product features in accordance with market needs, it inevitably ends up with inferior quality. Many manufacturers simply do not have the time to share their designs with their later buyers before they introduce them for sale. Naturally, one wonders whether they use them themselves.

In addition, markets in the rich industrialized countries are showing increasing signs of saturation. New consumer values are coming to the fore. In the future, customers will increasingly insist not only on quality, but also on endurance: "People aren't about to stop buying things. But instead of more and glitzier, they will want fewer and more durable."[48] This will be even more true in periods of recession or in markets in poorer countries where harsh economic realities preclude a rapid succession of new product purchases. Manufacturers who continue to insist on machine-gun sequencing of new products will therefore face increasing difficulties.

Product Continuity

In May 1991, Apple Corp. introduced its new operating System 7.0 for its line of Macintosh computers. Both the press and experts unanimously hailed it as a significant technical improvement over the previous System 6.X. Although its purchasing price was generally regarded as quite reasonable, two years after its introduction, far less than 50% of all Macintosh users had bought it. In the fast-paced personal computer business, two years is a very long time. The reason for its poor acceptance rate lay largely with the circumstances surrounding the System 7.0's introduction. Not only was it accompanied by very poor publicity on the part of Apple which left many potential computer users insecure with respect to the product's utility. Many users of the old system also suffered additional costs because the switch to the new system required some of their other software applications and files to be adapted. This led to significant increases in the effective costs of the new product which could easily reach $500. Finally, for the average Apple customer, the complete range of the new system's usefulness only became fully accessible after a considerable and time-consuming learning effort.[49]

---

48 Fischer, 1990.

For the sworn community of Apple users, all this was a bitter disappointment. In the past, they had repeatedly resisted very tempting offers by rival suppliers to lure them away from "their" Macintosh. On the other hand, the community lived largely on the renowned user-friendliness of the Macintoshs and therefore had little technical expertise nor any interest in acquiring it. No wonder, that many users preferred to stick to the old system for longer than Apple had planned for them to. At least they were familiar with its restrictions. Meanwhile, Apple has introduced System 7.5 and is already working on System 8.0.

The story of System 7.0 is a typical consequence of the Acceleration Trap. In committing themselves to a dizzying rate of new product introductions, manufacturers are increasingly overrating the ability to create a continuous stream of innovations as a crucial prerequisite of competitiveness. Having arrived at this conviction, it is apparently quite difficult to escape from it. In 1991, Japanese manufacturers of white goods (refrigerators, washing machines etc.), for example, could not even be moved by serious exhortations on the part of MITI to reduce wasteful production methods and switch to longer product life cycles in the face of difficult economic conditions. Although one could observe a brief lengthening of product life cycles in 1992, it did not last. In the case of brown goods (audio, TV, etc.), not even that happened. To the contrary, in business year 1993/94, the number of models simultaneously offered by manufacturers in the Japanese market again increased over the previous year.[50]

Such an attitude becomes particularly problematic if there are no obvious follow-up innovations in sight.[51] The technical advancement incorporated in every new product generation becomes more complex and more costly. Unfortunately, customers do not always regard this as "progress." Even such technology-intensive products as computers are no longer differentiated by their technical specifications, but tend to be viewed almost as commodities. The sophistication of product features like the resolution of a monitor, hard disk read/write speeds, the number and transfer rates of storage media, networking capacities and all the rest can hardly tempt a buyer. Nowadays, almost anybody with some technical background can build a working computer. The parts can be purchased anywhere. As technical

49   Galvin, 1993.

50   Kanno, 1993.

51   This was already pointed out in a review of Casios product policies in 1982 by Ohmae, 1986, p. 92.

progress in PCs concentrates increasingly in the components of systems, in processors and the like, the systems themselves become exchangeable. Anyone who has ever bothered to take a look at the insides of a PC can confirm this. By far the greatest share of its volume is just air. The rest consists largely of electronic components whose main difference lies in their manufacturers' logos printed on their sides or tops.

The same is true of cars and motorcycles. Nowadays, they are manufactured almost on a worldwide basis. In the first half of the 1950s there were less than a dozen countries that had the infrastructure, the capital and the know-how to afford an automobile industry. These were the "classic" automobile nations U.S., England, Germany, France, Italy and a couple of others. Today, there are at least 40 countries participating in this market with varying depths of value-added. They include most of Southeast Asia, Latin America, Northern Africa, India, Turkey and other countries on the verge of breakthrough to industrialization. True enough, some of them are still at the level of assembly, but their ambitions definitely range further and in the future could easily include vehicle development.

Technically, a supplier can therefore only hope to differentiate his product from that of his competitors if he can offer some *fundamental improvement* or at least something that looks like one. That is not only very expensive and risky, it can also easily lead the supplier into a technological wilderness where the compatibility with existing products is no longer guaranteed or where customers are faced with increasing comprehension difficulties. No wonder that they sometimes simply refuse to add another device to the many they have already invested in.

It is exactly this problem that suppliers of audio equipment like Sony, Philips and Panasonic are faced with while they are frantically developing new products to stimulate the market for consumer electronics which has been stagnating ever since the introduction of the compact disc. The compact disc replaced the LP record which previously replaced the shellac record. But what will come after the CD? Certainly, not every household has got a CD player yet. But because of long development times, companies need to think several years ahead about what will come next. Since 1990, the market has therefore witnessed the announcement of a whole range of new and different audio concepts with confusing names like DAT, DCC, MDD, and DAC from different suppliers that are only partly compatible with existing systems at best. Among each other they tend to have nothing in common except for the letter D (for digital).

Most recently, these efforts have been joined by the attempt to introduce digital VCRs and to replace another well established standard with a new one,[52] or alternatively to introduce digital video discs (DVD) where hopeful manufacturers only managed to agree on a partial set of common standards. There will be six different disc types for different usage types. As of this writing, compression algorithms for the video signal will be the same, but for sound compression they will not. As a result, video discs purchased in the U.S. will not run on a European disk player.[53] Just as with videocassette recorders in the 1980s, there is a danger that several formats will emerge. In any case, one of several marketings aims of DVD is to replace existing media like CD-ROMs. This would cut off CDs' market potential and the likelihood of their sustained support through software providers before it has been anywhere close to fully exploited. Something similar might happen with personal computers, which according to ideas of companies like Oracle could be replaced by network computers before the end of the century. Floppy disks are another case in point. Outside the world of mainframes, these "floppies" have become the primary mobile medium for temporary or permanent data storage. According to Fokus Magazine 32/93, a total of roughly 20 billion floppies had been sold by mid 1993. They contain an unimaginable volume of numbers, texts, images, sounds and knowledge from the worlds of science, society, business, and the arts. Part of this information, at least, is intended for permanent storage. In a few years, however, no disk drive will be able to read the disks. If they are not copied (and, with every new standard, recopied over and over again), the innovation infatuation of computer firms may therefore lead the historians of the future to regard the best known era in history as the worst documented phase of human development.

Macroeconomic Costs and Use of Raw Materials

We will finally turn to those consequences of the Acceleration Trap that lie outside the area of immediate corporate concern. There are numerous issues, but we will address only two. They touch on the ecological and macroeconomic aspects of shorter product life cycles.

To come straight to the point, the acceleration of product life cycles automatically leads to the wasteful use of natural, or national, resources. A

52 Innoue, 1993.

53 Ishizawa II, 1994; Hirose, 1995; Ishizawa IV, 1995; Mergler, 1996.

simple calculation shows this:[54] Let us assume that a factory (or some number of factories) annually produces and sells 100 machines needed in the economy. Let us further assume that these machines are subject to straight-line depreciation of 10% per year and that they are scrapped at no costs when their book value has reached zero. Under these conditions, the installed base, i.e. the number of machines sold and used in the economy, will grow until the number of machines scrapped and sold annually is the same. The scrap rate of 100 units per year equals the annual production volume of 100 units per year when the installed base has reached 1,000 units. This point occurs about 30 years after the factory goes on line. After that, the installed base remains at 1,000 and the factory produces only replacements for depreciated machines.

Assume now that the depreciation rate were doubled to 20%. This would correspond to a halving of product life cycles from 10 to 5 years. Running at full steam, the same factory would now only suffice to produce an installed base of 500 units. Already after about 15 years, it would only produce replacements for scrapped machines. Since the production capacity of the factory stays unchanged at 100 units/year, its *microeconomic* characteristics will be more or less the same. *Macroeconomically*, however, there are considerable differences. The country now needs twice as many factories plus the resources to operate them to guarantee an installed base of 1,000 units.

A similar set of considerations applies to the consumption of raw materials under conditions of short product life cycles. Today, the sheer volume of production and scrappage even in industries such as electronics, which in earlier times were considered ecologically sound, has led to serious waste disposal problems, not to mention the waste generated by the more raw material and energy intensive branches of industry.[55] No doubt, the reclamation of raw materials plays provides partial relief. It is also true that a lot of progress has been achieved in this respect recently, particularly as manufacturers are beginning to design recyclability into their products from the outset.[56]

But even if recycling can relieve many problems, it cannot solve them. In particular, any raw materials savings that can be achieved by recycling

---

54 The author first heard of this example in a lecture given by Dennis Meadows at the International Academy of the Environment in Geneva on June 29, 1992.

55 Naegele, 1989; Buhl, 1990.

56 Regarding this whole issue, see Schwanhold et al., 1993, p. 51 et seq.

can be destroyed again by shorter product life cycles and correspondingly shorter useful lives of products. Figure 5–7 reveals this. It shows the combined effects of cycle lengths and recycling ratios on the installed base of a good at a given point in time.

Figure 5–7 should be read as follows: Assume that in a country like France there is an installed and constant base of 120 million radios. If these radios have an average life cycle length, or useful life, (right axis) of five years, then it follows that every year 20%, or 24 million radios, are scrapped and replaced by new ones. If scrapping involves an average recycling ratio (left axis) of 50%, it further follows that one half of the scrapped radios is transformed into new radios or some other good. The other 12 million radios, corresponding to 10% of the installed base, end up on a dump, and it is this rate that can be read off on the vertical axis of Figure 5–7 for a combination of varying cycle lengths and recycling ratios. The labor input and the raw materials contained in these dumped radios, some of it quite valuable and/or extracted at some ecological cost, are lost for good.

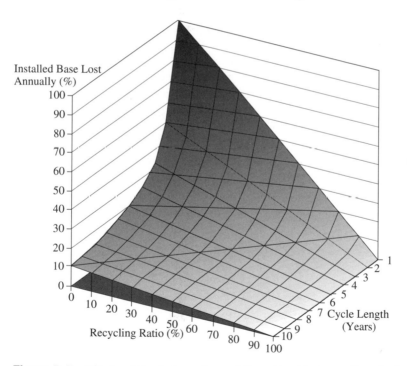

Figure 5–7 Effects of Cycle Lengths and Recycling Ratios on Installed Base, percent

An investigation of the three-dimensional surface of the figure shows that life cycle lengths impact raw material savings far more than recycling ratios do. In other words, the longer use and occasional repair of a product is better than its reclamation. For example, with 8-year life cycles and a 20%-recycling ratio, 10% of the installed base is wasted annually. To maintain the same 10% loss of installed base with 4-year cycles requires recycling ratios not of 40%, but of 60%! With 10-year cycles, even if *nothing at all* is recycled, the installed base loss is no higher than for 1-year cycles and a *90%* recycling ratio. Only with 100% recycling ratios are there no losses, irrespective of cycle lengths.

Unfortunately, the laws of thermodynamics disallow recycling ratios anywhere close to 100%. Even the best recycling technology is associated with some energy losses and the use of further raw materials (and therefore also of financial resources). According to the German Chemical Industry Association, for example, the cost of recycling household waste in 1994 was about $2,000 per metric ton. With increasing recycling ratios, there is a disproportional increase in recycling costs. Even under optimal conditions, recycling ratios for major commodities in practice, therefore, rarely exceed 60%.

The steel industry has perhaps one of the longest traditions of raw material recycling among all major manufacturing industries. According to the International Iron and Steel Institute, world production of raw steel in 1991 was approximately 737 million tons, as opposed to approximately 770 million tons in 1990. In 1991, about 414 million tons, or 56.2%, of total output was derived from scrap steel. In 1990, that value was 425 million tons, or 55.2%. In other industries, these values are usually significantly lower, unless they concern particularly valuable materials, precious metals etc. In plastics, a very sensitive area of the overall natural resources issue, recycling ratios are generally very low for technical reasons. Of the approximately 3.9 million tons of polypropylene consumed in the U.S. in 1992, for example, only 3% was derived from recycled material.[57] In addition, many countries, for whatever reasons, do not emphasize recycling that much anyway.

It is probably safe to say, that unless there are some very powerful legal or market incentives, recycling ratios will not increase very much. In Northern Europe and Japan, for example, where recycling in the private sector is far more widespread than in the U.S., households are beginning to regard

---

57 For further details including some very revealing statistics regarding this subject, see Kelly, 1994, particularly Figures 3 and 4 and pages 293-295.

the effort of sorting their trash by different colors of glass, tin, paper, bio refuse etc. into separate containers as a definite nuisance. Life before was so much easier. But this is presently not our primary concern. The crucial point is: recycling will only go so far. As far as coping with the effects of shorter product life cycles is concerned, it does grant some extra time. But in the long run it is a dead end.

As a last thought, only one more comment will be added: Even if one could recycle 100% of raw materials at zero energy expense, the share of materials tied up in the recycling process at any one time would be much higher with short than with long product cycles. For example, if the complete recycling process, i.e. the sorting of used materials, reprocessing, storing, reintroduction into the industrial process and marketing of new products, takes one year, then with 3-year product life cycles, 25% of all raw materials for that particular product/market would be in the recycling process at any one time (three years of utilization plus one year of recycling). With life cycles of nine years, this value comes down to 10% (nine years plus one). Naturally, the difference between 25% and 10% of raw materials enters product prices. Finally, with the acceleration from longer to shorter product life cycles, recycling capacities have to be expanded to cope with a higher recycling demand. No doubt, this creates jobs and perhaps it is an attractive investment. It does not, however, contribute much to the overall productivity of the economy.

Closing Comments

The list of consequences of the Acceleration Trap discussed above is by no means exhaustive. It could be expanded significantly, especially if one were to include societal dimensions. For example, no mention was made of the tensions arising in a society where even a 30-year old can no longer comprehend the consumption habits of teenagers. What are the psychological impacts if every purchasing decision in a free market *for* a good is automatically associated with 9,999 decisions *against* an overabundance of other ways to spend money? More and more, large high-tech corporations are discovering that they themselves are failing to keep up with the swift changes their own advanced technologies have wrought upon them. In industry, millions of employees are under constant and enormous pressure to learn and relearn, to change their fields of expertise or their professions and to adapt to varying work environments. This leads to substantial strains, not only for them, but also for their families, for corporations, for communities, the educational system and society at large.[58] Of course, it is true that nobody should, or wants to, do the same thing year-in, year-out. But it is also true that everybody needs at least some degree of stability in his or her working life. How else could they ever put whatever they have learned to use, or gradually hone their skills, or find satisfaction and pride in their achievements? This is just as much part of a humane reward system as fair salaries and wages are. A frequently quoted piece of wisdom these days is "In the future, the only constant is change." Or something to that end. In everybody's interest—including that of industry—perhaps it is time to question the wisdom of that particular statement.

Twenty years ago, Abernathy and Wayne in a classic article pointed out that "management needs to recognize that conditions stimulating innovation are different from those favoring efficient, high-volume, established operations."[59] Their analysis showed that an *exclusive* reliance on learning curve and cost digression effects can lead to a decreasing ability to respond to innovative competitors. They argued that innovation and customized, superior products are a better strategy than selling price competition, particularly if it has already been going on for some time. The essential message of the article is that price minimization does not guarantee market success for all times.

This, however, also works the other way. Seeking competitive advantage excessively in a constant torrent of new products at the expense of other instruments of business success can be just as dangerous. Innovation is a good thing at appropriate intervals and appropriate speeds. It is not an end in itself. Companies and industries would do well not to be deluded by the general glorification of innovations. They should beware, lest it become a fetish.

There is an old adage: In sufficient doses any medicine becomes poison.

---

58 For example, the scarcity of qualified workers for growing high-tech companies has led to what Labor Secretary Robert Reich has called a "paradox" in the work force. The need for new and constantly adapting skills has created two labor economies, one where wages are rising and the other where they are falling. Motorola, for one, has had to reject nine out of ten job applicants as unqualified for the company's factories. Source: Swoboda, 1994.

59 Abernathy and Wayne, 1974, p. 118.

Summary

Leaving the theoretical model of Chapter 4, Chapter 5 turns to "the real world" and gives some examples of the dangers a corporation is faced with if it falls into the Acceleration Trap. These dangers concern both the management and structure of a company and include among others:

- Late warning signals that the product range of a company is getting narrower;

- A decline in average sales per product;

- An increasing share of younger and therefore, riskier products;

- Severe and costly time pressures in the development of new products;

- A dangerous shortening of corporate time horizons;

- Drastic financial consequences of product failures.

Market adaptations to shorter product life cycles mean that the profits of innovation or technology leaders are becoming increasingly short-lived, or do not occur at all, because modern technology itself allows lightning-speed competitor reactions. Technology leadership positions today are not measured in years, but in months, sometimes weeks. In addition, one can expect a declining degree of innovation acceptance by customers if innovation rates begin to exceed the speed with which markets can digest change. Innovation saturation is no impossibility.

Since short time spans between innovations preclude cost digressions and economies of scale which would otherwise be possible, shorter product life cycles in the final analysis also increase suppliers' cost burdens. At the same time, suppliers have less time for an effective management and implementation of the innovation process. This reduces the effectiveness and the efficiency of R&D efforts, irrespective of whether technology is developed in-house or outsourced. The innovator should be aware, that a product innovation will regularly entail a reduction in the market value of products already installed in the market. The care for this installed base and its clients are part of manufacturers' responsibility. It serves not only the long-term relationship between supplier and customer, but also a national and social concern for the efficient use of scarce resources and raw materials.

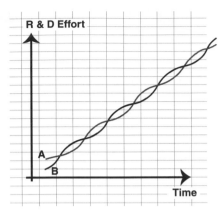

6

The R&D Spiral

One question deriving from the previous chapters is, why is all this happening? Why has R&D expanded at such colossal rates if its exaggeration leads to the consequences described above? Why do entrepreneurs, whose constant awareness and control of costs (at least in theory) is so diligent otherwise, saddle themselves with this burden? R&D costs money, a lot of money. And that is not all. Pharmaceuticals have to fulfill increasingly stringent requirements, legally, technically, and economically. Machine tools and industrial robots manufacturers are constantly enhancing performance characteristics with higher speeds, greater precision, increased efficiency. The density of electronic circuits on a microchip is approaching the ultimate barriers imposed by nature. In every area of technology, developers are fighting an uphill battle to push the limits of their fields or to find new fields. The cost of these improvements is exploding. Therefore, R&D efforts do not only cost a lot of money, but *more and more* money. In any company conducting R&D, it should be clear that these rising costs can only be justified if there is a corresponding expectation of profits. That, after all, is what business is all about. If something costs $100 now it must earn more than $100 later. Even if R&D's long lead times will not let this happen tomorrow, at some later time, in the foreseeable future, one does expect it.

Securing the Future

The most general justification of large R&D budgets is, briefly stated, "securing the future." Resistance to R&D budget increases is frequently overcome with slogans such as "Chemistry has a future because there is no future without it."[1] In economically difficult times, such slogans are also used to ensure that budgets are cut only gradually and unwillingly. "R&D," according to a plethora of industrial announcements, "is the foundation of our business/our jobs/our competitiveness, now and in the future." "It is the security(!) that we can achieve revenues when today's products can no longer be sold." "It is the guarantee(!) of our long term survival..." and similar statements.[2]

Such reasoning is not entirely unfounded. Any innovation that is based on technical change, cannot be had without some form of R&D, be it in-house or purchased externally. The only question is, how much R&D is needed to "secure" the future? Taken literally, attaining such security would require infinite means. A "secure future" is, strictly speaking, a contradiction in terms. By its very nature, the future is open and therefore insecure or at least uncertain, in today's world more so than in the past. If it were otherwise, the future would be some other notion, perhaps something like an "inescapable fate," but certainly not what we normally associate with that word.

But let us not split hairs. Let us not think of "securing the future" as the ambition to cast it in some fixed unalterable mold. Let us think of it in relative terms, i.e., as the need to get a *better* grip on the future, to have *more* of a say in shaping it, to concede the competition *less* freedom in determining our own destiny. And let us see R&D as a tool for pursuing this objective.

Under such eased constraints, however, any R&D operation will automatically be governed far less by considerations of the future and, by implication, more by those of the present. It means that the role of normative goals in R&D planning and priority setting will decline. The urgency of achieving certain results within a given time frame will fade. It further means that research objectives will be based less on what *ought* to be, than on what *is*, or even *was*. The reaction to *current* conditions and signals becomes a prime mover.

1   Coined by the Association of German Chemical Industries [Chemieverband].

2   See, for example, "Dynamik für morgen. Wer die Zukunft sichern will, muß schon heute neue Produkte entwickeln" ["Dynamics for tomorrow. Securing the future means developing products today."], Cannibol and Fischer, 1990.

Generally, such current conditions and signals can be of two different kinds. Either there is a market need that demands new or improved performance characteristics of products or processes, or some industrial R&D lab or other research institute develops new knowledge or technological capabilities. The former is demand driven and is usually termed "market pull innovation." The latter is supply driven. It attempts to identify an application for a new capability and is typically referred to as "technology push innovation." The details and the interactions of the constituent parts of these innovation models were explained earlier in Chapter 1. Their essential difference is that, in the case of "market pull," there is a need waiting for a technical solution, whereas "technology push" offers a technical solution for which a need still has to be found. Thus, in the one case, there is a problem looking for an answer, while in the other, there is an answer looking for a suitable problem.

A new technology, incidentally, can switch from one mode to the other. In 1961, for example, Theodore Maiman, then at Hughes Laboratories in California, built the first working prototype of a laser device. At that time, nobody really knew what a tightly focused beam of coherent light was good for. Initially, there was talk of modulating communications signals, of "death rays" to disable oncoming planes and missiles, and of tunnel boring machines that would melt their way through mountain rocks. Today, laser applications have realized some of these visions. Other unexpected ones range from supermarket scanners and eye surgery, over industrial welding, cutting and measurement, to music reproduction and document print. Hardly a week passes without the discovery of some new use for lasers. The problems lie more in adapting the laser's features to these applications than in finding them. For communications and imaging purposes or for high-density data storage, for example, it would be nice to have a durable laser that emits light at very short wavelengths, at the blue end of the visible spectrum or even beyond in the realm of the ultraviolet or x-rays.

In recent years, a third cause of growing R&D budgets has been added to the two mentioned above. Among the common justifications for exploding R&D budgets, this third reason plays an almost embarrassed role. Although its existence is not always readily acknowledged, it is in fact quite widespread and also falls under the heading of the various attempts to "secure the future." Its driving force, however, is not the recognition of a need for improved performance or of the potential of some new technology. First and foremost, it is based on the fact, or the belief, that some competitor, is, or soon will be, busy "doing something," either improving an existing technology, or creating a new one. In this way, "market pull" and "technology push" are joined by a third stimulus for increased R&D activities. We will call it "competition driven." It implies that a new R&D project is started, or the budget is increased, not because there seems to be a market, nor because it looks technically promising, but simply because somebody else has done so, or is threatening to do so.[3]

Driven by Competitors

How does this work? First and foremost, it requires an intimate knowledge of what the competition is doing. It is common knowledge today that the staffs of corporations in many of the technology intensive branches of industry are eyeing each other like hawks. In fact, aside from adapting products to local markets, one of the most important functions of the R&D facilities that large corporations maintain in other highly developed countries lies in the provision of a local "window on technology."

There is a good reason for this. Observing the R&D decisions of other organizations can often be a relatively cheap alternative approach to developing the underlying know-how oneself. Effective access to insider information on technical development programs in foreign countries or other companies is best achieved by becoming a member of the local research network. It is therefore no coincidence that the United States with its numerous and renowned R&D centers, its tradition of intellectual openness both at the university and the business levels and its excellent communications and transportation infrastructure has become the prime address for foreign R&D establishments. As of 1992, 141 Japanese companies maintained R&D facilities in the U.S., rising from a little over 20 in the mid 1980s. Predominantly, they were active in the areas of information, bio-, and automotive technologies. German companies had 35 laboratories in the U.S., more than half of these in the automotive and biotechnology fields, the U.K. maintained 13, France 12.[4]

---

3   "Competition-driven" in this context should not be confused with what is commonly referred to as "benchmarking". In recent years, the latter has developed into a sophisticated and often useful means for a company to discover its own strengths and weaknesses or is a contribution to the solution of previously identified crucial problems. Frequently, it does not only involve comparisons with direct competitors but transcends industrial boundaries.

4   Weiss, 1994.

Since the U.S. is the leader in most of the important high-tech fields, one finds proportionally far fewer non-national laboratories in France or Germany which also have smaller R&D establishments and are "protected" by a language barrier. The United Kingdom is a special case. In some important areas of knowledge, biotechnology, aerospace or solid state physics for instance, it is easily among the leading nations. In addition, it has the English language advantage. Both U.S. and Japanese companies, therefore, have good reason to go there first if they wish to establish any facilities outside the U.S. at all. Hitachi and Toshiba, for example, maintain research centers in the environment of Cambridge University. As a nation, Japan also has a lot of technology to offer these days, of course, but access there has never been easy for foreigners, so that only in very recent years one could witness an increasing number of companies setting up an R&D presence there.

There are also other, less formalized ways of information gathering, not only in industry but across the complete spectrum of R&D activities. Statements such as, "There is probably no exciting new performance curve [of superconductors] in any European laboratory that is not known the next day in all other interested labs,"[5] are indicative and hold equally well for the U.S. International scientific and technical conferences and meetings, for example, are extremely popular information nodes, not only because of the carefully selected exotic, climatic or cultural attractions of the chosen city or romantic island in which they normally take place.[6] The official program of presentations and workshops at such events can usually justify no more than 50% of the participation fees, at best. Whatever is shown or said in an official talk or lecture is always carefully predigested by the presenting organization to ensure that not too much precious know-how is revealed. Anyhow, the results presented in these papers are only rarely brand new. As a rule, they only report on what is already well established and is therefore a closed subject.

No, the really interesting information does not flow at the core of the conferences or in lecture halls, but at the periphery. That is where talk turns to subjects which are still in the idea stage or in preliminary phases of R&D. They are not completed yet and are therefore at the *current* center of developers' attention. Presumably no place on earth is used more frequently for the gathering of information on competitors' R&D (or any other) activities

5   Komarek, 1989.

6   Conspicuously often, meetings seem to be in Honolulu or Venice or St. Moritz, and only rarely in Belfast or Detroit or Kiev.

than the bars of conference hotels. That is where tongues are loosened and where "just between you and me," one or the other piece of valuable information slips across. Researchers in the same field often know each other personally and speak the same (technical) language. After all, one of the very principles of their profession rests on the open exchange and discussion of information. In a conversation with a colleague across organizational boundaries they may also find the ego boost they do not encounter in their everyday work environment at home.

Many large firms whose business is technical have recognized the importance of this informational shunting yard and are therefore quite eager to have their R&D staff participate in professional gatherings. In addition, they are also willing to undertake considerable other efforts to gain better insight into their rivals' R&D activities. Approximately one third of the high-tech chairs at the Massachusetts Institute of Technology, for example, are financed by Japanese firms, presumably not out of sheer altruism. The Japanese communications giant NTT even maintains an office in the Boston area, staffed by several highly qualified technology specialists, whose sole function is the acquisition of information on activities at MIT and Harvard and on the interaction of both universities with the many small (or formerly small) high-tech firms on Route 128. Other companies incorporate this as an additional function of their existing R&D laboratories abroad.

In the interest of success, many companies are willing to use every, repeat *every* trick in the book. The stories about Japanese R&D tourism to Silicon Valley have become legend. But there are more isolated cases too. The production manager of a new factory for chemical specialties in the American Midwest, for example, which was recently visited by the author, asserted that during construction the plant was overflown regularly by an airplane chartered by a competitor. The intent was to gain insight into processing technologies from aerial photographs of the plant layout.

Of course, it is not only innocent U.S. companies that fall victim to such sinister activities. Exactly the same game is being played among companies of the same nationality and with exchanged roles in Japan and Europe. On April 17, 1994, for example, the Japan Times reported that the CIA had supplied Detroit with industrial secrets on Japanese automotive technologies involving chemical catalysts, ceramic engines and long-lasting batteries. In February 1995, the French government expelled five Americans, including four diplomats, for spying on French technology, claiming that there were more U.S. than Russian agents in France. The

American Electronics Industry Association maintains an office in Tokyo, staffed by top line experts who read and speak Japanese. It is not only remarkably well informed, but also able to wield considerable influence. In the same vein, German firms like Daimler-Benz, Siemens, Volkswagen, Bosch, and the large and even mid-sized chemical firms maintain technology "listening posts" in Japan. Some of them also have branch offices in Korea, where they evaluate government and industry publications, tap into data banks, study press releases, maintain contacts with the right people and even go so far as to allow an occasional glimpse at their own technological lingerie in exchange for inside information.

The many pieces of the information jigsaw puzzle are collated at the firms' headquarters. This process is sometimes erroneously referred to as "benchmarking" or "identifying best practices in other organizations and learning from them." The puzzle pieces are evaluated and then become basic inputs for the firms' own R&D programs. It is not uncommon for this process to lead to R&D projects, which are based on nothing but a more or less precise analysis of what an important competitor is up to. Essentially, they are realized "just to be on the safe side."[7]

Imagine this fictitious, but quite plausible scenario: The American firm Silicon Graphics, well-known for its high-powered computer workstations, advertises in a U.S. newspaper for 20 biochemists. Something like that can hardly escape competitors' attention. Alarm signals go off in other computer firms in Japan and Europe—and naturally, in the U.S. The topic receives priority on the agenda of the next weekly meeting of R&D management. What is behind it? Why biochemists? Does SG have a biocomputer in the works? Are there any clues in the literature? What happened at the last conference? What has SG recently been patenting? What about the availability of biochemists? From which universities? Two assistants are assigned the task of gathering further details and presenting their findings within two weeks. At the same time, personnel will look into the labor market situation. Administration and logistics will check the availability of suitable laboratory facilities etc. etc. The rest is easy to imagine.

7   That this is indeed so is confirmed by a representative 1992 survey of industrial firms by the Japanese Agency of Industrial Science and Technology. 36% of all firms indicated that "competition with other companies" was their main incentive for technological developments. That percentage was second only to those referring to "user needs" (40%), see MITI, 1992, p. 18.

It does not always have to be a want ad that provides the initial spark for a new R&D project. Sometimes it is merely a side remark by a researcher friend working for a competitor about the purchase of certain laboratory equipment that triggers conclusions about new research directions. In other instances, it will be the remarkably frequent meetings in a conference lounge by managers from two competitors, whose technological interests would complement each other perfectly (why didn't we spot this before?). Unusual stock fluctuations, an odd remark by the head of R&D in an interview, or even a rumor, are enough to spark the R&D machinery to life. Basically, the machine's activities have little to do with satisfying actual or perceived market needs. They are determined far more by a sense of threat emanating from a business rival.

This orientation toward the level of technology or the activity of "the others" occurs not only in the context of industrial competition; one can also find it when countries or even continents compare themselves with each other.[8] It is regularly used to influence the definition of research programs and their budgets. Figure 6–1 shows a typical example. The table compares the current state and development trends for certain future technologies in the U.S. with those in Japan and Europe, with respect to both R&D and products.

Such tables have become very popular in all the major industrial nations in recent years. The Japanese, in particular, are extremely fond of regularly surveying firms and industry observers with respect to relative technology positions. The nice thing about such comparisons is that, depending on whether one wants to be seen in a leading or trailing position, one simply picks the appropriate technology fields. Since tables and graphs are always far more convincing than pure text or numbers and can be so easily copied, most of their readers do not bother to question the assumptions and definitions that underlie them, even if these should be contained in the accompanying text.

8 For example, it was interesting to note that toward the end of the 1980s, CERN, the European quantum physics research facility in Geneva, was developing the technology for the Large Hadron Collider (LHC)—a smaller but technically more ambitious version of the Superconducting Collider (SCC) then under construction in the U.S. By the time the LHC-plans were formally presented to the CERN Council for budget approval, the SCC had been cancelled. The immediate effect of this relieved competitive pressure was that some of the CERN member countries balked at the $689 million bill, see Anon.{16}, 1994.

	Compared to Japan		Compared to Europe	
	R&D	New Products	R&D	New Products
Advanced Materials	◆ ▼	▼ ▼	▲ ◆	◆ ◇
Advanced Semiconductor Devices	◆ ◇	▼ ▼	▲ ◇	◆ ◇
Artificial Intelligence	▲ ◇	▲ ◇	▲ ▲	▲ ◇
Biotechnology	◆ ▼	▲ ▼	▲ ▲	▲ ◇
Digital Imaging Technology	▲ ▼	▼ ▼	◆ ▼	▼ ▼
Flexible Computer-Integrated Manufacturing	▲ ◇	◆ ◇	▲ ▼	▼ ▼
High-Density Data Storage	◆ ◇	▼ ▼	▲ ◇	◆ ◇
High-Performance Computing	▲ ◇	▲ ▼	▲ ▲	▲ ▲
Medical Devices and Diagnostics	▲ ◇	▲ ▼	▲ ◇	▲ ▼
Optoelectronics	◆ ◇	▼ ▼	◆ ◇	▲ ◇
Sensor Technology	▲ ▼	◆ ◇	▲ ◇	◆ ◇
Superconductors	◆ ▼	◆ ▼	◆ ◆	◆ ◇

U.S. Level of Technology			U.S. Technology Trends		
Ahead	Even	Behind	Gaining	Holding	Losing
▲	◆	▼	△	◇	▽

Source: Emerging Technologies, U.S. Dept of Commerce, 1990

Figure 6–1　U.S. Levels of Technology and Technology Trends compared with Japan and Europe for 12 Emerging Technologies

For instance, what are "advanced materials" in Figure 6–1? The term can cover all sorts of things and involve the steel, electronic or chemical industries. Words like "Ahead" and "Behind" are also rarely explained. A typical statement in a company might be: "We are six months behind." Does that mean, that the leader was, where we are now, six months ago, or that will we be, where the leader is now, six months hence, or that it will take us six months to catch up? Each interpretation can lead to substantially different R&D measures and costs. Apart from that, what does "being behind" really mean? A six month lag between leader and follower in electronics or genetic engineering can be cause for alarm—or comfort, whatever the case may be. For nuclear power generation technology, it hardly matters either way. Even who the "enemies" in Figure 6–1 are, is not really clear. For example, is it Europe *per se*, or the European Union or European governments or

European firms? Does that include only firms with headquarters in Europe, or also those with significant revenues there (which would cover GM or IBM, for example)? What about transplants? No mention at all is made if licensing agreements have been taken into account.

On the other hand, the conveyance of technological information is not what these tables are all about anyway. Except in the rarest of cases, the addressees are not the scientists or engineers directly concerned. They usually do not need to be told who the respective leaders in their fields are. Rather, the tables are intended for the providers of financial resources, i.e., those who have the final say and can give the go-ahead. The general aim of such overviews is generally to support requests for funds. They work like a double-edged sword: Either they prove that one is in a trailing position and therefore needs more cash to catch up, or that one is in a leading position and therefore needs more cash to defend this position.

Nevertheless, even the scientists themselves cannot always detach themselves completely from such industry or company oriented comparisons. In the course of his work, this author has had numerous opportunities to do interviews in industrial R&D settings. In recent years, one of his favorite questions has been to ask—somewhat intrusively and persistently—a researcher at Company X, why he is working on a certain project. Amazingly often, the answer has been "I am doing it because Company Y is doing it." Perhaps one does not hear it every time and perhaps not always in these words. But this is what it often boils down to. Turning then to the scientists and engineers in Company Y with the same question, the answer is "because of Company Z." And since Z's researchers have based whatever they are doing on the threat posed by X, one finally arrives back at the starting point. There is an expression for such circular causality that feeds on an internal and uncontrolled logic of its own. It is an "escalation spiral" where one person's or organization's activity is largely dictated by that of another.

R&D and Arms Escalation—A Parallel

In 1889, the poet and later Peace Nobel Prize laureate Bertha von Suttner (1843–1914) described the same mechanism in its application to a completely different context. In her poem "Canon of the Great Powers," she set out precisely those rules which apply to the "competition driven" side of industrial R&D:

"My weapons are defensive,

Your weapons are offensive,

I must arm, as you are arming,

As you are arming, so I am arming,

So we arm

And arm and arm, on and on and on ..."[9]

The use of such comparisons is not new. Quite the opposite, the explicit or implicit analogy of military and industrial activity is used so often (including in this book) that by now it is taken for granted. Any further detailed discussion or justification is generally regarded as superfluous.[10] The parallels have become part of the everyday language used in press releases, financial reports and literature on business management. Everywhere, one finds mention of "marketing offensives," "concentration of forces," "competitive fronts," "market share gains," "product strategies" and many other activities and circumstances with a military flavor. Chief(!) Executive Officers(!) occasionally like to see themselves in the role of visionary field marshals. The same parallels also crop up in official documents. The reports of commissions and committees of inquiry submitted to government cabinets and parliaments often have a striking similarity, whether the subject is the industrial threat from Japan or the nuclear threat posed by the former Soviet Union.[11] The production capacities of automobile manufacturers are counted in the same way as rocket launcher sites or the numbers of Chinese military advisors in Third World countries. Occasionally, the very

---

9   "Meine Rüstung ist die defensive,

Deine Rüstung ist die offensive,

Ich muß rüsten, weil Du rüstest,

Weil Du rüstest, rüste ich,

Also rüsten wir,

Rüsten wir nur immer zu..."

Quoted by Bastian, 1991, author's translation.

10 See, for example, Rubner, 1991.

11 Ross et al, 1989 (for the semiconductor industry); Iklé et al, 1988 (for military deterrence), both reports to the U.S. government.

difference between military and civil items becomes blurred. In official statements of the 1960s, for example, the U.S. saw its long-term military air superiority threatened by the development of the (civilian) Anglo-French Concorde supersonic aircraft.[12]

One would be well advised to meet such popular equalizations of military confrontation and commercial competition with a certain skepticism. For one thing, there is one distinct difference between these two branches of human (or inhuman, if you will) activity, which renders their analogy fundamentally questionable. Simply put, victory in war depends on the successful destruction of enemy forces and/or the capability to absorb destructive measures by the enemy. The success of an industrial company, on the other hand, does not depend on the destruction of a competitor but on the creation of added value. It has been rightly pointed out that the former rests on "destructive capacity" and the latter on "distinctive capability."[13] In other words, the *military* strength of a country depends on the volume of available means, whereas the *economic* strength of a firm is a function of its competitiveness.[14] The latter can, but does not necessarily, depend on scale effects. Specialization, for example, can help a small firm's long term survival. Specialization in the military sphere, however one might imagine such a thing, would seem to be a somewhat dangerous strategy.

In spite of all this, the use of the military analogy for purposes of this particular study is not without merit. The reason for this has little to do with the choice of vocabulary. The analogy is meaningful because we do not compare the *whole* range of military and entrepreneurial activities in all their manifestations and characteristics. Our aim is rather to concentrate on only one narrow field. In the business case, this field is research and development, and in the military case, armament. Common to both is that they do not constitute the traditional core of entrepreneurial competition or military contest. Rather, they are both essential preparatory phases before either can take place. A war cannot be conducted without prior weapons procurement, and in high-tech industry, one cannot survive without preparatory R&D, irrespective of whether one carries it out oneself or buys it in. Also, scale effects apply to both cases. The more I arm, the longer or more intensively I can wage war; the more R&D I engage in, the more I can use technology as

12 Horwitch, 1982, p. 4.

13 Kay, 1993, p. 364 et seq.

14 For an excellent discussion of the question whether the term "competitiveness" can justifiably applied to national economies, see Krugman, 1994.

an instrument of achieving competitive advantage (providing, of course, that I procure the right weapons and develop the right technology).

The parallels do not end there. Even a superficial survey of some of the publications regarding the arms races after World War II[15] and prior to World War I[16] reveals an astonishing degree of agreement between mechanisms and trains of thought between the worlds of the military and of industrial R&D practice.

It is a well-known phenomenon that removing one's viewpoint from the current focus of interest to a different frame of reference can substantially facilitate the appreciation and understanding of it. The reason for this is that basic issues are detached from their factual backgrounds and are placed into a more general context. In the following pages we will make use of this effect to explore some of the parallels between industrial R&D and the process of military armament. If the parallels hold, then perhaps industry could profitably learn from the findings of military strategists and think tanks.

Escalation Dynamics

To begin with, how does such an arms (or a research) race come about in the first place? The basic mechanism was explained above: Two or more parties determine the intensity of their own activities based on those of the other party or parties concerned. Country or Company A compares its own actions with those of Country or Company B and reacts appropriately. If A sees that B's armament or R&D efforts are growing, then A will increase its efforts too. Simultaneously, B compares its efforts with those of A and reacts in like fashion to increase (or decrease) its efforts. After a few rounds, this leads to a constantly increasing (or decreasing) escalatory spiral.

A simple representation of this escalatory interdependence is modelled in Figure 6–2. At the top of both circles, the levels of R&D (expressed, for example, in dollars per year or employees) or of weapons (e.g. nuclear warheads or tanks) are shown. Both values are compared with one another as well as with the desired relative values (intersection of both circles). Actual and desired levels are brought in line with one another. The new levels are then compared again with those of the rival etc....

15 For example, Evangelista, 1998; York, 1970; Carlton and Shaerf, 1975; Axelrod, 1987.

16 Fischer, 1964, p. 15 et seq.; particularly p. 43 et seq.

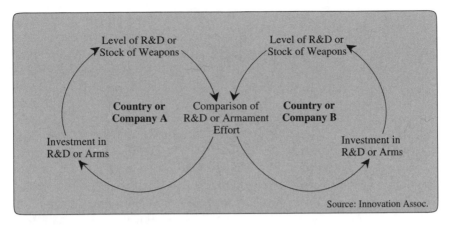

Figure 6–2 Escalation Mechanisms in R&D and Armament Efforts

Historically, there have been many escalatory arms races. They range from the rivalry between Sparta and Athens in the 5th century BC, Carthage and Rome in the 3rd century BC, over the Anglo-German race for naval superiority in the first decades of the 20th century to the U.S.-Soviet arms race up to 1990. Invariably, these races consisted of the same steps:

- Each country estimates the opponent's weapon strength.

- That strength is compared to one's own desired superiority (or tolerated inferiority).

- Desired strengths are compared to actual strengths.

- The gap between actual and desired strengths is closed.

After a certain procurement delay, a larger weapons arsenal than previously becomes available. This, in turn, serves as a departure point for the same steps of the enemy. One should note that, in such situations, weapons procurement guidelines are not set, for example, by whatever is needed to reduce enemy territory to rubble, but by the arsenal of weapons which the enemy has, or will have, at his disposal.

Interestingly, in such situations the estimate of the opponent's strength or potential does not even have to be correct. What counts are not the objective facts, but the *perceived* truth. The enormous efforts that went into development of the American atomic bomb during World War II, for example, were originally not carried out with the aim of bombing Japan or Hiroshima but for fear of "the" German atom bomb. For whatever reasons, however, there was no serious effort to develop such a bomb in Germany during the war.[17] Germany therefore found itself in a nuclear arms race of which it was probably not even aware, and America was racing a competitor who in reality did not exist.

As we know today, these types of assumptions were repeated quite often in the years following World War II. First encounters with the Soviet-built MiG-15 fighter planes in the Korean War, for example, led U.S. military planners to the erroneous conclusion that it was superior to Lockheed's F-86 "Shooting Star" and to the initiation of new American fighter designs.[18] The Soviet Union, for its part, began to develop its own uranium bomb in the 1940s only after the American bombs had exploded over Japan. In the case of the hydrogen bomb, it did not even wait for the first American device to explode. The mere suspicion—this time a correct one—that such an American program existed was enough to authorize its own program.[19]

Irrespective of whether the perception of the rival's activity is correct or not, the decisive point is the link between this perception and one's own activities. Almost compulsively, it leads to reactions based on simple formulas. It is also such cookbook reactions with which companies frequently support their R&D decisions, regardless of whether competitors' R&D plans and activities have been correctly fathomed or not.

Unfortunately, such external perceptions and linkages often come about in subtle, inconspicuous, even unconscious ways. For example, probably a majority of companies today determine their R&D budgets by looking at the average ratio of R&D to sales of all companies in their particular branch of industry or of their major competitors. Presumably, there is a certain comfort in knowing that one is spending just about as much as everybody else. "Well, if we are putting in the same effort as the other guys I suppose we can't be all wrong," the CEO might utter. That is true, but only to the extent that the other guys are not reasoning along the same lines. If they do, the system becomes very unstable. Since every company contributes to the average budget and if this, in turn, becomes the yardstick for

17 See Brix, 1994, p. 348.

18 Source: Private communication of Deutsches Museum, Munich, Aviation History Section, November 1994.

19 See Evangelista, 1988, p. 240 et seq.

everybody's budget, then an increased R&D allocation by just one single company can trigger the escalation spiral to start spinning.

Exactly the same thing can, and does, happen in the military sphere. In South East Asia, for example, the defence budgets of most countries have risen during the 1980s and the beginning 1990s, although not as much as the respective Gross National Products (GNP). Then in 1993, the Malaysian government suddenly decided to increase its defence budget from 2% to 6% of GNP over the coming years. This meant the end of the region's relative armament calm. The Malaysian government explained its initiative with "the fluid and unpredictable security situation" prevailing in Asia since the end of the Cold War, a diplomatic euphemism for the unpredictability of the People's Republic of China. Malaysia's additional weapons purchases, however, caused other countries in the region to become nervous. Neighboring Thailand decided to revoke its already publicized intention to reduce military expenditures. Among other things it bought a small aircraft carrier in Spain. Indonesia, for many years one of Malaysia's friends, suddenly recalled certain confrontations in the 1960s which had nearly led to war and decided to buy 39 decommissioned warships of the former East German navy.[20] Significantly, the average growth of defence budgets in Thailand, Singapore and Malaysia between 1989 and 1994 was between 13% and 15% annually. South Korea plans to double its defence budget in the five years to 2001. Taiwan's budget will grow by 20% in the year 1996/7. Not to be outdone, the official mainland Chinese defence budget in 1994 grew by over 21% to Yuan 53.3 bill. (ca. $6.3 bill.). The *inofficial* budget is probably a lot larger. Even Australia has given up its tradition of a purely self-defence oriented military arrangement and is pursuing a more active role in South East Asia. The region has suddenly become a very attractive market in the international weapons bazaar.[21]

Figure 6–3 illustrates a frequent result of the escalation spiral. While there is always a certain delay in A and B's reactions to each other's budget increases, there is nonetheless a continuous increase in absolute expenditures. At the same time, the *relative* positions of both parties remain more or less constant. If it is A's strategy always to have the larger R&D budget, and B's to match it or at least to come close to doing so, then their relative

20 Anon.{10}, 1993.

21 On 27 November 1995, The Nikkei Weekly sported a headline in its Asia/Pacific section "Arms race breaks out across Southeast Asia." Regarding this whole issue, see: Ota, 1994; Anon.{24}, 1994; Anon.{25}, 1994.

strengths will not change in the future. The participants in such races usually seem to forget that if all rivals increase their R&D budgets by the same percentage, it will be very difficult for any one of them to gain a significant lead. In the final analysis, Figure 6–3 shows us how individual rationality can turn into collective irrationality. What makes sense if one company does it (it gains a lead or catches up with the leader), ceases to make sense if everybody does it (not everyone can be ahead of everybody else)—a classic instance of the Tragedy of the Commons.

"Though this be madness, yet there is method in't."[22] Namely, if the growth of R&D leads to success (a correlation which, as we have seen in Chapter 3, can often only be shown with great difficulty) then the rule, that outspending the rival is the surest path to glory, has proved itself once again. If it fails, one can at least claim to have tried everything. This effectively excludes the possibility of assigning any blame if R&D costs tend to grow. In addition, inflicting pain or efforts on oneself, i.e. spending money, always conveys the feeling that "at least we are doing something," whereas refraining from such efforts can easily imply that one is shying away from facing the issues.

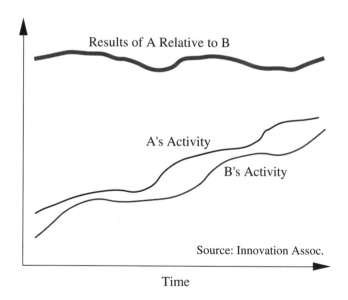

Figure 6–3   Escalation Results in Arms and R&D

22 W. Shakespeare, Hamlet I, 2.

In doubt, therefore, a company will rather pursue a new technology than run the risk of neglecting it. As long as this in accordance with the company's interests anyway, there is nothing wrong with it. But if it is not, the consequences are manifold: duplicated or unnecessary projects, needless developments, R&D for its own sake, and, in the end, more technology than the supplier can sensibly employ to satisfy current or potential market needs. It is also reminiscent of the military sphere: beyond a certain point, additional weapons do not confer additional security, but only increased costs. The associated risks, on the other hand, increase immeasurably.

In the business world, one can observe numerous companies following the principle of R&D escalation as a deliberate strategy. Some of the large Japanese corporations regard permanent technological leadership as an essential pillar of corporate policy. At NEC, for example, the determination to be Number One in every field of company endeavor borders on religious dogma. Toshiba, too, has repeatedly expressed a jealous ambition to maintain a constant lead in memory chips. This aim is becoming increasingly difficult to fulfill in view of growing competition from Korea. In 1992/93 Samsung replaced Toshiba as the leading producer of DRAM chips. This, in turn, has resulted in massive investment programs by Japanese manufacturers.[23] "We can't tell [Korean electronics manufacturer] Samsung and the others to stop investing," said Hajime Sasaki, executive vice president of NEC. But he said Japan's biggest chipmaker was 'prepared to make the investment necessary to keep up.'[24] The escalation is in full swing ...

Similarly Sharp, which marketed the first pocket calculator with a liquid crystal display (LCD) in the beginning of the 1970s, has taken care never to lose its lead in LCDs. Such decisions are not always cheap to uphold if they are not borne by rapidly rising demand. In the case of LCDs, at least, that seems to be no problem. The world market is presently growing at over 25% per year. However, other firms, such as NEC, have also developed the ambition to become leaders in the field. Little wonder that between 1987 and 1993, Sharp's LCD R&D team grew from approximately 150 to 1,000 employees. In February 1995, a 3-year investment program of ¥130 bill. (approx. US$ 1.3 bill.) was launched for the development of color and monochrome LCDs, ¥10 bill. more than originally planned. Meanwhile, NEC has also doubled its budget.[25] Both companies are said to be spending $1 bill. on

23 Anon.{14}, 1993.

24 Anon.{20}, 1994.

25 Hirose, 1995; Nakamoto, 1993; Naide, 1993; O'Toole, Thomas P., 1993 I.

new LCD facilities, while other companies like Seiko-Epson, Toshiba, Hitachi, Casio and Sanyo and even Korean and U.S. companies are entering the fray.[26]

Japanese companies are by no means alone in such intentions and actions. The U.S. giant General Electric thinks along similar lines. 3M, perhaps one of the most innovative companies in the world and also termed an "ideas pressure-cooker", has recently been placing even more emphasis on the introduction of new products than it traditionally has anyway.[27] In Germany, Siemens has not shrunk from a carefully masterminded deployment of the company's notoriously large coffers in the struggle for leadership in public communications networks. Part of this strategy is founded on the anticipation that sooner or later others in the field will simply lose their R&D stamina. So far, the plan seems to be working. "Eight years ago there were about 25 firms competing in the field; now there are only seven really important firms."[28]

A particularly instructive example of such escalation dynamics revolves around Intel Corp.[29] In 1971, the firm invented the microprocessor, which is the heart of every present day computer. Between 1978 and 1991, the company did not have an exclusive monopoly in microprocessors but did hold a very dominant market position. This was largely based on its relationship with IBM. IBM's personal computers were world market leaders, were sold by the millions and moreover gave rise to legion upon legion of PC-clones (identical or operational copies of IBM-machines produced by other manufacturers). All of these PCs, together some 90% of a worldwide total of 140 million units in use in the beginning 1990s, used Microsoft's DOS operating system. DOS, in turn, only ran on the x86 series of Intel microprocessor chips. Intel developed several generations of increasingly powerful 86-series chips to drive the DOS-PCs. The 8086 processor (1978) contained 29,000 transistors and could process 16 bits of data simultaneously. The fourth generation 486 which was introduced ten years later consisted of 1.2 million transistors and could process 54 million instructions per second.

26 Anon.{27}, 1994.

27 See Anon. {29}, 1995.

28 Ludsteck, 1993 I.

29 Information on the Intel case is based largely on Anon.{11}, 1993; Anon.{21}, 1994; Anon.{22}, 1994, corporate annual reports, and the Intel Forum accessible through the Compuserve® computer network.

Intel's quasi-monopoly was reflected in its financial results. In 1992, the production of one 486-chip cost about $20–30. It was state of the art and sold for ten times that amount or more. In the same year, the firm's revenues were $5.8 bill., approximately 60% of which was microprocessors. Net profits were a handsome $1.1 bill. All of this was achieved by a workforce of only 26,000. Intel's per capita *profit* after taxes was higher than the per capita *revenues* of many other companies generally regarded as financially healthy. Because Intel had the time to delay the development and introduction of new microprocessors until the market asked for them, corresponding R&D costs were considerable but easily financed. Selling prices remained relatively high. Nevertheless, they were reduced by about 12% annually to keep customers happy. The world of Intel seemed almost too good to be true.

Unfortunately, things that seem too good to be true, usually are. Rich pastures will always attract further eaters. For one, relations with IBM cooled after it became increasingly clear that Intel was building its market success on the back of IBM's market dominance. IBM also began to look at other alternatives and started to cooperate with Apple and Motorola in the development of its own "Power" microprocessors.

For another, in 1991, a new Intel challenger had shown up in the shape of AMD (Advanced Micro Devices), a longtime Intel licensee. AMD offered its own version of the 386 processor which was both cheaper and more powerful than Intel's. It was immediately able to win a considerable share of the market. Intel reacted by suing for patent infringement. Legal proceedings lasted for a several years. They ended in January 1995 in a compromise after both parties had spent millions of dollars in lawyers' fees. In addition to legal action, Intel was also obliged to take the technological initiative. Because greatest profits could be made where the company still had a (technology) monopoly, new products had to be found quickly. The result was the 486 chip, a product against which neither AMD nor Cyrix, another rival that had appeared on the scene, could compete at the time.

But Intel could not stop there, since both AMD and Cyrix were already working on follow-up products to their 386-chip. The range of applications for the 486-chips was broadened as quickly as possible. By the end of 1993, Intel offered at least 30 different versions of the 486. In addition, the development of the next processor generation, the Pentium (actually, the 586, with 3.2 million transistors able to process 250 million instructions per second), had to be speeded up. It was announced at the beginning of 1993, one year earlier than expected, and was accompanied by an $80 mill. promotion campaign to accelerate its market acceptance. Unfortunately, the first few million Pentiums to be delivered contained a fault that caused arithmetical errors under certain circumstances, perhaps a mistake that could have been avoided if the processor's development cycle had followed the original schedule. In any case, Intel's competitors, and particularly IBM, were most happy to take advantage of this opening.

Another problem with this rapid technological advance was that increasing chip power was not exactly cheap, neither in R&D nor in manufacturing. For example, a factory for the 386-chip cost about $200 mill. A 486-chip factory cost on the order of $1 bill., and for the Pentium (586) Intel was looking at $5 bill. The compulsion to stay in the lead caused Intel's R&D budget to skyrocket. In 1994, it reached $1.1 bill., 42% over 1992 and 3.5 times that of six years earlier. With $2.4 bill., Intel's capital investment in 1994 was almost double that of 1992. Since products were now being aggressively pushed into the market instead of waiting for the demand to materialize, the cost of sales was also going through the roof. In 1994, it reached $5.6 bill. or 71% over 1993 while sales grew by "only" 31%.

All this was bad for profits, of course. In 1994, Intel's operating income stagnated for the first time since 1986 and stayed at a little under $3.4 bill. That was still a very handsome profitability, of course. Compared with previous years, however, and even if one discounted the $475 mill. extraordinary charge Intel took for the faulty Pentiums, it was a throwback: Between 1987 and 1993, Intel's operating income grew at an average of 55% per year.

In 1995, Intel's results were back on track again. Net revenues grew by 41% to $16.2 bill. Operating income grew even faster by 55% to $5.25 bill. But the race continues. In November 1995, the sixth generation Pentium Pro Processor (originally dubbed the P6) which in turn is twice as fast as the Pentium[30] was introduced in the market, while the seventh generation chip, due to enter the market in 1997, was in advanced stages of development. Intel's rivals, in the meantime, are not standing still either. Both AMD and Cyrix have announced their own versions of the Pentium. Because their developments started later, they can avoid some of the R&D-dead ends Intel encountered and at the same time enhance their processors' performance for additional attractiveness. This, in turn, will force Intel to introduce its fol-

---

30 It also follows slightly different architectural principles taking it somewhat closer to the competing RISC-type microprocessors developed by Motorola.

low-up chip even earlier and to reduce prices for the products already on the market earlier than planned.

Intel has won another round. But not the war. The technology escalation wheel continues to spin. More predators are showing up, UMC from Taiwan, for example, or NexGen from Milpitas Ca. South Korean competitors like Samsung, Hyundai and LG Semicon have announced plans to enter the non-memory chip market. The IBM/Motorola/Apple alliance to develop RISC-based processors is also moving along. They are all hot on Intel's tracks and have money to spend. Since the company has room for price reductions on the one hand, and also the cash for technology improvements on the other, it will probably be able to keep its lead for a while yet. But the days of quasi-monopoly are over. That would only work if the PC market continued to grow sufficiently fast (something Intel has no direct control over) and if users were willing to go along with an endless series of P7s, P8s, P9s and P-whatnots. Whether, and to what extent, that will be the case remains to be seen. In any case, there is a striking similarity with the runaway naval escalation during the years of crisis leading up to World War I in Europe. At the time, Great Britain insisted on maintaining the largest naval fleet in Europe,[31] Germany insisted simultaneously on its right to acquire its own showpiece navy. It did not do either one very much good. Except for one major battle, neither fleet saw much action during World War I, not did they contribute very much to its outcome.

Overkill

Once one has embarked on the escalation road, it becomes very easy to overshoot the target. In the microprocessor arena this seems to be about to happen. In the military arms race, it has become abundantly familiar in recent decades. At the height of the Cold War, both the U.S. and the Soviet Union had sufficient nuclear weapons at their disposal to have made planet Earth uninhabitable many times over. Yet still more warheads were added to the arsenals. Not without reason were the Superpowers' efforts at the time appropriately dubbed the "Race to Oblivion."[32]

---

31 At the time, Great Britain demanded the so-called "two-power-standard" according to which the Royal Navy had to be at least as large as the second and third largest European navies put together. The parallel with the post-cold-war U.S. policy of maintaining armed forces large enough to lead two wars simultaneously seems more than superficial.

32 York, 1970.

Such excessive armament occurs for several reasons. One of the principal ones is that no effective brake exists to stop rivals from mutually and repeatedly attempting to outdo each other. Such a brake could be recognized by its ability to stop the arms or R&D effort at a time when further efforts cease to provide a corresponding gain. One example from the history of the nuclear arms race where such a brake was lacking may serve to illustrate this:

Between 1950 and 1960, the average explosive power of U.S. nuclear warheads increased by a factor of roughly 1,000. Over the same period, the maximum speed of the delivery systems that carried the warheads to their targets (subsonic aircraft) remained more or less constant at about 1,000 kmh (650 m.p.h.). The increase in destructive potential meant that the population in the Sino-Soviet area immediately threatened by U.S. warheads increased from a few million to several hundreds of millions. Since the method by which this grisly statistic is measured is of no concern to us, we will ignore it.

In the following decade between 1960 and 1970, the explosive force of U.S. warheads underwent only a slight increase. But now the speed of the delivery systems increased by a factor of about 30 as intercontinental ballistic missiles travelling at 25 times the speed of sound replaced manned aircraft. The numbers of threatened population in "enemy territory," however, remained largely unchanged. The reason for this was that by 1960, a certain "saturation point" had already been reached. The increase in weaponry beyond this point was most fittingly termed "overkill."

Overkill came in two shapes. On the one hand, there were soon more bombs than appropriate targets. On the other hand, the destructive potential of a single bomb had become greater than necessary for the razing of even the largest cities. The overall result was that the arms growth from 1960 to 1970 had achieved practically nothing.[33]

So much for the arms race. In R&D, one can also observe a tendency for overkill, even though the phenomenon is not always as clearly discernible as in the military sphere. R&D overkill manifests itself in various ways. In one respect, there are products whose technical functions go far beyond what is usable or useful, or whose performance potential can never fully be exploited even by the most demanding of customers. Some examples may serve to illustrate this:

---

33 See York, 1970, p. 47 et seq.

- Millions of digital stopwatches all over the world can measure time to an accuracy of one *thousandth* of a second. A human being, unfortunately, is physiologically incapable of taking advantage of such precision. Registering a signal and reacting to it by exerting pressure on a button simply takes too long. Under the most favorable circumstances, a nerve signal from the eye to the brain, its processing there and the triggering of a fingertip response takes on the order of tenths of seconds. The indications of hundredths or even thousandths of a second is pure technology ballast with not the slightest practical value.

- Occasionally, a stopwatch will be able to perform this amazing function at no less than 200 meters (ca. 600 feet) under water. In his own interest, the author urgently advises even the most daring of his readers to refrain from testing such features personally.

- A number of bicycle manufacturers offer "super high tech" bicycles with 12, 18, 21 or 27 or even 36 gears. Now, the ratio progression of these gears is not linear, but is dictated by the size, respectively the relationship of diameters, respectively the number of teeth on the two sprockets selected by the rider out of a possible combination of 3x12 or 4x9 over which the drive chain runs. Sounds complicated? It is. It can result, for example, in the 16th gear coming before the 15th or even the 14th. A household calculator, best with a π-function, would be needed to determine the optimal gear for every speed range and situation.[34]

- Many of these household pocket calculators, in turn, are capable of working with figures which exceed, *by many hundreds of orders of magnitude* the number of electrons in the universe. What practical need can there be (except perhaps in the most exotic corners of combination theory and probability calculus) for such hand-held number crunchers? In a household, surely not any.

- In the living rooms and studies of the industrialized world, one finds audio devices whose faults are not only inaudible, but scarcely measurable.

- On the streets, there are cars whose engine, driving potential or road hold never come close to full exploitation.[35]

- The oversized (1 gigabyte is now the norm) hard disks of untold millions of PCs carry increasingly massive software programs whose

34 Bollschweiler, 1993.

possibilities are only exploited to a few percentage points. Their 1,000-page manuals, on the other hand, are usually incomprehensible. In any case, only the fewest of users are willing to read them or even look up something in "the new and improved version" every one or two years when a new generation is introduced in the market.

- In hospital examinations, expensive diagnostic equipment is frequently used only because it happens to be available, not because it results in improved medical care or because it is medically necessary.[36]

- Modern washing machines offer so many settings and wash programs that an average person is no longer capable of operating them.

- The remote control of the Sony SLV-E7VP video recorder (the author has one. It is no exception) comes with 59 pushbuttons plus two slide controls with a total of eleven possible settings.

- The instruction book for the Canon Wordtank (an electronic dictionary) is 220 pages long in every one of the eight languages it serves. It is several times larger than the Wordtank itself.

- From here it is only a short step to the Boeing 747, whose technical documentation is said to weigh more than the complete aircraft.

- In 1993, the world's fastest elevator (45 km/h) was installed in a 70-story building in Yokohama, Japan. It is only allowed to reach its top speed on the 27th floor, however, so as not to leave its passengers' stomachs on the ground. A mere 15 floors (some two to three seconds) later the brakes must cut in to ensure that they are not ejected through the roof.[37]

All these products or behaviors originated as the result of efforts to incorporate increasingly sophisticated levels of technology into products.

---

35 A nice example of this: The 1996 Honda CBR 900 RR motorcycle received a 99.8% perfection rating in Germany, up from the 99.6% for the 1995 model. The differences between old and new are minimal: a slightly adjusted sitting position, a 0.2" reduction of gas tank height, adjusted shock absorbers, reduction of tyre weights by ca. 0.5 oz. All in all, a wonderful piece of engineering, developed with significant efforts and offered at unchanged prices. The only drawback: Actually using only a part of the bike's capacities implies a permanent state of illegal driving. Source: Böhringer, 1996.

36 Bayles 1993.

37 See Anon.{12}, 1993.

The idea is to outdo the competitors by adding more and more performance and features instead of comprehending what the market really wants, even if the market itself is not always capable of specifying its wishes precisely. For the end users it is of small consolation that they "do not have to buy" such technologically oversized products. More often than not, they have no choice. As already indicated, supply is by no means always determined by what the market wants, but also by the actions of competitors. All too often, the customer can only purchase all of the features or none.

A second dimension of overkill has to do with time. Frequently, it is possible to determine when or what kind of market needs will arise for specific performance parameters. In the market for industrial adhesives, for example, a fairly constant rate at which users have demanded product enhancements has become apparent in recent years. In these cases, improvements have been readily absorbed by buyers. Often they have even participated in defining a new product's characteristics. In other cases, however, manufacturers have simply not waited for the right time to come. In the race to outperform the competition, they will introduce products or product features well ahead of the time when demand has sufficiently materialized and that any new products can really be of any practical use. Many spreadsheet and word processing software programs, for example, offer so-called "macros". These are recorded series of commands, keystrokes and mouse clicks of freely variable lengths that users of programs can define themselves in order to automate repetitive tasks and to customize their software. Such features have been available for at least ten years, but only now are average PC users gradually beginning to become aware and take advantage of them to any significant degree.[38]

Similarly, there is no obvious reason why the world should need a fourfold increase in the storage capacity of microchips every one to two years. The products and services based on these chips are all too often premature, or insufficiently tried and tested, or both. Intel's problems with its faulty Pentium processor which had to be rushed to market faster than originally planned are an obvious case in point. And memory chips and processors are no exception. Examples abound in other fields of technology, too. They include various teletext or consumer information services like BTX (or Prestel), ISDN (Integrated Services Digital Network), digital audio cassettes, bubble memory devices, Japan's HDTV and many others.

38 Crabb, 1994.

One frequently misapplied justification for such premature products or total failures is that the pace of change in modern societies, rapidly evolving markets, and the inconsistencies in consumer demand leave no alternatives to rapid-fire product innovations. What this kind of argument tends to overlook is that the hectic rate of change in the market is not so much the cause of suppliers' behavior patterns, as its effect. Nature probably intended human beings to feel comfortable with a far more moderate rate of change than the one they must cope with in their business or private lives today. Left to themselves, the habits of individuals, groups and organizations would therefore tend to appreciate a far slower turnover rate than present-day technologies allow.

A third dimension of overkill, and one which keeps escalation alive, is the widespread conviction that offence is fundamentally better than defence. In the world of the military, particularly after World War II, this became the predominant military doctrine fairly soon. It was understood that in the nuclear age and given a choice, the protection of one's own population was in principle ethically and emotionally perhaps more acceptable than the destruction of a foreign population. However, this could only be seen as a realistic course of action if one's own defence was 100% reliable. A single enemy bomb or missile that made it, or even might have made it, called the whole concept into question. Since it was impossible to give any guarantee for an untestable defence system, it was therefore better to rely on attack from the outset.[39] One predictable result of this was that whenever there was the suspicion (whether correct or incorrect) that the enemy was acquiring some awful new weapon, military planners of the other side would decide that it was better to get it first, "just to be on the safe side."[40]

More or less the same is true in industrial competition. Typically, a firm will no longer wait until it is reasonably certain that the rival is busy developing the next technology generation. Because often enough it has witnessed the rival pressing ahead with some new technology thereby forcing the extension of one's own R&D efforts, a company will assume that this is a permanent state of affairs. By now, perennially short product life cycles do not leave much time to think anyway. Simply assuming that the rival will do whatever one would do oneself, if one were the rival, makes it extremely

39 Carlton and Schaerf, 1975, p. 9 et seq.
40 See York, 1970, p. 31 et seq.

tempting to forestall him, "just to be on the safe side." This is what euphemistically is often called "preemptive strategy". Its result is not only that the spiral continues to spin, but does so at increasing speeds.

Escalation Drivers

In his farewell address to the American people in January 1961, President Dwight D. Eisenhower coined a term which was rapidly to become an integral part of political language: "In the councils of government we must guard against the acquisition of unwarranted influence, whether sought or unsought, by the *military-industrial complex*" [author's emphasis]. At that time and since then, the military-industrial complex has basically been regarded as consisting of two different notions. On the one hand, there was the fear of excessive political influence by a military "establishment" that cooperated closely with a large weapons industry. On the other hand, it warned of industrial machinations intent on involving the country in war in pursuit of economic interests.[41]

It should be clearly stated that despite the numerous parallels between the R&D race and various arms races, the author does not imply the existence of a civilian R&D-counterpart to the one actually or presumed to exist in the military arena. Any "scientific-industrial complex," or clandestine conspiracy of researchers and engineers across company-, industry- or national borders aimed at annual R&D budget increases, would be hard to imagine.[42] The R&D profession sees the open publication of its findings as one of its decisive success criteria. In contrast to the military, where secrecy is an important precondition of success, research and science do not flourish under cover.

Then again, R&D's enormous escalation in recent decades does beg the question who is behind it or has an interest in its continuation. Specifically, there are at least three aspects of the fear of the military-industrial complex which also hold for the R&D arena: In the course of the American/Soviet arms race, the vast expenditures, the complexity of numerous weapons programs, as well as the lack of any truly effective congressional (and—presumably—Communist Party) control, led to an atmosphere in which costs could grow largely unchecked. Bizarre overbillings (e.g. the

41 See New Grolier, 1992, under "military-industrial complex."

42 Interestingly, however, in recent years there is talk of a "medico-industrial complex," see Anon.{19}, 1994.

famous military toilet lid for $6,000) were often paid without question. Bribery, bid-rigging and the sale of information became such common occurrences that after a while they even failed to arouse widespread indignation. In its place, emerged an attitude of powerlessness that shrugged off the determination to get a grip on things.

It is this feeling of lacking control and of helplessness which can also be observed in many industrial concerns when it comes to R&D. In many cases, it has even reached the boardrooms. Quite frequently, the chief financial officer of a company or its CEO will attempt to gain control of R&D. Particularly during recessions such as the one affecting almost all industrial nations after 1991/1992, this has become a common occurrence. Usually, however, both CEO and CFO will lack the expertise to decide where one could, or should, cut the budget. If they go ahead and cut anyhow, as many of them do, they run the risk of being accused of gambling away the company's future. If they do not, they have achieved nothing. In either case, they have to rely on the advice of the head of R&D who is himself a researcher. There are only very few companies where this role is not the prerogative of a scientist or technician. As exceptions, they serve rather to confirm than refute the rule.

No doubt, there are certain advantages to having a technologist run a corporation's technological development. At the very least, he or she will be familiar with the typical day-to-day operations of an R&D department. One may wonder, however, whether these are really sufficient grounds to give that person the job. Just because someone is, or was, a good laboratory researcher does not mean that he will also be a good R&D manager or that he is capable of correctly judging R&D's contribution to sustained corporate success. The Peter Principle according to which a person is promoted until he reaches his "level of incompetence" does not stop at laboratory doors.

Apart from that, as a researcher the head of R&D will not be able to make any significant scientific or technical contributions anyway. The spectrum of technologies covered by any large or even mid-sized industrial concern today is far too broad to permit a full grasp by any one person. The narrow specialization in the natural and engineering sciences would never allow this. At best, the head of R&D will manage to stay roughly abreast of what is going on in his own area of specialization, if his time permits, that is. But even if he could keep up, the very fact that he concentrates his attention on one particular field of technology, would place grave doubts on his ability to achieve a balanced view of the whole range of technologies in which the company is involved. Even worse: As a researcher, he will be obliged to pass judgement on the role of research in his company as a whole. Since it is very difficult to be objective in affairs close to one's heart and mind, it is fairly obvious that this will not help in keeping R&D and its associated expenditures under tight control. In view of this, it might be well worth considering whether a non-R&D professional as head of R&D might not serve a corporation's technology *and* business interests far better. It would ease the integration of the R&D function with those of production and marketing and at the same time enhance the level of mutual understanding between members of diverse disciplines within R&D.

Moreover, it is becoming increasingly apparent that among the numerous means with which industry controls its costs and finances even in very large and complex operations today, there is none so far that would allow an equally effective control of R&D. To this day, accountants and academics are grappling with the problem of measuring the returns from money invested in R&D. Even for the smallest corporate investments, for example, a $30 rake for the gardener in the factory courtyard, there are procedures designed to keep track of billing, bookkeeping, depreciation and audit. The purchase of a photocopier or filing cabinet for a few thousand dollars regularly requires at least three competing offers plus a precise investment analysis which takes every detail into account, including the calculation of an internal rate of return. In R&D, all too often this is not the case. There, projects can sometimes cost hundreds of millions, run for many years and still not be subject to any really meaningful subsequent, let alone preceding control. Who can credibly and objectively state that the results of some R&D project (some of them good, some of them not so good, some of them on time, some of them late) were worth the project's costs? Even with foresight, who, outside the group of research personnel directly involved and therefore biased, would be in position to say if some extravagantly expensive piece of equipment is absolutely necessary? Even if it costs $1 mill. and is only used for 10 minutes per month, any critical questions from outsiders can always be silenced effectively by the technical expertise residing exclusively within the lab. Various attempts to install some form of effective R&D controlling have regularly failed for the simple reason that any controller would have to have an enormously wide range of expertise. It would have to include not only the relevant scientific and technical aspects of R&D work, but also its financial and managerial implications.

If controlling is to be more than just some form of subsequent control of proper resource utilization, and if it is to include an advisory function which ideally would also participate in the definition of goals, then things look rather bleak in R&D. Any R&D controller who could perform this function not just for one, but for a whole range of different technologies would have to be a Superman. It remains to be seen whether experiments with so-called technology audits will be successful or not. Daimler-Benz is currently attempting such audits, in which the actual need for a particular technology is examined by a panel of both internal and external experts.[43]

To repeat, it is this feeling of helplessness in which R&D has even surpassed the military-industrial complex. To give an example, in 1991, the R&D efforts at the Japanese electronics giant Hitachi reached 10.7% of sales for the first time. The company was always one of the largest R&D spenders in Japan, and perhaps the world. But for the first time in 1991, the sense of such rapidly rising R&D costs was hesitantly questioned. In a newspaper article, one of Hitachi's sales directors anonymously and respectfully remarked, "It is never clear whether we're getting adequate results based on our investment. We *may* need to establish a system to evaluate the effect of our R&D spending." The technical side quickly and very clearly rebuked him: "Anyone who argues that allotting more than 10% of sales income to R&D spending isn't cost effective is talking nonsense. *We are spending what's necessary.*"[44] But who knows what is really "necessary"?

Today, in military matters, at least in the Western democracies, there is invariably a political, non-military control authority which supervises and steers all armament efforts to some, more or less satisfying, degree. It is a moot point whether this structure was born out of the war experiences of the 19th and 20th centuries or is founded on the fear of the enormous destructive potential of modern weaponry. The military, in any case, does not claim ultimate decision making powers. Because war—and preparing for it—is far too important to be left to the generals, the Supreme Commander is always a civilian.

---

43 Cf. Hess, Interview with H. Weule, VP Technology Daimler-Benz AG, 1993; According to discussions of the author with a senior member of R&D at Daimler-Benz, there are already complaints that the audits were no more than routine exercises and really not worth their costs.

44 Matsumoto, 1990, emphasis added.

In industrial R&D, this is not the case. The organization of R&D, its choice of technologies and areas of enquiry are regularly left to the scientists and engineers themselves. Who else is there? They are the ones who decide on budget allotments or the procurement of laboratory equipment. They are even the ones to assess each other. The system of "peer review," where colleagues of the same or related fields pass judgement on papers published in technical journals, research grants and laboratory equipment, has been frequently criticized. The critics' main points are the counterproductive mingling of technical issues, personal considerations, aspects of career development, and the competition for scarce R&D funds.[45] In recent times, the same is increasingly being said of the "Science Citation Index," (predominantly in academia) and the "Patent Citation Index" (more relevant in industry) which claim to serve as indicators of the R&D productivity of individual researchers. Not only are such systems easily misleading and/or misled, they have also drawn criticism in that they involve only "members of the club" and are therefore biased. There are no external controls. Accordingly, they do not offer any guarantees that whatever the R&D department is doing is really necessary, nor whether it is doing it with the maximum degree of efficiency and effectiveness.

The result of all the "special circumstances" which, it is claimed, set R&D apart from other users of funds, is that many CEOs or company boards only approve an R&D budget or turn it down. They do not participate in *shaping* it. No doubt, there are numerous and important exceptions to this, particularly in companies where the CEO does have the necessary technical background or—even if not—is competent and confident enough to tackle the problem anyway.[46] But lacking this or any other capable authority, the "R&D-Establishment" will decide the distribution of its financial allocations largely by itself. It is little wonder, then, that R&D costs are under permanent growth pressure. By doing so they will also cause other companies— even if they are under strong leadership—to increase their R&D budgets too. To use a metaphor, it is difficult to lose or even maintain one's weight if one holds the key to the icebox.

45 See, for instance, McCutchen, 1991, p. 27 et seq.

46 The attractiveness of not having a researcher as VP R&D is not meant to imply that no former researcher should embark on a senior management career. Quite the opposite, this can make a lot of sense. Regularly, a researcher will not achieve this leading position without extensive business experience anyway. This should provide a sufficient basis for a well-balanced view of the whole breadth of corporate issues of which technology is only one.

Nevertheless, to blame only the scientists for all this would be misplaced. After all, they are only doing what they are supposed to and paid for. Obviously, they supply the initiative for many new programs and the pursuit of new ideas and concepts. Any accusation that they are doing this with some malevolent intent or against better judgement would be misplaced. Neither is it their aim to destroy the profits earned in the company's production or marketing departments. The same is true of the designers of the increasingly sophisticated or powerful weapons which serve more to reduce than increase the safety of their countries or the likelihood of world survival. Their motivation also is not some homicidal mania, or thirst for blood, or malice, or some other base or depraved intent. In a way, that is a pity, because, if it were the case, the "evil" could be dragged to the light of day and something could be done about it.[47] Unfortunately, this is not so. Weapons experts are usually convinced that their new concepts of defence or destruction really serve the well-being and security of their nation, just as a company's researchers and technicians are certain that all the expected results of their work are essential to the long-term well-being of their employer.

On the other hand, this does not mean that the scientists and others involved in R&D are saints. Nor, equally, are they innocent fools. They are—perhaps to the disbelief of many—perfectly normal human beings. They are subject to the same temptations, suffer equal animosities and harbor the same ambitions. They are no better and no worse, but just as greedy or generous, timid or courageous, opportunistic or confident, aspiring or indifferent as the rest of us. Most of them, in fact, are fairly harmless and, on average, perhaps a little more analytically minded than the rest of the population, which in turn might have been a decisive factor in their choice of profession. Finally and importantly, by no means are they inherently smarter, even though there are some very smart ones among them. While scientists' motivational structure, therefore, might differ from that of the average business professionals, their overall values are largely the same. Salesmen know that it is in the interests of their employers to sell more than in previous years. Engineers harbor no doubts that better quality makes good sense. Equally, technology developers are borne by the conviction that their findings and development results are something worth having and that financing them is therefore worthwhile.

Indeed, it would be astonishing if this were otherwise. All R&D professionals have invested many years of their lives in learning and mastering

47 York, 1970, p. 234 et seq.

their fields of specialization. If they are lucky, their active years will grant them the opportunity to contribute to the advancement of these fields by some small and perhaps even large amount. Over the years, the fields *must* become the center of their professional and even private existence. Under these conditions, will they be the ones to cut the budget?

Moreover, the scientists and engineers in the Western (and many of the Eastern) industrialized nations have had this self-assurance virtually thrust upon them. One of the great science fiction authors, Arthur C. Clarke, once said: "Any sufficiently advanced technology is indistinguishable from magic." That is true. We have let ourselves become enchanted by the feats and wonders that technology has wrought in these two centuries. The innumerable technical products and services for industry and consumers, the airplanes, antibiotics, ballpoint pens, cameras, cars, computers, concrete mixers, contraceptives, credit cards, detergent concentrates, electric bulbs, express trains, fertilizers, nylon stockings, plastic buckets, robots, sewing-machines, space ships, sun glasses, video recorders, x-ray machines, and zip-fasteners have made our lives safer and easier. Whenever need was greatest, technology came to the rescue. It ended wars and warned of hurricanes. It saved our children from disease and caused food to grow in barren deserts. It made us rich, enabled us to speak with remote corners of the world and unveiled the secrets of distant stars and planets. It was pure magic.

All these miracles bestowed a special aura upon the technicians and scientists who made it all possible. They became the high priests of the modern era, endowed with special insights only partially granted to other mortals, at best. Their august pronouncements are received in rapt devotion. Whatever emanates from the mouth of the scientist, already bears the proof of truth. Whoever begins a statement—however preposterous—with the words "Recent scientific findings have shown that...," will not encounter much disagreement. In his aptly titled book "Technopoly," Neil Postman has termed this tendency as *scientism*. According to this, "science," which basically was never more than just a set of standardized rules of procedure, has been promoted to something far greater. Even in nonscientific areas, these procedures and their results have acquired a status of irrefutable, eternal truths. Research and science have had the belief or even the desperate hope pinned upon them that they are the source of all Truth and Wisdom even in normative, moral or ethical matters, and that they contain the solutions to all problems. This is not only often the case within industrial corporations, but even more so outside them. Journals like *"The Futurist"*, for example, have developed, and are spreading, a positivistic message that is almost entirely free of even the slightest doubts regarding further technological developments.[48] The same is true of books like John Naisbitt's *Megatrends 2000* or Alvin Toffler's *Future Shock* In this way, R&D, especially R, takes on an almost religious character. In the Middle Ages, we believed with unshakeable faith in the authority of the Church. Today we believe with unshakeable faith in the authority of Science.[49] Even those not involved in a corporation's technology development efforts cannot always shake off this conviction,[50] and to the extent that these non-technologists do not shake it off, the technologists themselves begin to believe in it too.

Table 6–1 Some Sources of Motivation and Criteria of Success in Industrial Corporations

R&D Personnel	Non-R&D Personnel
Patents	Revenues
Publications	Costs
Knowledge	Profits
Technical Performance	Market Shares
Professional Recognition	Added Value
Scientific Honors and Prizes	Rewards, Bonuses
R&D Resources	Investment Funds

The conclusions from all this are not particularly complicated: There are two kinds of escalation drivers. Table 6–1 shows that on the one side, there are the scientists and engineers engaged in R&D. Due to their education and the nature of their activities, they have an objective interest in further progress of their fields. On the other side, there are all the others in a

---

48 See Toffler, 1995.

49 See Postman, 1992, p. 64 and 156 et seq., especially p. 174 et seq.; for a—well-balanced—view from the other side, see Waldegrave, 1994, and Hausen, 1994.

50 In some quarters, there still seems to a widespread belief in the ultimate form of "technology push", i.e., that all one needs to do is give scientists and engineers whatever they need and they will come up with some profitable new product; viz the following quote: "If Japan is to get an edge on other nations in such endeavors [of building new industries, author's note], the manufacturing sector must move quickly to seek out individuals with creative ideas, and then provide the environments these original thinkers need to bring such ideas to fruition."
Source: Yoshikawa, 1994.

company who are not involved in R&D. Their interests can usually be expressed in monetary terms, be it revenues, costs, or the difference between the two. There is a distinct discrepancy in attitudes resulting from these two kinds of motivational dimensions. It may also be the reason why researchers often complain that their findings are not utilized in the production and sales departments, while the production and sales people accuse the researchers of busying themselves with matters of no practical value.

To put it simply, the motivation of R&D-employees lies in their technical knowledge or inventiveness. Their criteria of success are expressed in technology dimensions, in patents, published papers, technical performance parameters or peer recognition. They tend to contribute *actively* to R&D escalation because it will improve their chances of professional and personal fulfillment.

The non-R&D employees boost R&D *by omission* in that they do not sufficiently harness the R&D effort to the organization's benefit. Their omission occurs in two ways. Either they assume out of good or even blind faith in technology that it will create a continuous stream of wonderful new products or processes which will lead the company into a golden future. This (admittedly declining) faith is founded on the conviction that there is a technical solution to all problems, even where further technology can no longer be justified.[51] Or they do not have this faith in the first place but instead have given up on the attempt to install a planning and decision making mechanism which will successfully relate what the market really needs with what the corporation really can and wants to do.[52]

It is not always possible to place an individual employee unequivocally into one of the two categories of Table 6–1. In the development of process technologies which are more directly concerned with business-related issues such as costs, for example, there is a distinct overlap between the two columns. Therefore, it should only be taken as an indicator to understand some of the basic difference between both categories. More importantly, the distinction underlines the urgent need to combine the two columns into a common system of values and goals and to translate the success criteria of the one side into terms that are meaningful to the other. The more important R&D becomes in a company, the more essential it is to forge bridges of understanding between both worlds. To date, such bridges are still few and far between.

51 Shiraki, 1992; Masuko, 1992 I; Ludsteck, 1993 I.

52 See von Braun et al, 1990, p. 564 et seq.

Escalation Fatigue

At present, the only effective curb for both the arms and R&D races is a shortage of money. It is an effective brake, but three factors argue against its use:

- It is dangerous to speculate on the competitor's exhaustion.

- The brake kicks in late, if not too late.

- It is the worst conceivable way of saving money.

Firstly, it is dangerous in the sense of an old hunting rule: Never corner a wounded animal. It could suddenly turn very aggressive. With hindsight, the U.S. arms strategy of the Reagan era, designed to involve the Soviet Union in an arms race which it could not sustain economically, was a prime example of this. In more than one sense, the West was playing with fire. Threatened with economic and political bankruptcy, the Soviet Union might have placed all its bets on one card and struck out as long as it felt that it still had a reasonable weapons parity. The Japanese attack on Pearl Harbor in 1941, in many respects followed such thinking. The Japanese leaders were certainly aware that their country was hopelessly inferior to the U.S. But with every day that passed without surrendering to the rigid sanctions imposed by the U.S. and U.K. to end the Japanese intervention in China, the situation worsened. In such desperation, stubbornness can easily turn into an attitude of defiance: "It can only get worse, and who knows, we may even be lucky. Now or never!"[53]

Such situations are not limited to the hostilities between countries or the relationship between predator and prey. Companies too, if they are unable to keep up in R&D, may choose to resort to aggression. Instead of giving up, they will frequently prefer to escalate even further before they are weakened irrevocably. If they can no longer finance the development of a new product generation or cannot realize it for some other reason, they are left with little choice. Sales of the old product range are then pushed as aggressively as possible. Its attractiveness is promoted by all available means.

It is a familiar phenomenon that one of the first effects of the introduction of a new technology is the improvement of the performance characteris-

---

53 Axelrod, 1987, p. 163 et seq.

tics of the older technology in danger of being substituted. Ever since electronic imaging has begun to loom as a serious contender for the photography market, for instance, traditional chemical films have become better and better. This can throw any introduction plans for a new technology seriously off course. It can even scuttle them altogether. Galliumarsenide, another example, was hailed as the better and more advanced microchip material than silicon for many years. It never really took off, because silicon-based technologies kept getting better than previously had been thought possible. Even slight improvements of the old technology, justified or not, can be puffed up as major breakthroughs. Easily then, a murderous price war erupts which causes all market participants to suffer, including the technology leader.

The Japanese firm Seiko-Epson is a good example of this. The company manufactures watches, semiconductors and computer peripheral equipment such as printers and disk drives. It also offers a range of personal computers. After an explosive growth rate in the second half of the 1980s, Epson's share of the Japanese PC market between 1990 and 1992 declined from 8% to 6%. This market share loss was primarily due Epson's declining technology position vis-a-vis market leader NEC. At the same time, foreign manufacturers such as IBM, Dell and Compaq were aggressively forcing their way into the Japanese market. Epson was obliged to introduce massive price reductions and, despite a rapid profit decline, offered its low-end PCs 25% cheaper than NEC's comparable machines. NEC, in turn, also reduced some prices, but for the time being still relied on its technology lead. The overall effect of this and of the inroads of U.S. PC manufacturers in the Japanese market was that NEC's PC local market share dropped from 60% in 1993 to 40% by the end of 1995. The business also became less profitable. Even as these lines are being written, the battle continues and Seiko-Epson's fate is undecided.[54]

Secondly, the financial brake kicks in late or too late because a country's or a company's arms or R&D expenditures cannot simply be switched on and off like a light bulb. In the world of the military, this has been a topic in newspaper headlines since the end of the Cold War and has influenced the urgency of major weapons programs. "Crisis in the Arms Industry," says *Die Zeit*, a leading German Weekly, or "Arms Industry Bewails Peace Dividend," Germany's *Süddeutsche Zeitung*. Similar headlines could be seen all over NATO countries. At the end of President George Bush's

---

54 O'Toole, Thomas P., 1993 II; Onishi, 1993; Patton, 1994; Fulford, 1996.

term in office, the U.S. defence budget amounted to approximately 5% of GNP. It is now moving toward 4%, and there is no obvious reason why it should stop there. According to plans in the Clinton administration, the defence budget in Fiscal 1997 will amount to $249 bill. compared to $278 bill. in fiscal 1994. Further cuts are planned until 1999. Accordingly, the Aerospace Industries Association estimates that total aerospace employment between 1989 and 1994 declined from 1.331 mill. to 827 thousand.[55]

Such developments are not confined to the United States. According to European Commission estimates, defence spending in Europe will fall by 25% between 1991 and 2000, severely cutting the 650,000-member work force currently employed in the industry. Both France and the U.K. each lost more than 100,000 aerospace jobs between 1993 and 1995.[56] In Germany, large corporations like DASA (Deutsche Aerospace) with tens of thousands of employees as well as mid-sized companies like Heckler & Koch, manufacturer of the G3 rapid fire gun, are suffering.

One frequently trodden path out of such difficulties is conversion, the switch to civilian or at least dual-use products which have applications in both the civil and military fields. Successful conversion is no easy task, however. For one, there are already well established manufacturers in the civilian markets who will not exactly welcome further competitors with open arms. For another, successful market entry does not end with prototype development. The fundamentals of product manufacture, marketing and company management are quite different in the civilian marketplace, even if the civilian and military products are similar. The private buyer of an airplane, for instance, has completely different purchasing decision criteria than the procurement office of the armed forces.

The difficulty of mental, financial, managerial and physical "retooling" has proved itself many times in the past. In the 1970s, for example, a whole host of American aerospace and electronics firms attempted to diversify from the defence into the civilian markets. Boeing tried speedboats, Grumman ventured into busses, Raytheon went for data terminals. All three projects ended in disasters. Automobile maker Daimler-Benz's recent attempt to branch out into a whole host of new technology fields at the same time (aerospace and defense among them) resulted in a $4 bill. megadisaster

55 See Benson, 1993; Lopez, 1995.

56 Butterworth-Hayes, 1994, p. 35, 36.

in 1995. TRW, another U.S. aerospace company, is one of the few which converted successfully. But that attempt started already in the 1960s.[57]

Sometimes the search for civil applications of military technologies can lead to exotic results. Based on its guiding and propulsion systems used in fighter aircraft, for instance, Japan's leading defence contractor Mitsubishi Heavy Industries has developed a device that determines the sex of *ayu*, or sweetfish, by the shape of their fins,[58] hardly a mass market, but perhaps expandable into other fields. England's GEC-Marconi was also successful. From parallel processing technology developed for defence applications, the company has built a range of in-flight entertainment systems. Overall however, the conversion process has proved painfully difficult for almost all of the companies that have attempted it.[59] This is particularly true in Russia where the conversion of a previously government-pampered industry believed to have given jobs to over 3.5 million employees has practically failed completely.[60]

In large part, these conversion difficulties stem from the near impossibility for large organizations to change their methods and ways of thinking while using the same management, employees and technologies. For this reason, a number of firms, General Dynamics among them, have refrained from conversion altogether. Instead, they have focused even more on their own specialization by buying other companys' defense related businesses. For General Dynamics this has worked so far. In whatever way one goes about solving problems of this kind, however, any adaptions to such fundamental changes in company technology policies tend to take a lot of time.

The same kinds of problems invariably recur in the attempt to reduce the R&D budget or to convert R&D expenditures into something else.[61] Basically, a company's R&D effort is characterized by two types of costs. Neither of them can be easily or quickly changed. One of them is materials, principally laboratory buildings and equipment. The other is employees. In many respects, and more so in continental Europe and Japan than in the U.S., both have taken on the nature of fixed costs. Machines and other equip-

---

57 Anon.{13}, 1993.

58 Takahashi, 1995.

59 Butterworth-Hayes, 1994.

60 Anon. {26}, 1994. According to other estimates there were as many as 16 million employees, Butterworth-Hayes, 1994, p. 38.

61 On the attempt to do this with National Laboratories, see Shulman, 1995.

ment are part of the balance sheet. It takes time to depreciate them to zero. Selling off used equipment is usually difficult and will hardly realize its book value, even if a buyer can be found. To adapt and deploy it for other purposes (conversion!) is usually not possible without considerable further expenditures, if at all. After all, a measuring device is always a measuring device—or scrap.

Similar difficulties arise when a laboratory is converted into a factory or some other building. In the electronics industry, some of the exorbitantly expensive semiconductor development laboratories (clean or ultra-clean rooms that can easily cost hundreds of millions of dollars to build) have occasionally been utilized as offices for lack of alternative uses. Some employees may have found it amusing to have nitrogen or helium outlets at their desks. The rental charges for these "offices," on the other hand, were hardly a laughing matter.

R&D *people* are not easily "convertible" either. For support personnel (technicians, lab assistants, secretaries, etc.) this might be possible. But to change a scientist or development technologist into a production engineer or even a salesman, will only be successful under favorable and probably exceptional circumstances, even if the scientist or engineer in question should cooperate enthusiastically. Naturally, it is not impossible to do so and there are numerous examples of scientists with business talents who have gone on to become successful operational managers and even company presidents. However, this is hardly a change that can be achieved very quickly. Given the particular traditions in Japanese industrial organizations, perhaps it is easier there than in Europe or the U.S. to shift people from R&D into completely different jobs. It is, therefore, quite frequently attempted in Japan, but it would be a delusion to assume that is always a success story, let alone an optimal solution.

It would also be a mistake to assume that a reduced R&D budget will automatically generate additional liquid funds. Quite the opposite. In 1992, Henkel KGaA in Düsseldorf, the fourth largest chemical firm in Germany, for example, decided to reduce personnel in its corporate research and process development laboratory by 25%. The aim was to lower overall R&D costs which, just as in many other companies in the industry, had risen faster than sales in previous years. Simultaneously, market-oriented R&D in the operational divisions was to be strengthened. Wherever possible, personnel from corporate R&D was therefore shifted into product or application development and production engineering. Layoffs could largely be avoided.

Where necessary, they were achieved through normal employee fluctuation and, in some cases, by offering early retirement. The whole changeover took a year and a half, and the first result was an *increase* in R&D personnel costs. Over the long run, R&D costs will no doubt decrease and cumulative savings will add up to more than the costs of restructuring, but "the skid marks are very long," the vice-president of R&D remarked thoughtfully.

The third reason mitigating against the slowing of the R&D escalation through an increased scarcity of funds rests on two pillars. The first results from the way companies (and other organizations) normally implement cost cutting programs. Such programs are typically the result of liquidity shortages, reduced profits or revenue shortfalls. The general order goes out to cut costs throughout the company. This includes R&D, of course, and so instructions are issued to reduce expenditures by, say, 20%. Naturally, such measures are labelled as a process of "focusing" or "strategic realignment," but in very many cases, and irrespective of words, they boil down to across-the-board cuts.

In Fall 1993, for example, the Japanese electronics giant Fujitsu Ltd. announced that in business year 1993/94, its R&D budget would be cut by 5.2% or ¥16 bill. to ¥280 bill. As a reason for the cut, the company specified weak domestic demand and the rising value of the yen. Neither has anything to do with R&D, nor can a reduction in R&D do anything to ameliorate the situation. The cut was no more than a *reaction* to the corporation's declining profits and weak sales. Given the same conditions, other companies react differently. Matsushita, another Japanese electronics giant, whose total revenues in the same business year was predicted to fall by 4% and gross profit by as much as 11%, was also forced to cut costs. The company announced, however, that irrespective of other measures the R&D budget would be the same as the previous year. In relative terms, therefore, it was even rising. In all Western industrial countries, there seems to be this curious divergence in company reactions to a recession. For whatever reasons, the majority appears to favor the Fujitsu route.

Even if one can think of no other way, the only thing that can be said about such blanket R&D cuts is that they are definitely the wrong way to go about it. Cutting *all* projects by 20%, means that non-crucial projects will continue to consume resources. At the same time, those projects which are vital to the long-term survival of the company are not receiving the resources they need. In either case, one can therefore rest in the assurance of having made a mistake.

The second pillar goes deeper. The reader will recall as was pointed out earlier that companies regularly claim the needs of the future to justify the buildup of R&D in the present ("R&D secures the future"). R&D budget cuts that are based on current difficulties put this argument to its ultimate rest. Any relation that the R&D program might have had to the future before, are severed once and for all. Irrespective of whether a company's difficulties come in the shape of reduced revenues, falling profit margins or declining cash flows, they are results of *past* developments. Using them as fundamental guidelines of the future, renders any goal orientation, that might have existed before, invalid at a stroke. Long-term action is replaced by short-term reactionism.

Such short-term reactive thinking is particularly harmful in R&D. It has been pointed out before that, among all corporate activities, R&D has the longest time-horizon. It is often far longer than that of personnel policy or even major construction projects. Development times for a new pharmaceutical product, for example, can easily be in excess of ten years. These long time-horizons can lead to profound effects if budgets are suddenly changed. An average advertising campaign, for instance, can be terminated relatively quickly and easily and with no great loss if the company's liquidity demands it. Only the direct campaign results are jeopardized. For R&D, the case is quite different. If a project is suddenly suspended, then not only are future results sacrificed. Large previous investments are lost as well. In addition, a half completed project is really not good for anything. Equipment has to be written off. Researchers have been employed and trained in vain. Teams are disbanded. In addition, the state of knowledge or development up to project termination or delay can only rarely be preserved, only to be warmed up at some later date if needed.

There are two reasons for this. One is that the half-life of technical knowledge has become very short indeed. Even the latest findings do not remain new for long. A number of young physicists in industry and at research institutions, for example, have complained to this author that even younger researchers, who had graduated only two or three years after them, had mastered software techniques which were totally unfamiliar to them. Due to increasingly short product life cycles, many of today's technologies are developed with a view to specific needs at specific times, i.e., for "windows of opportunity." Only within this time frame will the products have an edge. A new type of catalytic converter, for example, can therefore not be left half completed on the shelf for five years and then taken up again. By then, a competitor will have long entered that market with a similar device or some other technology that will take its place.

Currently, it is generally surmised that the totality of human knowledge doubles roughly every three to five years. Around the year 1900, by comparison, the doubling time was on the order of a century. Today, there is a new medical finding every five minutes, a new physical interrelationship is discovered every three minutes, and a new chemical compound is formulated every 60 seconds.[62] Even if far more than 90% of these discoveries are of no commercial value, it does show that discoveries age rapidly. Moreover, even with the best possible documentation, the really crucial R&D results are stored in the heads of teams and individual human beings, who in turn are also difficult to store.

The same considerations apply if specific items are to be put up for sale. A brand name, plant and equipment, even whole divisions and subsidiaries of a company can be sold off relatively easily and liquidity thus improved. To sell an on-going R&D project, on the other hand, is almost impossible, quite apart from the problem of finding a market value for it. Even if the whole project and its interim results were perfectly documented (which is practically never the case for incomplete projects), the problem still remains how to integrate this knowledge into the purchasing organization. The successful transfer of technology is one of the most difficult of all management tasks. The successful transfer of *incomplete* technology is even more difficult. The decisive knowledge is in the heads of those researchers working on the project anyhow, and these researchers—or their heads—are rarely at the disposition of company management.

The consequence of all this is a realization which for some corporate managements is quite unpleasant: Once a company has embarked on an R&D (ad)venture, it is very difficult to bail out. No doubt, in limits R&D projects can always be speeded up or stretched, and good project management can certainly improve both project effectiveness and efficiency. But fundamentally, they cannot be discontinued without losses. In this respect again, they are similar to major weapons programs, particularly with respect to their cancellation halfway through completion.

---

62 Volk, 1993. As a matter of interest, at the end of 1993, Japanese researchers registered the twelve millionth chemical compound.

The American taxpayer only recently experienced the same painful effect in connection with the Superconducting Collider which was intended to detect Higgs-Boson particles and other exotic constituents of matter. It took three attempts before the Congress finally decided not to build the 54-mile long particle accelerator ring because of its expected cost of $16 bill. At that time, however, $2 bill. had already been spent. That is why near the small town of Waxahachie, Texas one can now find an empty, useless, curved tunnel as a 16-mile-monument to how R&D decisions should *not* be taken.

Metaphorically, one can imagine the R&D process as an oil pipeline. The length of the pipeline corresponds to project lead times. The oil corresponds to the project. If one decides that the oil is not needed, while it is flowing through the pipeline, the only thing to do is to turn off the pumps. That way, further transportation costs are saved, but the oil stays in the pipeline and nobody benefits from it. One cannot get it back either, short of drilling a hole in the pipeline, which will also cost money and possibly only result in the oil seeping into the desert. It might be possible to turn up the pumps. The oil will then arrive at the other end sooner, but at a higher cost. Turning the pumps down, reduces costs but delays the oil in reaching its destination. Whatever one does, once the oil is in the pipeline numerous degrees of freedom have been foregone or lost.

Real decision freedom therefore only exists at the beginning of the pipeline. Only there can one decide the oil's quantity, type and composition. Naturally, a project can always be stopped and if in doubt a company with little financial choice will do just that. It should only realize that every day by which that decision is delayed will increase its losses. It would be far better, therefore, not to be faced with such decisions in the first place. Once taken, R&D decisions, in many respects, are particularly strong tethers. Initial R&D project selections are crucial long-term decisions for the company as a whole. Strategy is formulated at the beginning of the pipeline. To a large degree, everything that follows is only execution. For this reason the question *what* to do R&D on, i.e., what to feed into the pipeline, attains particular importance. It is this question to which we will devote our attention in the last chapter.

Summary

Large R&D budgets are usually justified by the need to secure the future of the corporation. This happens either by claiming future market needs which require specific technical solutions, or a technological breakthrough which initiates a search for a market need that can be met by the solution. That, at least, is the theory.

In reality, however, many R&D efforts are based far more on the desire to keep up with the competition. Not only does this require significant and costly analysis efforts to understand competitors' R&D activities. In addition and more importantly, it can, and does, also very easily lead to a spiraling escalation of R&D costs. In this respect, there is a striking similarity to many historic military arms races. The similarity holds true not only for the typical interactive dynamics of escalatory processes where the activity level of one party determines that of the other. It can also be observed in the tendency to overshoot goals and perform more R&D (or buy more arms) than is actually required in a given business (or military) situation. In the military setting, this process has come to be termed overkill. But overkill can also be observed in civilian R&D whenever products are developed ahead of time or with exaggerated performance levels. As an additional parallel, even the strategy of participants in the R&D race is suggestive of the military arms race situation: Offence is always favored over defence. And since all parties behave in a similar fashion, none can achieve a sustainable advantage.

An important contributor to the R&D escalation is the fact that R&D operations are only rarely managed with a view to the interests of the organization as a whole. One reason for this often lies with the top management of R&D, usually an individual who is a member of the R&D community him- or herself. Another is the dearth of effective instruments for R&D control. A third is a frequent semi-religious belief in the scientific or technological solvability of all problems in general, and of entrepreneurial problems in particular. For the active members of the R&D community, this creates an atmosphere of almost unconstrained R&D budget growth potential. For all others, it is reason enough to forego sufficiently determined attempts to participate in the formulation of effective R&D policies.

Just as in the military arms race, an end of the R&D escalation only occurs for lack of funds. Lack of funds, however, is a particularly blunt instrument of R&D control. For one, it is extremely dangerous to speculate that the competitor will be the first to give up. In any case, this will not happen before significant costs have been incurred by all parties. For another, a reduction of R&D efforts will often initially lead to increased R&D costs. These are associated with the diseconomies of refomulating goals, redirecting human and capital resources and writing off previous investments. Finally, measures of this type reduce corporate strategy in general, and R&D strategy in particular, to a reactive posture which prefers to consider past developments as an input to R&D planning rather than one of normative or visionary goal setting for the future.

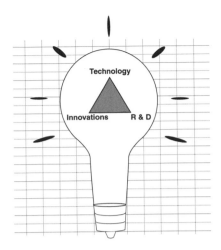

7

Conclusions

A book about the innovation war and its inherent dangers is confronted with one main difficulty: The subject is not readily accessible to an outside observer. The industrialized world has grown accustomed to regarding as technical progress what in fact is often only technical change.[1] In the same vein, the word "innovation" invariably has a positive flavor. Just like health, wealth and an impeccable reputation, it is considered a goal perpetually worth striving for. Any attempts to qualify this view, are therefore not always benevolently welcomed. Also reports, documentations, statistical overviews, or case studies on R&D are regularly characterized by great enthusiasm. Whatever elements of critique they might contain, will more likely refer to a lack of sufficient funding than on excessive haste or spending. Only very recently has reporting on R&D occasionally begun to be presented in forms that might serve to cast certain doubts on it.

The blame for such attitudes which promote R&D to some exalted level of sublimity can be levelled at no one in particular. They are part of the spirit of our age. They did, however, render a lot of the background research to this book to something of a jigsaw puzzle. It rests on many small data

---

1 Depending on one's perspective, one can indeed view many of the technologies of earlier centuries as more "progressive" or advanced than those of today. From the point of view of efficient energy utilization, for example, the ancient wind-powered water drainage system used in Dutch land reclamation in many respects was—and partly still is—far superior to the system of diesel- or electrically driven pump arrays that replaced it.

points, on examples and counter-examples. It tries to consider singular events and long-term trends, quantitative surveys and qualitative guess work. It attempts to take into account the views of experts and of lay persons, including researchers under the clear desert skies of Arizona in search of remote galaxies, overstressed laboratory managers in the industrial heartlands of the Ruhr valley, and virtual reality players in the amusement arcades of Tokyo's Roppongi district. And it tries to distill from all these inputs an overall and more or less coherent image.

In addition to these many little details, every one of the preceding chapters is concerned with different issues. This may easily obscure whatever overview might arise. To use a metaphor: A house consists of bricks, the way a town consists of houses. It is not easy to develop a feeling for the layout of the town from the arrangement of bricks. For this reason, we will now leave the level of bricks and turn to the arrangement of houses by asking what conclusions can be drawn from all of the above. To this end, we will briefly recall in 33 hypotheses the first six chapters and then derive some recommendations for the organization and structuring of R&D from them.

Hypotheses

R&D as an Established but Risky Industrial Activity

1. Industrial R&D is coming of age. In a systematic form, it has been practiced for more than a century.
2. R&D's basic justification rests on the realization that to sustain a company's long-term survival, it must not only look after today's products and production, but also after those of tomorrow.
3. Already in its early years, R&D was entrusted to experts and was thus professionalized. Since then, it has also become the subject of rigorous analysis. In spite of this, there are still no exact or generally accepted and workable definitions of what constitutes technique, technology, science, basic and applied research, and experimental development.
4. The same is true of the innovation process. There are at best vague notions of which inventions will end up as successful innovations. It is also unknown how, and to what extent, scientific and technical breakthroughs affect a company's commercial success.

Excessive Growth in R&D Spending

5. Since World War II, the sums invested in R&D have risen constantly and rapidly. Since the middle of the 1960s, R&D growth in the technically advanced branches of industry has outstripped sales growth by significant margins. In many companies today, R&D represents a substantial proportion of total costs.

6. In the highly developed industrialized nations, up to 3% of GNP is spent on R&D.

7. The influence of the government, both as a regulatory agent as well as an active participant in R&D, is very strong.

8. The aim of the R&D struggle among companies, industrialized nations, and regional economic groupings is the domination of whole branches of industry.

9. Ever since World War II, the United States has led the world in technology development. This is increasingly being challenged by the technological ambitions of Japan and the European industrialized nations. In more recent years they have been joined by a number of advanced Third World nations.

10. Especially in recession-prone periods, both private and government-financing of R&D is gradually approaching its limits. Nevertheless, many companies maintain their levels of R&D spending even under conditions of low, or negative, sales growth.

11. To achieve even a slight technology-based sales lead it has become necessary to disproportionately expand R&D spending. For the case of 30 major electronics companies described in Chapter 3, it proved difficult, if not impossible to discover a positive relationship between R&D growth and sales growth. This held true even if one assumed a delayed effect of R&D spending increase on sales growth.

12. As R&D investment increases, doubts regarding the optimal allocation of funds also arise. In a number of companies and industrial branches, have R&D budgets apparently reached, or even exceeded, reasonable upper limits. In spite of this, many companies, not only in the so-called high-tech industries, regard a high level of R&D spending as a crucial prerequisite of long-term corporate survival.

13. Technological progress alone, however, will stimulate a stagnating or saturated market only to a very limited degree.

14. R&D lead times, interest rates and the marketability period of a new technology are critical factors in the formulation of R&D plans. Par-

ticularly, overextending R&D lead times can have disastrous financial consequences.

The Dangers of Continuous Acceleration of Product Life Cycles

15. Increasingly, R&D aims at securing future revenues by supplying new products earlier. The introduction of new products leads to the obsolescence of older products. The earlier availability of new products thus leads to a faster obsolescence of existing products. Put differently, excessive R&D prematurely cuts off revenue potentials.

16. Incessant growth in R&D output causes a general acceleration of product life cycles. Indirectly, it also contributes to the acceleration of other economic, political and social changes.

17. In order to keep up with shorter product life cycles, companies have to increase their R&D budgets or improve R&D productivity. This leads to a further acceleration of product life cycles.

18. Since they seem to be accompanied by growing revenues, shorter product life cycles initially look attractive. Revenue growth does not last, however. This would only be possible if one could shorten product life cycles and increase R&D expenditures or R&D productivity indefinitely.

19. Aside from a theoretical lower limit, a product life cycle also has a practical lower limit. This is considerably larger than zero and differs among products and industry sectors. Since customers do not have an unlimited capacity to accept innovations, their resistance to further product life cycle acceleration will increase as this limit draws near.

20. The discontinuation of product life cycle acceleration leads to a decline in sales volume. The more cycles have been accelerated previously, the larger this decline will be. This is the most important effect of the *Acceleration Trap*. The mechanisms of the Acceleration Trap are metaphorically summarized in Figure 7–1 with the image of a garden hose.

21. The Acceleration Trap's danger lies in its ability to delude. It feigns real growth in sales, where in fact only later sales are prematurely realized.

22. The workings of the Acceleration Trap are not easily visible. They are superimposed by other developments and can frequently be of a long-term nature. However, a body of empirical evidence is emerging that confirms the suspicion that many of the sparkling so-called "growth

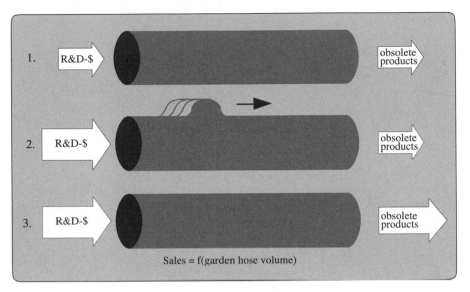

Sales = f(garden hose volume)

Figure 7–1 Principle of the Acceleration Trap. Consider the product spectrum of a company as water in a garden hose. As long as products are in the hose they contribute to revenues. R&D investments fill the hose by supplying a continuous stream of new products. Products leaving the hose are obsolete. 1. Under steady-state conditions, inflows equal outflows, i.e. new and obsolete products balance. 2. An increase in R&D is like turning up the tap. New products lead to a wave of additional revenues travelling through the hose, whereas obsolescence rates remain unchanged for a while. 3. Later, the speed of obsolescence catches up with the speed of innovation. Revenues go back to where they were before. Only transition times (product life cycles) have become shorter. The company is stuck with high levels of R&D spending, however: Turning the tap down, would lead to declining revenues.

markets" are in reality rather lackluster "acceleration markets."

23. Once a company or an industry has begun to seek its fortunes in an acceleration of product life cycles, it becomes increasingly difficult to back out without significant sacrifices both in sales and sales growth. With every passing day, both the acceleration as well as its discontinuation become more expensive.

24. Market growth offers no immunity from the effects of the Acceleration Trap. Similarly, intensifying innovation activities will serve more to increase entrepreneurial risk than the prospects of business success.

- Shorter time horizons.
- More innovation failures.
- Narrower product spectrum.
- Long-term market share losses.
- Steep increases in cooperation costs.
- Greater pressure on development times.
- Larger share of younger, and thus riskier products.
- Smaller production runs, loss of learning curve effects.
- Raw material inefficiencies, poor use of natural resources.
- Less attention to detail and quality in the development process.
- Neglect of existing customer base and of installed product base.
- Tighter deadlines, thus more potential for friction in cooperation.
- Less enduring technology leadership, thus declining innovator profits.
- Declining effectiveness of technology as means of differentiation in market.
- Expanded use of inferior R&D resources, thus deterioration of R&D effectiveness.
- Increasing costs of crucial R&D components (experts, tools, capital, gov.approval etc.).
- Concentration of R&D resources on shorter time spans, deterioration of R&D efficiency.
- Habit-forming effects of frequent innovations implies need to maintain high R&D budgets.

Figure 7–2   Some Negative Consequences of Technology-Induced
Faster Product Life Cycles

25.   In business and literature, shorter product life cycles are generally
associated with more dynamic business conditions and therefore
frequently applauded. Unfortunately, they also entail a whole series
of damaging effects and risks. Some of these are listed in Figure 7–2.

Competition-Driven R&D Growth

26.   It is becoming increasingly apparent that to a large extent R&D
growth is determined by the desire of companies just to keep up
with competitors. Aside from "market-pull" and "technology-
push," the more present-day orientation of "competition-driven"
has become an important input for R&D investment decisions.

27.   In the interest of investigating their competitors' R&D efforts, companies, industry associations and even governments are willing to
go to considerable (formal and informal) efforts. The results of such
investigations often serve as a justification for increased R&D budget demands.

28.   In this context, the correct assessment of a competitor's R&D activities is not essential. The simple *belief* that the competitor is increasing his efforts is sufficient to stimulate one's own additional efforts.

R&D Escalation Model

29. Competition-driven R&D growth leads to an escalation spiral similar to an arms race. Given the right setting, a small initial spark can set off the spiral's spin.

30. In absolute values, such escalatory processes typically lead to drastic spending growth by all participants. Relative spending, however, remains fairly constant so that no one achieves lasting advantages.

31. Escalation can easily lead participants to overshoot targets and develop more technology than can easily be consumed and digested by markets. Just as in the military arms race, one can observe numerous phenomena of overkill.

32. Even during economic periods of recession, a number of forces and circumstances contribute to keeping the R&D escalation alive:

   - A sense of helplessness regarding R&D matters, generally viewed as extremely complex by outsiders.

   - A very strong predominance of members of the R&D community itself in the control of R&D.

   - A dearth of financial methods and tools for effective external R&D control.

   - A strong reliance on technology and a belief in the technical/scientific solvability of many, if not most entrepreneurial problems, both within corporate management and even more so outside it. The advancement of technology and technological "progress" is still clouded in a shroud of mystique. This leads R&D demands and R&D performance levels to be regarded with greater lenience and benevolence than other investment-intensive or long-term activities.

   - The traditional orientation of R&D employees' motivational structure toward the expansion of knowledge and the improvement of existing technologies. Financial aspects are assigned only insufficient weight in this structure.

33. The only—and very recent—effective means of bringing the R&D escalation to an end seems to be a shortage of cash. Unfortunately, it is also a very poor instrument because:

- It is dangerous to speculate that rivals will run out of funds first.

- The investment in one's own previous R&D effort is usually irretrievably lost.

- Basing R&D decisions on present cash flows or corporate profitability implies an R&D orientation that reacts to values of the past. It should, instead, be following normative goals for the future, or perhaps even be instrumental in setting such goals.

Ending the R&D Escalation

Perhaps the most important question the reader might have on his mind at this point is how to find a way out of the escalation spiral. Industrial firms frequently point out that, in this respect, they have little choice. Either, so they claim, they run with the pack as long and well as they can so as to keep up with the R&D investments of their competitors, or they go under. A third way, for instance, an "understanding with the enemy" such as nations might manage to achieve in a war, was out of bounds for an industrial enterprise. The Fair Trade Commission, various antitrust authorities and other watchdogs of the free enterprise system would never allow it.

We will not go into any of the legal or regulatory questions regarding an understanding among competitors to brake the R&D race. The main reason for this is that an explicit or implicit "understanding"—however one might legally or ethically interpret such a term—is not necessary. A promising start would already be made if the parties concerned were to become aware of the existence of the escalation. The knowledge of their participation in the escalatory spiral, its costs, and its consequences would already constitute an important first step toward rethinking. Just a one-time act of conscious perception which—with all due modesty—might lie in the reading of these lines could suffice to initiate a process of deliberation which at least *might* put a check on budgets.

Escalation control mechanisms can further arise tacitly, both in the military and the competitive industrial arenas, if one party understands the interests of others and can relate to their situation. A well-known example of such tacit processes is the so-called "prisoners' dilemma" that originated in game theory.[2] The dilemma assumes the following situation: Two villains, A and B, are caught red-handed committing a crime. At the sheriff's office

---

2   See for example Star and Urban, 1989, who demonstrate the dilemma in a different setting.

their attorney explains their situation to them. If both of them say nothing, they will each get a year in prison. If one of them confesses, he can get away with one month and the other will go to prison for ten years. If they both confess, they will both go for five years. A and B are not allowed to communicate. What should they do?

Obviously, the best overall result would be for both to remain silent. For A and B individually, however, it would be even better to confess, *provided* the other one does not because then they would both get five years. Confessing also protects each one them from a ten-year sentence in case the other one should confess. The core of the dilemma is that cooperation (remaining silent) leads to good results and mutual selfishness (confession) to bad ones, with egoism being a very tempting proposition.

The prisoners' dilemma can be very easily translated into an R&D dilemma. Every company participating in the R&D race can gain significant advantages if it advances at a fast pace and the others do not. But if all participants or the majority move at the same fast pace, then they will only incur high R&D costs, and none of them will can cash in on a technology leadership position. So what is a company to do? If it "cooperates," i.e., becomes aware of its situation and does not invest in any R&D race without sufficient payback, it will avoid substantial costs. But if only one or very few other companies increase their R&D budgets, it runs the risk of losing out. So it will have to increase its R&D budgets too, and in the long run all will be worse off than before.

There are various strategies one can follow if one is caught in a prisoners' dilemma. Naturally, the situation is not always the same. For example, it can become more complex if there are more than just two modes of possible behavior (i.e., not only "remaining silent" or "confession" but also "partial confession"), or if there are more than two parties involved. But normally, this will not change the basic dilemma. What does make a difference, however, is whether the two participants are strangers to each other or whether they have gone through the same experience before. The more they are familiar with one another the better they can guess each other's actions, even without communicating. They know the other party's behavior patterns from past experience and can rely on the other party knowing theirs. Under these circumstances, the communication barrier presents much less of a problem. In industry, where competitors have been familiar with each other sometimes for decades, this situation is more or less the norm. An implicit or tacit "understanding", therefore, is not so hard to achieve. Since the behavior of corporations tends to be far more consistent and calculable than that of crooks, one probably does not even need a telephone or a postage stamp.

Observations of a great number of simulated and real prisoners' dilemma situations have shown that, in the long run, aggressive strategies (in our examples: immediate confession/aggressive R&D spending) frequently lead to the worst results. Mutual restraint, on the other hand, that does not seek to outdo whatever the opponent has done and remains assertive but non-aggressive instead, is associated with the highest likelihood of "cooperative" solutions where everybody profits. The situations and simulations where such "tit-for-tat" strategies were developed usually concerned other settings than a race for a leading technology position. They included military arms races, price wars, distribution issues, rebate and advertising campaigns, and other conflict situations that easily give rise to escalation mechanisms. There are, however, no obvious reasons why they should not be equally valid in the R&D arena.

Recommendations

Positioning R&D

Chinese Communist Party Chairman Mao tse-Tung is claimed to have said, "You cannot overtake the runner in front of you by following in his footsteps." Mao may have been wrong in many things, but applying this wisdom to R&D looks like a good piece of advice. In any case, one would do well to handle any competition-driven finding of R&D priorities with marked restraint. Otherwise, it can lead all too easily to a rapid accumulation of similar or duplicated R&D efforts without any corresponding profits.

The greater part of the books and articles addressing the question which paths to follow in R&D express the opinion that companies should be guided only by the demands of the market place. That makes sense. After all, the final aim of whatever is developed in the R&D laboratories is to turn it into products that can be sold there. Nevertheless, in a pure form, such an attitude is probably just as dangerous as an R&D program that is exclusively competition-driven.

A firm that is only driven by the market and only develops some new product for which it receives, or believes itself to be receiving, signals from the market can easily and unexpectedly be driven to the brink by just that market. This is not only true because the market will only begin to send demand signals for some new technology *after* the availability of this technology has been sufficiently well established. Under the circumstances, this can only have been done by a competitor. Also, particularly high-tech markets are quite capricious. Whatever the trade journals and information networks of the world acclaim as "the technology of the future" to which all R&D resources are to be devoted, can prove to be tomorrow's chimera. A firm that has bet all its R&D resources on this one illusive technology can then suddenly find it has run out of options.

Similarly, technological euphoria and an unequivocal conviction that a new technology in some way or other will always find a market can very easily lead to misjudgments and failed developments. Technology is not an end in itself. Whoever lets himself be dazzled by it can hardly operate profitably. In such instances, the prospects for commercial success are largely a matter of chance.

So what is to be done? Naturally, R&D priorities and budgets should not be governed by just one of the three factors, technology, market or competition. All three—and others—have to be considered, both in their respective contexts and their mutual interaction. In practice, there is no straightforward or universal way of converting them into R&D budgets and project lists. Cookbook approaches rarely work where ingredients, spices and outcomes have to be balanced and weighed against one other and where final results are subject to uncertainty. There is no one right way to go about it.

All present-day companies are probably aware that R&D can no longer be pursued just for reasons of corporate image, or intellectual curiosity, or propriety, let alone vanity. For that, it has simply become far too expensive. Particularly researchers (but not only they) constantly need to keep in mind: *R&D investment today belongs to the most costly, most uncertain and longest term activities an industrial firm can engage in.* Unfortunately, this activity is also necessary. For this reason, R&D demands the most careful preparatory groundwork it can get. The conflict between well-founded and necessary R&D work on the one hand, and an unjustifiable cost explosion, on the other, makes this abundantly clear. The real need is for a more thorough selection process that in the end, arrives at those projects which are really essential for the well-being of the company.

If, in addition, companies can learn to view R&D not as a sufficient but only as a necessary condition of business success, they will also be able to base the size of their R&D budgets on what is minimally necessary, rather than what is maximally possible. *The idea is not to spend at least what the company can afford, but at most what it absolutely needs.* In all other areas of investment and spending (for example, travel costs), this principle goes without saying. Why not in R&D? The bitter truth is that a company or even a whole industry can lose money, market shares, revenues, and its future if it does not spend enough on R&D. But the same thing can happen if it spends indiscriminately, or simply too much. In the future, therefore, it can, and will, no longer be decisive to spend as much, or more, than others. Under the constraint of limited resources, what counts will be the ability to put together the *right* R&D program for the company—and then to stick to it.

Generations of R&D

In their excellent book, Roussel, Saad and Erickson[3] have given a number of useful guidelines as to how R&D can be incorporated, both on a corporate and divisional level, in a company's strategy, its organizational structure, decision making and culture with greater effectiveness. They distinguish between three stages—or generations—of R&D integration.

In First Generation R&D, researchers and their facilities are largely isolated add-ons to the rest of the company. Corporate management realizes that the company needs to hire some creative talent that will develop future products. It gives them the required laboratories and then hopes for the best. In this situation, the worlds of R&D and business are two distinct entities. Essentially, R&D management decides the technologies of the future and business management for its part decides everything else.

In Second Generation R&D, there is at least some interaction between R&D and previously specified business needs. It is largely restricted to the project, or individual business level, however. The strategic orientation of R&D is therefore only partial to certain market segments or specific business aspects at best. There is no overall integration of R&D into the company aggregate.

3   Roussel et al., 1991.

This only happens in Third Generation R&D where the R&D function becomes a constituent part of the overall company framework. There, "general managers and R&D managers work as partners to share and pool their insights in deciding what to do, why and when. In so doing, they take account of the needs of each business and of the corporation [as a whole]."[4] The concept of three generations of R&D, the way in which they are distinguished from each other, and their underlying principles are summarized in Table 7–1.[5]

According to the authors, only very few forward looking corporations have progressed to the Third Generation so far.[6] Nevertheless, the distinction of three separate levels of R&D integration in a company is a useful one. Among other benefits, it provides a clear frame of reference for a company pondering the role, position and management of its R&D setup in the organization's overall structure. One might wonder, however, whether the con-

	First Generation R&D	Second Generation R&D	Third Generation R&D
Management and Strategic Context	• No long-term strategic framework • R&D is an overhead cost	• Transition State • Partial strategic framework	• Holistic strategic framework
• Philosophy	• R&D decides future technologies • Business decides current technology objectives	• Judge-advocate management/R&D relationship • Customer-supplier business/R&D relationship	• Partnership
• Organization	• Emphasis: cost centers, disciplines • Avoid the matrix	• Centralized and decentralized • Matrix management of projects	• Breaks the isolation of R&D
• Technology/R&D Strategy	• No explicit link to bus. strategy • Technology first, business implications later	• Strategic framework by project • No integration business- or corporatewide	• Technology/R&D and business strategies integrated corporatewide
Operating Principles	• Lacking combined business/R&D insight • Fatalistic	• Distinguish between types of R&D • Combined business/R&D insights at project level	• Combined business/R&D insights across the spectrum
• Funding	• Line item in annual budget • Fund what you can afford	• Funds based on needs, risk sharing • Different parameters by R&D type	• Varies with technology maturity and competitive impact
• Resource Allocation	• At the discretion of R&D • No upward visibility	• To fundamental R&D by central R&D management • To other R&D jointly by customers and suppliers	• Based on balancing priorities and risk/reward
• Targeting	• Is anathema for fundamental and radical R&D • Business and technological objectives sequential	• Consistent business and R&D objectives by project for incremental and radical R&D	• All R&D has defined business *and* technological objectives
• Priority Setting	• No strategic priorities • Priorities vary with operational circumstances	• For fundamental R&D by central R&D management • For other R&D jointly by customers and suppliers	• According to cost/benefits and contribution to strategic objectives
• Measuring Results	• Expected results not defined precisely • Measurement often misleading	• Quantitative for incremental results • "Market intelligence gap" for radical R&D	• Against business objectives *and* technological expectations
• Evaluating Progress	• Ritualistic and perfunctory • Periodic	• Formalized peer reviews • Good communications with businesses for incremental and radical R&D projects	• Regularly *and* when external events and internal developments warrant

Table 7–1 Strategic Concepts and Operational Principles of "Third Generation R&D"

4 Ibid. p. 6-8.
5 Ibid. p. 31, 36 and 39, [partly condensed for space reasons].

cept could not be usefully complemented by further two, or perhaps one and one half, generations.

The first of these would belong at the beginning of Table 7–1 and is therefore best termed Zero Generation R&D. Its logical underpinnings go back to the origins of industrial R&D in the 19th century, to a time when technical progress and the improvements of products and processes was largely based on the trial and error attempts of individuals, masters of crafts, experienced workmen on the factory floors and others who frequently had not even received any formal technical training. Although this type of activity lies outside the realm of what today is generally referred to as "R&D" (including the definitions used by the authors of "Third Generation R&D"), one should not forget that this was the root of all attempts to employ technology as means of differentiation in a competitive market place. Equally, one should not assume that this original form of "R&D" is one of a bygone era that ended with T. A. Edison. To this day, there are millions of small and medium sized enterprises, even in the highly industrialized regions of the world, that do not purport to engage in some high-tech activity, but whose business is still of a technical nature and subject to technical change. Just because they do not have an explicit R&D budget or a clearly defined R&D department does not mean that R&D—in whatever shape—does not exist there.

In these enterprises, products and processes are improved, or even new ones invented, in some corner of the factory or repair shop and often more or less on the side. Perhaps this only happens because a passionate technician has some spare time and is willing to invest it in an idea. Perhaps it is a fickle customer demanding some special version of a standard product which leads to a new product line. More often than not, in such loosely organized enterprises the costs of technical improvements will be regarded as production costs or simply as part of the general costs of doing business. They are decided on the spur of the moment and more or less informally. There is no listing or choosing of priorities. There is just a job that needs to be done. The downside of all this, of course, is that there is no sense of direc-

6   Ibid. p. 35. In fact, Roussel et al. name only two: Merck and IBM, the latter only for the Proprinter development which arguably was really only a case of good Second Generation R&D. This lack of technology strategy input from the top levels of companies especially among U.S. corporations is confirmed by a study by Roberts, 1994 p. 6, who found that the Chief Technology Officer of a corporation is a member of its board in 95% of the cases he studied in Japan, whereas in European firms this value only reached 55% and an astonishing low of 20% in the U.S.

tion and no control over where the company's technology base is headed and where its emphasis lies. Accordingly, R&D results are not measured because, strictly speaking, there is nothing to measure. In the final analysis and although there is no *evaluation* of technical change, there is still *change* and the technical adaption to a changing business environment.

The idea, or existence, of a Zero Generation R&D attains even larger significance if one sees it in the wider perspective of the world-wide changes occurring in industry today. More and more companies in the rich countries are transferring labor-intensive production facilities into countries with lower labor costs. They are not doing this with their R&D laboratories anywhere close to the same extent. Ample reference to this was made in Chapter 2 above. But as independent companies in the developing countries or subsidiaries of multinational corporations take on a greater share of world production, it is almost inevitable that they will gradually hone their methods anyway. Already now, the Malaysian Peninsula is turning into South East Asia's high-tech corridor. Intel Corp. produces Pentium chips there, Sony precision parts for compact disc players. The skills and the technical knowledge of local workers has become highly sophisticated. Sooner rather than later, they will learn to improve production processes, and ultimately some inventive individual or work group will come up with an idea for a new product or process that goes beyond, or differs from, the specifications received from the headquarters or customers in the industrialized world.[7] Possibly, it is tuned to the conditions of the local market place or to customers in other advanced countries. Whatever the reason, this kind of change can then become the crystallization point of independent local R&D activities and of future R&D Generations in these countries too. This was how industrial R&D in North America and Europe originally arose. There is no reason why it should not happen again in today's Third World countries. With the benefit of having a model to learn from in the rich countries and the ambition to become fully industrialized nations, it will probably also come about faster. In many areas of the world, especially in South Korea, Taiwan, Singapore and other countries it has already become apparent.[8]

The other additional, full or half generation R&D would be added at the end of the spectrum described in Table 7–1. We will call it Fourth Gener-

---

7   See Davis, 1995.

8   It is indicative for this trend that in 1993 South Korea, Taiwan and Singapore were already spending 2.0%, 1.8% and 1,2% of their respective GDPs on R&D. Their ambitions certainly go still further.

ation R&D. It parallels the Third Generation in most respects, and expands on it in one very important dimension:

Third Generation R&D is largely governed by those factors which are directly subject to a corporation's control or influence (e.g. organization, cost allocation, managerial structures) or at least can be evaluated with well-known instruments (e.g. market size, competitor activities, customer satisfaction). In contrast, Fourth Generation R&D additionally seeks to include such factors in the decision making process which lie outside the immediate corporate or business realm. It considers societal changes, political developments on a national and international plane, environmental issues, shifts in values, attitudes and beliefs and many other external determinants of business. It looks at needs for products and technologies in a more reflective mode. It searches beyond a given or perceived market demand, and it integrates business/R&D strategy not only into a corporate horizon but into one encompassing the whole of an industrial society in which the industrial firm is just one of many forms of citizenship.

Shaping R&D

In this way, the R&D function can also become instrumental in the realization of corporate social responsibility. In many respects, industry has not met this responsibility at all or if so, only to the minimum degree it could get away with. Environmental auditing, corporate ethics reporting and a few other instruments are only used at the insistence of society at large and rarely with a deeper conviction on the part of industry of their need. Industry in general, and the high-tech industries of the dawning 21st century in particular, would do well to open their eyes, ears and mouths to the rest of society and to involve it both at home and abroad to a far larger degree in its long-term thinking and decision making than has been the case so far. In fact, this would also be good business. Nothing sells like societal acceptance, or as The Economist put it some time ago, "How to make lots of money, and save the planet too."[9]

To some, all this might sound like naive and wishful thinking. In the author's conviction, it is difficult to conceive of anything else in the long run. In a chaotic world that is increasingly beset by religious and ethnic strife, political convulsions, environmental and raw material crises, group egoism, migration pressures, economic and labor market predicaments and a multi-

---

9   The Economist, 3 June 1995, p. 65.

tude of contradicting tenets, opinions and ideologies, problems of sheer governance have come to the fore. The various past and ongoing attempts by national and international bodies to come to grips with these enormous problems have only very rarely drawn on the capacities and experience available in industry in any extensive way. That is indeed amazing. Not only do many of the thorny and interwoven problems facing the world today find their origin directly or indirectly in the industrial development of the last two centuries. In many respects, the industrial firm is also perhaps better equipped than other bodies to tackle them.[10] It has at its disposal managerial talent, technical and financial resources, experience in coping with complexity and—perhaps more important than anything else—an enormous pool of established and emerging technologies.[11] It is only a matter of time before society at large will demand that this potential be employed in contributing to finding solutions. There can be little doubt that the industrial R&D function with its long time horizons, its capacity for interdisciplinary cooperation and its insights into scientific and technical matters will be one of the prime candidates for supplying such contributions.

All this means that the task of defining the right R&D program requires many more factors to be taken into account than just the three mentioned so often on these pages: competition, market, technology. These factors can roughly be categorized into four groups.

- The constraints outside the corporation and beyond managerial control.

- The R&D constraints within the corporation.

- The indicators and tools for management and control of R&D.

- The varying, and sometimes conflicting, goals to which R&D contributes.

These four groups and some of their component elements are shown as concentric areas in Figure 7–3. The outermost area of Figure 7–3 includes those factors in the company's operating environment which are not subject to immediate control by corporate management. Since they can have sub-

10 For a very enlightened article arguing along similar lines, see Tickell, 1994.

11 In addition, industry is not subject to many of the constraints hindering other institutions from addressing long-term problems effectively. For example, it is not bound by four-year terms of legislature, although interest rates can play a similarly dictatorial role in reducing time-horizons, of course.

stantial influence on an R&D program, however, they obviously still have to be considered in defining an R&D program. The second area covers factors which have an immediate influence on R&D but are not part of it. These factors are endogenous to the company and can therefore be shaped by a corporation and its management. The factors shown in the third area are typically those used to directly shape and steer R&D. They come in many forms. Apart from R&D-specific instruments, they also include many classic and general management tools not included in the figure. The goals in the fourth area, finally, supply the standards for the use of the control variables and the shaping of the corporate R&D environment. The range of goals is not as large as that of the control variables. Nevertheless, a company will only rarely have one single R&D goal such as sales maximization, for example, or profit maximization. A due balancing process is therefore essential.

Among all these, there is a special subset of variables listed in Table 7–2 which management would do well to keep in equilibrium. Maintaining this

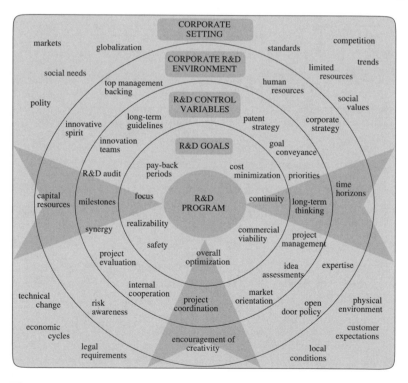

Figure 7–3   Elements Shaping the R&D Program

equilibrium serves to prevent R&D from drifting into an ill-balanced orientation which could lead to an inefficient use of resources, to duplicate efforts, or to missed opportunities. They include following dimensions:.

Table 7–2 Balancing R&D

Basic R&D	↔	Applied R&D
Divisional R&D	↔	Corporate R&D
Domestic R&D	↔	International R&D
Exploratory Research	↔	Continuous Development
In-house R&D	↔	Outsourced R&D
Product Technologies	↔	Process Technologies
Regional/decentralized R&D	↔	Centralized R&D
Revolutionary Innovation	↔	Evolutionary Improvement
Short-term R&D	↔	Long-term R&D
Strategic R&D	↔	Operational R&D

Maintaining such balance is not only a matter of convenience but has deep implications. Take the product and process technologies mentioned in the sixth row of Table 7–2, for example. Put simply, the former govern *what* a company makes, the latter *how* it makes it. Both are of central importance for a manufacturing firm's business success, but in different ways.

In the advancement of process technologies, learning from experience, particularly with respect to costs and quality, plays an important role because learning effects can be seen fairly readily.[12] Improving quality—or processes—in many respects, therefore, is a permanent goal. It finds its original expression in the Japanese quality concept of *kaizen* as a frame of mind that ceaselessly and unendingly aims for quality improvement. Of necessity, it assumes a certain degree of continuity. Classic Western thinking, on the other hand, basically regards an innovation as a one-time change that is complete in itself. The variation associated with innovation thus tends to conflict with kaizen's need for continuity. More innovation means less continuity, whereas better quality among other things also requires a certain degree of constancy. Continuous improvement enriches given products, but also tends to cement their existence. It reduces the

12 Senge, 1990, p. 23-24, makes some very insightful observations in this regard.

likelihood of unexpected breakthroughs or of revolutionary new products. A permanent succession of revolutionary new products, on the other hand, impedes the attainment of high degrees of quality.[13] Finding the correct balance between both goals is therefore crucial. It finds its embodiment, for example, in how a corporation divides its R&D resources between the advancement of product and process technologies.

Preparing for R&D

The foregoing section's list of factors influencing a corporation's R&D selection process is complex and far from complete. In different companies and at different times, individual factors carry different weights. They often overlap, some of them are difficult to define, and occasionally they tend to qualitatively or quantitatively blend with one another. Some of the terms (e.g. "synergy", "corporate strategy", "project management") cloak whole hierarchies of sub-terms and concepts. Forging a handy R&D tool from them and using it is no easy task.

On the other hand, if it *were* an easy task, many of the problems mentioned in the chapters of this book would not exist. Also, the difficulty of a task is no reason not to tackle it—if it is important enough. Considering the magnitude that R&D has reached in many companies as well as the role it plays for their future, this importance is hard to deny. R&D has become simply too expensive to be started wantonly or inconsiderately. Quite the contrary, it requires meticulous planning, advance review and re-review. Its every financial and technical aspect must be subject to thorough inspection and every previous assumption questioned. This assessment should involve both R&D personnel and other departments. Their work commences long before actual the R&D process is initiated, and it does not end with budget approval or project begin.

This thought is illustrated in Figure 7–4. In any R&D project—or any other complex non-repetitive undertaking, for that matter—the level of information about a project at any one time normally conforms with the stage of the project. The further a project progresses, the better its critical parameters can be recognized and the clearer it becomes what is really important. Anybody who has ever built a house can confirm this. When you are finished you finally know how to do it best. Unfortunately, complete information at the end of a project is largely useless. The house is completed,

13 More on this in: von Braun, 1995, p. 248.

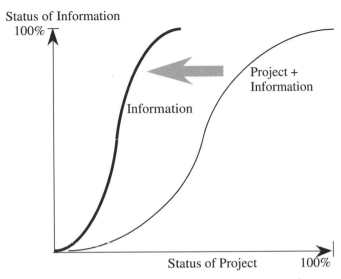

Figure 7–4 Decoupling of Information Status and Project Status

and one rarely needs a second one. But every day, by which relevant project information would have proceeded the corresponding stage of project implementation would have been of immense value.

In view of the enormous leverage effects associated with early decision making in R&D, a limited effort to achieve such earlier information would be worth its cost many times over. All and any sources of information and understanding such as idea visualization, brainstorming, portfolio analysis, systems simulation, information networking and any other traditional or new[14] tools that can contribute to early information assembly should be used for this purpose. Traditional and vague justifications which where often used in the past to discount the many uncertain aspects of R&D are simply not good enough any more. Statements such as, "We cannot afford not to work in this area" or "The project promises a lot of useful side effects which we cannot even begin to estimate," even if true can not be used to justify R&D expenditures.

This is not to say that the risks associated with R&D can ever be reduced to zero. We cannot even come close. Some (significant) degree of uncertainty with respect to technology, timing, finances, outcomes or mar-

14 For some new ideas, see Urban et al., 1994; and Frenkel et al. 1994.

kets is an inherent part of any R&D activity. Since R&D's very function is to develop products and processes which as yet do not exist, it is not possible to determine every detail in advance. Industrial practice, however, has by no means reached anywhere near a point where it might need to worry about this remaining uncertainty. Attention should rather focus on attitudes regarding technology in general, its potential, its costs, and its dangers. In all too many corporations these are still far too uncritical. Presently at least, one can safely say that the problem of *how* one arrives at the optimal R&D program should not fail to be addressed because this cannot be done unequivocally. In practically all the companies that the author has had the opportunity to look into, there could at least have been a *better* solution.

It is simply unacceptable that R&D funding for long-term programs—as is often the case—is cut because *momentarily* there is a cash crunch. If at some previous point in time one has arrived at the conviction that a certain project is crucial for the future of the company (or the country, for that matter), then this evaluation should not change just because of a slimmer profit margin (or of lower tax revenues). For example, a number of Japanese companies cut funding for energy-efficiency research projects in the years since 1992 because oil prices have happened to decline. Such practices are more an indication of poor or insufficient project conception than prudent management. Cancelling a project only for reasons of this kind—with everything else unchanged—is simply nonsense and contradictory. On the other hand, if the original decision *for* the project was merely made because the company was flush with liquidity at the time, then it was nonsense from the outset and should never have been started.

"50% of our R&D spending is useless," is a statement ascribed to many CEOs these days, "I just don't know which 50%." If that is true, then there is enormous room for improvement. Many companies are willing to invest substantially and/or bear significant consultants' fees just for a chance to improve the productivity of their factories, their inventories, their overheads or other functions by a mere 10%. Why not do the same for R&D? Most medium-sized companies today maintain at least ten, and sometimes one hundred, financial administration specialists on its payroll just for purposes of cash and liquidity management, credit administration and exchange rate optimization. In addition, they often pay substantial bank fees for the same purposes. All this is done in the mere hope of improving the company's margin at year's end by a few fractions of one percent. Siemens Kapitalanlagesellschaft, for example, a capital investment company established in January 1993, has a payroll of 12 employees whose job is to manage a little under DM 6 bill. (approx. $4 bill.) of liquid cash.[15] If this makes sense, as it undoubtedly does, then would it not also make sense to invest a few man years for the more complex R&D issues and their far greater rationalization potential? If the result of such an investment were to reduce a CEO's certainty of 50% useless R&D to 30%, it would surely be worth the effort many times over. Or let us put it another way: If a company has come to the conclusion that technology is an important element of its business and it ends up spending 10% of sales on R&D, would it not be prudent to spend, say, between 0.5% and 1% of the R&D effort (or between 0.05% and 0.1% of sales!) to seriously, objectively, and systematically consider the question, *what* to do R&D on?

For what purposes and how these funds should be invested in each individual case cannot be generalized here. Among other things, such considerations depend on the structure and size of a company and the industry in which it operates. In practice, it could be a small group of specialists who can serve as a bridge between the laboratory, on the one hand, and the rest of the company on the other. Or it could be the fees for external technology experts or specialized consultants who offer a whole range of tools for such purposes. Or it could be the time spent by top management, the sales/commercial, or the strategic planning departments on the orientation of the R&D program along the future needs of the company. Or it could be a mixture of all these and other activities. Whatever the means, the main goal is to reduce the uncertainties attached to R&D. As indicated above, every little bit of information improvement helps.

Deciding R&D

If one is willing to commit the necessary funds to this decision making process it is also possible to find approaches to many of the problems referred to above. The goal of this process is to identify those R&D directions which are crucial for the long-term survival of the company. *Vice-versa*, it should eliminate as early as possible all those projects which are not. That can be a demanding task. On the part of top management it requires:

- A clear notion of the company's long-term direction and chances including the social, economic, political and physical environment in which it operates.

15 Waller, 1993.

- The courage to make painful and occasionally unpopular decisions.

- Imagination, determination and endurance.

- An awareness of the company's true strengths and capabilities.

- Carefully tuned R&D resolution processes involving the whole company and not only R&D insiders.

- Procedures for the continuous verification of assumptions and observations on which R&D decisions were originally founded or which might influence these.

Among the many instruments available to a company approaching these requirements one could name, for example, an in-house capacity for very long-term analyses. This might be something like a corporate early-warning system that reacts to weak signals and which could point both to future dangers and future opportunities. The main purpose of such a capacity would not be to forecast what *will* happen but what *could* happen. Scenario techniques and their associated consistency controls are a highly effective tool for such purposes.

In spite of all the reports and worries about the increasing speeds of economic and social developments, it is remarkable how many evolutionary threads tend to move fairly slowly and often also allow reasonably accurate forecasts. These can play a decisive role in R&D decision making. Take demography, for example: The maximum number of 70-year-olds in 30 years is known. For industries whose business is in the development of instruments and other items in the health care sector, these are important data. It may sound trivial, but many companies that should, do not use this kind of information, in spite of its easy availability.

The same is true in many technology fields. It is amazing how slowly some fields of knowledge develop from original technical or scientific discoveries to widespread industrial applications. Much of what is offered in the markets of the industrialized world today as the latest technology generation was already the subject of discussions at universities some 30 or more years ago. Some examples:

- In mass production, there has been talk of the ultimate "lot-size 1" since the 1970s.

- Nuclear power plants have been around for about half a century. The complete control of the full fuel cycle is still evasive, although the underlying problem was known from the outset.

- The electron particle was a scientific discovery in the year 1899. It became the basis for a major industry only after World War II.

- Systems thinking and network approaches were concepts dating back to the 1960s or even earlier, but only recently are some companies beginning to grasp the power of such tools and are putting them to profitable use.

- Gene therapy and underlying research has been promising goods for at least a decade. It has yet to deliver.

- High-temperature superconductors were a scientific breakthrough in 1986. At the time, there was a lot of talk of new industries arising and old ones falling. So far at least, there are designs for prototypes, at best. Actual products are still years away.[16]

This is not to imply that the R&D-people are not doing their homework or that they are incompetent. It just turns out, that both breakthrough and evolutionary technical developments have the habit of being more difficult to realize than is normally previously anticipated. At least they are regularly associated with significant delays. In the author's view and in spite of views to the contrary,[17] such delays will rather tend to become longer than shorter. One of the main reasons for this is not so much technical, but rather our lack of understanding of economic and social systems and how these interact with technological developments. Who is in a position to say, for example, what the Internet's societal effects will be in the long run? Another reason can be found in the sheer *volume* of new technology that has arisen over the last one or two centuries and continues to do so in the present. Our industrial and market systems as well as our educational, social and professional infrastructures are increasingly less able to digest the growing accumulation of knowledge with the same speed as it is being created. In previous centuries, one could always turn to parents, teachers or "the elders" and their accumulated experience or wisdom of many years for advice. Today, teachers and trainers in many fields of science or technology have to work hard just to maintain a two hour

16 For some details, see Nairn, 1995.

17 See Winton, 1995: "Gates sees accelerating personal computer market."

lead over their students. In some respects, that is not all bad, in others it places enormous strains on both sides. It also leads to smaller and smaller forks, branches, twigs, and offshoots of knowledge specialization. All this compartmentalization is becoming more and more difficult to accommodate. And precisely *because* they have already digested so much and are expanding so quickly in so many different directions and dimensions, the industrial, economic and social systems on the receiving end of the technology generation process are becoming more and more unwieldy. Thus, in any number of fields there is a growing mismatch between the gathering of information and the ability or willingness to use it.[18] In effect, we are experiencing information overload or, as the author heard some time ago, "Too much data, not enough knowledge."

To indicate just one aspect of this, a few decades ago, researchers could still read the individual articles in the important journals of their particular fields. As the number of publications increased in every field of knowledge, researchers' reading habits were necessarily reduced to abstracts and journal digests in increasingly narrower fields. Later, even that proved to be too time consuming. One could therefore observe a widespread tendency to skim only the titles of recent publications and follow up on only one or two journals. Today, aided by powerful data banks, on-line services and so called search engines (essentially, high-tech software devices that allow access to further high-tech information),[19] perhaps the next step will be a reduction to

18 To give only two examples:

a) Today's genetic analysis technologies allow many new tests that screen for nascent diseases which might afflict an individual at some point in the future. What is often lacking, however, is any treatment for such pre-diseases. Essentially, one is generating information that *cannot* be acted upon.

b) Countless terabytes of scientific information gathered in space by satellites, probes or other means of observations is never subjected to an even cursory overview, let alone a thorough evaluation, but is just stored in the basements of space research centers. Here, one is generating information that nobody *wants* to act upon. In all likelihood, such occurrences are more prevalent in basic or fundamental research facilities than in industrial R&D centers, although they are by no means unheard of there either. Technological "overkill" as described in Chapter 6 frequently starts in the laboratory.

19 On 3 April 1995, for example, Oracle Corp. announced the availability of "TextServer3 with ConText", a software product that stores, analyzes and retrieves electronic documents by their content or actual meaning. It can search by "theme" instead of keyword occurrences and offers "speed-reading" and automatic summarization. As Oracle Corp. puts it, the idea is that "companies can surf the tidal wave (of information) rather than be overcome by it." See PRNewswire Florence, Italy, 3 April, 1995.

tidy groupings of titles restricted to very precisely defined areas. While such information gathering techniques are no doubt extremely effective, one should not forget that they also remove the individual researcher from the original sources and hinder unplanned cross referencing or lateral mental connections. In the final analysis, they contribute to automating the R&D process itself. Of necessity, they also give R&D an outlook that becomes more and more shortsighted. They carry the danger of extinguishing the very essence of what sets R&D apart from so many other activities and also from what makes it so stimulating: the spark of creativity.

Looking toward the horizons of the future, the emerging technologies 30 years or so hence are the subjects of discussions already today, especially among younger scientists who are unbiased by decades of experience in other well established fields. The least a company might do is listen to some of these discussions. Here too, a corporate or industry-specific early-warning system could be of invaluable help. It could either perform its own analyses or take intelligent (not slavish) advantage of the many sources on long-term trends which are abundantly available in the professional literature, at research institutes, think-tanks and from data banks, often at surprisingly low costs. In a properly processed form, this kind of information can lead to important insights into the path a technology is likely to take, where its ultimate limits are, and then enter the definition of long-term R&D programs.

With respect to technology demand, it is a simple but useful rule that today's existing or emerging problems are tomorrow's business opportunities. From this it follows that the institution of a Fourth Generation R&D is not merely the manifestation of a politically sensitive and potentially costly corporate social responsibility scheme. It also makes eminent financial sense. Making a business of solving the ailments and problems of individuals or of society in general has great motivating power, both for suppliers and customers. That is what a "market" is all about. There is nothing immoral to it. Doctors and insurance companies have been doing it for a very long time.

Of course, such problems are not always the same. They are subject to change over time and differ by culture, geographical region or state of development. But at least some parts of their solutions will have to rely on technology.[20] From a plethora of problems becoming visible today we will name only four examples in widely disparate areas:

- We know that the damages resulting from natural disasters, especially climate-induced (i.e., at least partly man-made) catastrophes such as hurricanes, cyclones, floods etc. are on the rise, even in traditionally temperate zones such as Europe.[21] One reason is that there are more frequent disasters. Another is that the density of values and properties in an increasingly populated and industrialized world is growing. A hurricane today will therefore have more harmful consequences both in terms of lost lives and health, as well as damaged or destroyed physical and social structures than the same hurricane did a few decades ago. Since there is little reason to believe that this trend will suddenly be reversed there should be ample opportunities for the development of technologies for disaster readiness, management, mitigation, rehabilitation and prevention.

- The problems of an ageing society in many countries should spur the development of many new technologies, not only in health care. An equally pressing demand would be the provision of tools that allow meaningful and productive lives for elderly citizens and do not disjoin them from the rest of society. For instance, making computers and networks more accessible and amenable to them might be a step in the right direction. Is the concept of a "virtual retirement home" realizable?[22]

- Reducing the required material and energy inputs in everyday products while at the same time allowing for longer product lives could prove to be a very worthwhile R&D endeavor. Escaping the Acceleration Trap will also require some rethinking of R&D into new directions.

- In the use of the oceans and continental shelves for the production of food, technology has so far largely supplied tools that are more in accordance with a civilization of hunters and gatherers than with some more modern type of society. Although the tools themselves have become very advanced, they still consist of nets, harpoons, tracking and stunning devices etc. They are appallingly dysfunctional when it comes to any form of husbanding of stocks. With

20 See Meyer-Krahmer, 1994, who argues that the avoidance of future ecological disasters depends crucially on the availability of the right technological innovations.

21 See for example Quarantelli, 1994; Munich Re, 1988.

22 Kaiser, 1995.

increasing technical sophistication, their use almost automatically leads to an exhaustion of resources and in due course to international fishery disputes. On land, the problem of poor productivity of resource use typical of nomadic hunters and gatherers was solved thousands of years ago with the invention of agriculture. Aquaculture, on the other hand, is in its infancy at best. Essentially, what is lacking is an ocean-equivalent of the plough share (actually, a whole bundle of technologies) which would allow a more sustainable exploitation of the ocean's resources.

Industry management would do well to remember that "progress" is not only measured in terms of technical performance characteristics. It does not occur just because some device has become cheaper, smaller, faster, harder, softer or denser. It is not even enough for it to be socially and environmentally acceptable. Ideally, new technology should also *enhance* social and societal advancement.[23] That would be true progress.

Methodologically, there is a multitude of organizational, technical, analytical and other measures and mechanisms to identify those technologies which will, or can, become decisive for a company's future. Some forward-looking companies, for example Microsoft, have already begun to implement them. We will not go into them here, since more often than not they are founded on the specific situation of an individual enterprise. In the end, one finds that they have only a few, but vital elements for the determination of major R&D directions in common:

1. *Incorporating R&D into the company.* As indicated earlier in this chapter, this is not only important because successful innovation increasingly also builds on the initiatives of the production, marketing and sales departments which in one way or another were involved in the conceptual phases of an innovation. It is also generally true that the individual elements of business success closely interact. Looking only at technology can easily lead to its overvaluation.

At issue is not the development of a corporate strategy, on the one hand, and to additionally afford an R&D strategy, on the other. Both belong together. They are building blocks of the same structure. That is to say, an R&D strategy cannot be developed by the staff of the VP Technology in iso-

---

23 For some further examples of technologies along this line of preference, see Kaiser, 1995.

lation from the rest of the company. Nor can it be decided over the heads of the R&D people. By its very nature, it is a process that has to be embedded in a dialogue among all levels and pillars of the organization. This dialogue carries much of its dividend already in the fact that it occurs at all. The longer and more intensive it is, the more rewarding it becomes.

2. *The consideration of critical skills and the interaction between technologies and R&D fields.* In the area of production, it is usually not easy to change established procedures. Similarly, sales and marketing people tend to have a hard time entering new or unfamiliar distribution channels. The same is true of R&D. Over time, a company typically develops certain technology fields where it commands particular strengths and where success is more likely.[24] Outside of these fields, it will often encounter problems. This can involve very basic dimensions of differentiation. For example, a company that has grown accustomed to developing goods that are measured in tons or pounds might have difficulties developing products that are measured in unit numbers or in bits and bytes. If the same company feels at home in organic chemistry, it might be well-advised to outsource any technology needs in the areas of optics or precision engineering, instead of doing so itself.[25] Perhaps it should forget about them all together. Such "technology families" can be the source of considerable synergies in R&D. The definition of such families and an accurate understanding of their present and potential future reach is proving to be a particularly useful criterion in the R&D decision process.

3. *A long term approach.* This is perhaps the most important feature of a successful R&D orientation. It implies not only a true awareness that even under rigorous control and optimal organization, most R&D work will not be completed within a month, let alone overnight. The importance of long-term thinking goes far deeper. In the final analysis, it rests on the realization that the future is nothing we are helplessly exposed to. "If you don't make history, you are history," is a popular saying these days. In a world of almost six billion people, that amounts to a lot of history, perhaps more than we care to experience. But it is good to bear in mind that although the future, i.e. tomorrow's history, is not certain, it *can* be shaped. The future is what you make of it.[26] The further the view of the future and the determination to shape it goes, the more effective a lever such thinking will be. For R&D, this is more valid than for anything else in a company.

24   See Roberts et al., 1991.

25   For a nice example of this in the textile business, see Rodger, 1995.

4. *Focus*. A corollary of any strict R&D selection process is that the manpower and resources will be made available promptly and with no constraints to those remaining areas of technology which have passed the test of strategic relevance. The technology developers themselves need to be reassured that the company backs their work, views it as its very own and uppermost concern, and is determined to bring it to a successful conclusion. More than anything else, a project or even a complete R&D program that has taken all selection hurdles has to be able to count on the unconditional support of top management.

All this can, and will, happen only if the company is borne by the conviction that R&D and its tasks are in accordance with the goals and visions of the company as a whole. Given that (and a little bit of luck), the integration of R&D and ultimately R&D success will follow automatically.

26 As Akio Morita, legendary chairman of Sony Corporation, said: "Our plan is to lead the public with new products rather than ask them what kind of products they want. The public does not know what is possible, but we do. So instead of doing a lot of market research, we refine our thinking on a product and its use and try to create a market for it by educating and communicating with the public." Quoted by Pearson et al, 1995, p. 312.

Bibliography

Abernathy, W. and Wayne, K.: Limits to the learning curve, in: Harvard Business Review, Sept./ Oct. 1974, p. 109-119.

Abernathy, W. et al., The new industrial competition, in: The McKinsey Quarterly, Summer 1982, p. 2-25.

Allen, Thomas J.: Distinguishing Engineers from Scientists, in: Managing professionals in innovative organizations, Ralph Katz ed., Ballinger Publ. Co., New York 1988, p. 3-18.

Altenmüller, G. Hartmut: Die Universitäten unter dem Andrang von Studenten, in: Spektrum der Wissenschaft, March 1992, p. 123-124.

Ammon, Ulrich: Deutsch als Wissenschaftssprache, in: Spektrum der Wissenschaft, January 1992, p. 117 et seq.

Anon.{ 1}: Conceptions of Technology, in: The New Encyclopædia Britannica, Chicago 1979, Vol. 18, p. 21-24.

Anon.{ 2}: National Research Council 1940: Forschung in USA, in: Das Reich (No. 12?), 20 October, 1940.

Anon.{ 3}: Herausgeber und Schriftleitung: Zur Einführung, Wissenschaft und Industrie, Vol. 1, No. 1, 15 July, 1922, p. 1.

Anon.{ 4}: Die Forschungsanstalten der Firma Krupp, in-house publication, Essen 1934.

Anon.{ 5}: Siemens gibt bei Chips nicht auf, in: Süddeutsche Zeitung, 27 January, 1991.

Anon.{ 6}: MITI agency promoting basic-research projects, in: The Nikkei Weekly, 23 November, 1992.

Anon.{ 7}: Forschung mit sinkender Produktivität. Arthur D. Little: Kürzere Durchlaufzeiten mit falschen Produkten, in: Frankfurter Allgemeine Zeitung, 21 May, 1991, p. 18.

Anon.{ 8}: Car dealers fear stalled growth signals trend, in: The Japan Economic Journal, 13 October, 1990.

Anon.{ 9}: Gillette. Blade-runner, in: The Economist, 10 April, 1993, p. 66.

Anon.{10}: Russia muscles in, in: The Economist, 17 July, 1993, p. 59-60.

Anon.{11}: The coming clash of logic, in: The Economist, 3 July, 1993, p. 21-23.

Anon.{12}: Uplifting, in: The Economist, 10 July, 1993, p. 81.

Anon.{13}: From guns to gadgets, in: The Economist, 2 Ocotober, 1993, p. 15; resp.: Still waiting for the bang, ibid. p. 69-70.

Anon.{14}: Japans Halbleiter-Hersteller starten Großangriff. Neue Kapazitäten für 16-Megabit-Chips sollen Siegeszug der Südkoreaner stoppen, in: Süddeutsche Zeitung, 7 October, 1993.

Anon.{15}: So much for the cashless society, in: The Economist, 26 November, 1994, p. 23-30.

Anon.{16}: Big physics, on the cheap, in: The Economist, 24 December, 1994, p. 109.

Anon.{17}: The shock of the not quite new, in: The Economist, 18 June, 1994, p. 85.

Anon.{18}: The second wave, in: The Economist, 7 May, 1994, p. 71-72.

Anon.{19}: The virtual heart of the medico-industrial complex, in: The Economist, 22 October, 1994, p. 99-100.

Anon.{20}: Chipmakers Raise Stakes, in: International Herald Tribune, 2 December, 1994.

Anon.{21}: Pentium pretenders, in: The Economist, 15 October 1994, p. 78-79.

Anon.{22}: Intel's chip of worms? in: The Economist, 17 December 1994, p. 63.

Anon.{23}: Sony R&D efforts follow shift to manufacturing overseas, in: The Nikkei Weekly, 24 October, 1994.

Anon.{24}: China's new model army, in: The Economist, 11 June 1994, p. 55-56.

Anon.{25}: South-East Asia's happy little village, in: The Economist, 23 July 1994, p. 51-52.

Anon.{26}: Umstellung der riesigen russischen Rüstungsindustrie auf die Produktion ziviler Güter so gut wie gescheitert, in: Süddeutsche Zeitung, 14 August, 1994.

Anon.{27}: Crystal Diplomacy, in: The Economist, 30 April, 1994, p. 72-73.

Anon.{28}: How to turn junk mail into a goldmine - or perhaps not, in: The Economist, 1 April, 1995, p. 63-64.

Anon.{29}: The mass production of ideas, and other impossibilities, in: The Economist, 18 March, 1995, p. 76.

Anon.{30}: Biotechnology mergers: Unseemly couplings, in: The Economist, 13 May 1995, p. 78-79.

Anon.{31}: Nongame software deficit hits 20-1, but games even score, in: The Nikkei Weekly, 6 November, 1994.

Anon.{32}: 3M: And then there were two in: The Economist 18 November, 1995, p. 82-83.

Arai, Hiroshi and Kyoshi, Ando: South Koreans gamble on 16M chip, in: The Nikkei Weekly, 28 June, 1993.

Auriol, Laudeline and Pham, François: What Pattern in Patents? in: The OECD Observer No. 179, 12-1992/1-1993, p. 15-17.

Axelrod, Robert: Die Evolution der Kooperation, R. Oldenbourg Publ., Munich 1987.

Backhaus, Klaus and Gruner, Kai: Epidemie des Zeitwettbewerbs, in: Die Beschleunigungsfalle oder der Triumph der Schildkröte, p.19-46, Backhaus, Klaus, ed. Schäffer-Poeschel Verlag, Stuttgart, 1994

Bastian, Till: Bald auch noch die "schwarze Bombe"? in: Die Zeit, 26 September, 1991.

Bayles, Fred: Study: If doctors have easy access to medical gadgetry, they will use it, Report by Associated Press, 19 August, 1993, with reference to a publication in the New England Journal of Medicine of the same day.

Bayus, Barry L.: Accelerating the Durable Replacement Cycle with Marketing Mix Variables, in: Journal of Product Innovation Management, September 1988, p. 216-226.

Bayus, Barry L.: Are Product Life Cycles Really Getting Shorter? in: Journal of Product Innovation Management, November 1994, p. 300-308.

Bayus, Barry L.: Speed-To-Market and New Product Performance Tradeoffs, unpublished paper; Kenan-Flagler Business School, University of North Carolina, August 1995, 42 pages.

Beam, A. and Mitchell, R.: The Computers That Refuse to Die, in: Business Week, 21 July, 1986, p. 89-90.

Beckmann, Johann: Anleitung zur Technologie, oder zur Kentniß der Handwerke, Fabriken und Manufacturen, vornehmlich derer, die mit der Landwirtschaft, Polizey und Cameralwissenschaft in nächster Verbindung stehen. Second ed., Verlag der Witwe Vandenhoeck, Göttingen 1780.

Benson, Johan: Interview with Wolfgang Demish, in: Aerospace America, June 1993, p. 6-8.

Betts, Paul: Airbus welcomes chance for wider role, in: Financial Times, 6 September, 1994, p. 8.

Böhringer, Ulf: Alles super - aber gut wozu? in: Süddeutsche Zeitung, 21 February, 1996.

Bökers, H.: Wie neue Software-Versionen sanften Druck ausüben, in: Süddeutsche Zeitung, 26 September, 1989.

Bollschweiler, Michael: Größter anzunehmender Wirrwarr, in: Süddeutsche Zeitung, 14/15 August, 1993.

Boslet, Mark: High-Tech Cos. Go All Out to Recruit Qualified New Employees, in: Dow Jones News Report, 10 April, 1995, 11:16 AM.

Botskor, Iván, Der Fernseh-Schock, in: Bild der Wissenschaft 7/1994, p. 37.

Brandin, David and Harrison, Michael: The Technology War, John Wiley & Sons, New York 1987.

Brix, Peter: Book Review of Operation Epsilon: The Farm Hall transcripts with an introduction by Sir Charles Frank, OBE, FRS, in: Interdisciplinary Science Reviews, 1994, vol. 19, no. 4. p. 348-349.

Buchanan, Robert A.: History of Technology, in: The New Encyclopædia Britannica, Chicago 1979, vol. 18, p. 24 et seq.

Buhl, E.: Gefährliche Wracks, in: highTech 8/90, p. 26-28.

Burton, John: High Hopes, in: Financial Times, 19 May, 1994, p. 10.

Buskirk, B. D.: Industrial Market Behavior and the Technological Life Cycle, in: Industrial Management and Data Systems, Nov./Dec. 1986, p. 8-12.

Butterworth-Hayes, Philip: European conversion goals hijacked by events, in: Aerospace America, April 1994, p. 34-38.

Butterworth-Hayes, Philip: Sales, not subsidies are the sticking point, in: Aerospace America, June 1993 p. 10-12.

Canibol, Hans Peter and Fischer, Manfred: Dynamik für morgen. Wer die Zukunft sichern will, muß schon heute neue Produkte entwickeln, in: Wirtschaftswoche Nr. 9, 23 February, 1990, p. 144-146.

Carlton, David and Schaerf, Carlo (ed.): The Dynamics of the Arms Race, John Wiley and Sons, New York-Toronto 1975.

Chimelli, R.: Zukunftspläne in einem Ozean von Zeit, in: Süddeutsche Zeitung, 10 February, 1993.

Clifford, M.: New kids on the block, in: Far Eastern Economic Review, 7 May, 1992, p. 60 et seq.

Cole, B. C.: Getting to the market on time, in: Electronics, April 1989, p. 62-67.

Coleman, Brian: Airbus May Fuel Flap With Plan for Military Plane, in: The Wall Street Journal Europe, 6 September, 1994.

Cookson, Clive and Green, Daniel: Robots invade the laboratory, in: Financial Times, 11 November, 1995.

Crabb, Don: Macro Economics, in: Compuserve Magazine, July 1994, p. 20-22.

Crawford, C. Merle: The Hidden Costs of Accelerated Product Development, in: Journal of Product Innovation Management,Vol. 9, 1992, p. 188-199.

Curtis, Carey C.: New Product Development Cycle Time: Investigation of Cycle Time and Accounting Measures, Determinants of Cycle Time and the Impact of Cycle on Financial Performance, Unpublished Doctoral Dissertation, University of New Haven, Connecticut, USA, July 1993, 252 pages.

Curtis, Carey C.: Non-Financial Performance Characteristics in New Product Development, in: Journal of Cost Management, Vol. 8, Fall 1994, p. 18-26.

Cusumano, Michael A.: Diversity and Innovation in Japanese Technology Management, in: Research on Technological Innovation, Management and Policy, Vol. 3, p. 137-167, Rosenbloom, Richard S. ed., JAI Press Inc. 1986.

Cusumano, Michael A; Mylonadis, Yiorgos; Rosenbloom, Richard S.: Strategic Maneuvering and Mass-Market Dynamics: The Triumph of VHS over Beta, Sloan Working Paper #3266-91, Massachusetts Insitute of Technology, March 1991, 45 pages.

Dash, Sanford M.: CFD: Where can it take us?, in: Aerospace America, February 1992, p. 48-51.

David, Leonard: India's space program picks up the pace, in: Aerospace America, August 1995, p. 32-45.

Davis, N. W.: Customers await better, cheaper ISDN software, in: The Japan Economic Journal, 3 December, 1988.

Davis, Neil W.: Asian nations seek wings of their own making, in: Aerospace America, March 1995, p. 4-7.

Dorr, Robert F.: Bills, Buffs and Broncos, in: Aerospace America, November 1995, p. 8-10.

Drews, Jürgen: Arzneimittelforschung und ethische Verpflichtung, Lecture given at the Carl-Friedrich-von-Siemens-Foundation, Munich, 22 June, 1993.

Easingwood, C. J.: Product lifecycle patterns for new industrial products, in: R&D Management, No. 18, 1988, p. 22-32.

Edmondson, Gail: Grabbing Markets from the Giants, in: Business Week, 19 December, 1994, p. 27.

EIRMA (European Industrial Research Management Association): Increasing the Speed of Innovation, Workshop Report V, Paris 1994, 75 pages, English version.

Eisele, Michael: Wettbewerbstheoretische Analyse der Verkürzung von Innovationszyklen, Unpublished Diploma Dissertation, University of Mannheim, Germany, Sommer 1993, 93 pages.

Ellis, Lynn and Curtis, Carey: Speedy R&D: How Beneficial? in: Research. Technology Management, Vol. 38 No. 4 , July-August 1995, p. 42-51.

Euler, Karl-Joachim: Eine Entdeckung verändert die Welt, 150 Jahre Elektrotechnik, Special edition of Elektrotechnik, 1981, p. 10 et seq.

European Patent Office: Annual Reports 1989-1993, in house publication (Munich).

Evangelista, Matthew: Innovation and the Arms Race. How the United States and the Soviet Union Develop New Military Technologies, Cornell University Press, Ithaca-London 1988.

Fischer, A. B.: What Consumers Want in the 1990's, in: Fortune Magazine, 29 January, 1990, p. 48-52.

Fischer, Andrew: Making bright ideas shine. Successful inventions are one in a million, in: Financial Times, 25 March, 1993.

Fischer, Fritz: Griff nach der Weltmacht, 3rd reprint, Droste Publishers Düsseldorf, 1964.

Fisher, J. C. and Pry R. H.: A Simple Substitution Model of Technological Change, in: Technological Forecasting and Social Change, Vol. 3, 1971, p. 75-81.

Forbis, J. L. and Mehta, N. T.: Value-based strategy for industrial products, in: The McKinsey Quarterly, Summer 1981, p. 35-52.

Freeman, Christopher: The Economics of Industrial Innovation, 2nd reprint., MIT Press, Cambridge, 1982.

Frenkel, Ammon; Harel, Erez; Koschatzky, Knut; Grupp, Hariolf; Maital, Schlomo: Indentifying the Sources of Market Value for Science-Based Products: The Case of Industrial Sensors, International Center for Research on the Management of Technology, Working Paper WP # 111-94, Massachusetts Institute of Technology, 1994, 28 pages.

Fulford, Benjamin: Price war forces PC industry restructuring, in: The Nikkei Weekly, 26 February, 1996.

Galvin, Christopher J.: Taking the System 7 Plunge, in: Compuserve Magazine, July 1993, p. 20-24.

Goldhar, J. D.: In the Factory of the Future, Innovation Is Productivty, in: Research Management, Vol. 29, March/April 1986, p. 26-33.

Gomory, R. E.: From the 'Ladder of Science' to the Product Development Cycle, in: Harvard Business Review, Vol. 67, No. 6, Nov./Dec. 1989, p. 99-105.

Götz, Birgit: Multimedia wird unser Leben verändern, Marktforscher prophezeien "explosionsartiges" Wachstum, in: Süddeutsche Zeitung, 23 March, 1993.

Gradyl, Barbara: Oracle sees info-highway reality, Interview with Lawrence Ellison, Reuters Financial Report, 14 March 1995.

Graham, Margaret B. W.: RCA and the VideoDisc, The business of research, Cambridge University Press, New York-London 1986.

Griffin, Abbie and Page, Albert L.: An Interim Report on Measuring Product Development Success and Failure, in: Journal of Product Innovation Management, Vol. 10, 1993, p. 291-308.

Gross, Neil and Carey, John: In the Digital Derby, There's no Inside Lane, in: Business Week, 19 December, 1994, p. 18-26.

Gruner, Kai et al.: Die Verkürzung von Produktlebenszyklen - eine computergestützte Anlayse von Einflußfaktoren, Working paper No. 17/1994, Betriebswirtschaftliches Institut für Anlagen und Systemtechnologien, Westfälische Wilhelms-Universität, Münster, Germany.

Hartmann, Hans: Forschung sprengt Deutschlands Ketten, Union Deutsche Verlagsanstalt, Stuttgart, 1940.

Hausen, Harald zur: Science and the Public. The German Situation, in: Interdisciplinary Science Reviews, Vol. 19, No. 1, 1994, p. 42-48.

Hayashi, A.: Hyundai's Headache, in: Electronic Business, 6 February, 1989, p. 25 et seq.

Herbst, Ludolf: Das Kalkül der Konzerne, in: Süddeutsche Zeitung, 19/20 August, 1989.

Hermann, Armin: Opfer müssen gebracht werden. Vor 100 Jahren begann mit Otto Lilienthal das Zeitalter des Fliegens, in: Süddeutsche Zeitung, 11/12 May, 1991.

Hess, Wolfgang: Ein Prüfstand für Forscher, Daimler-Benz führt die Qualitätskontrolle in der Forschung ein. Interview with VP R&D H. Weule, in: Bild der Wissenschaft 10/1993, p. 90-91.

Hirose, Toru: Matsushita's videodisc vote stuns Sony, in: The Nikkei Weekly, 30 January, 1995, p. 9.

Hirose, Toru: Sharp expands production base to meet soaring LCD demand, in: The Nikkei Weekly, 6 February, 1995.

Hofer, Peter: Das teure Objekt der Begierde, in: Bild der Wissenschaft 7/1994, p. 32-36.

Holzwarth, Franz: Zeit verkürzen heißt Leistung steigern, in: Siemens Zeitschrift, No. 2, March/April 1993, p. 6-11.

Horwitch, Mel: The Role of the Concorde Threat in the U.S. SST Program, Working Paper No. WP1306-82, May 1982, Sloan School of Management, M.I.T. Cambridge, USA.

Ikegami, Teruhiko: Developers tout photo standard, but critics see few benefits, in: The Nikkei Weekly, 24 October, 1994.

Iklé, Fred C., Wohlstedter, Albert et al. (The Commission on Integrated Long-Term Strategy): Discriminate Deterrence, Memorandum for the Secretary of Defense and the Assistant to the President for National Security Affairs, Washington D.C., January 1988.

IMEDE/World Economic Forum, The World Competitiveness Report, 1989.

Inoue, Yuko: Major manufacturers agree to set digital VCR standards, in: The Nikkei Weekly, 5 July, 1993.

Isaka, S.: Feverish competition spurs video innovation, in: The Japan Economic Journal, 1 September, 1990.

Ishizawa, Masato: NEC developing multi-platform software, in: The Nikkei Weekly, 18 July, 1994 (Ishizawa I).

Ishizawa, Masato: Sony fires 1st salvo in videodisc standards war, in: The Nikkei Weekly, 19 December, 1994 (Ishizawa II).

Ishizawa, Masato: Sony to blaze its own videodisc trail, in: The Nikkei Weekly, 27 February, 1995 (Ishizawa IV).

Ishizwawa, Masato: Chip makers develop 1-Gigabit DRAM, in: The Nikkei Weekly, 20 February, 1995, (Ishizawa III), p. 1, 23.

Japan Company Handbook, First Section, Winter 1993, Toyo Keizai Publishers, Tokyo.

Jonash, Ronald S. et al.: Product and Technology Management: Learning to Juggle in the Age of the Paradox, in: Prism, Arthur D. Little Publishers, Third Quarter 1994, p. 13-35.

Jopp, Klaus, Großwildjagd im Teilchen-Zoo, in: highTech, March 1991 p. 44 et seq.

Josephson, Matthew: Thomas Alva Edison, in: The New Encyclopædia Britannica, Chicago 1979, vol. 6, p. 308-310.

Kaiser, Gert: Guter Rat ist teuer, in: Bild der Wissenschaft 2/1995, p. 70-71.

Kandiah, Peter: Malaysia to make home-grown chips, in: The Nikkei Weekly, 13 February, 1995.

Kanno, Kenichi: Appliance makers reduce range of goods, extend product cycles, in: The Nikkei Weekly, 24 May, 1993.

Kaplan, Gadi u. Rosenblatt, Alfred: The expanding world of R&D, in: IEEE Spectrum, October 1990, p. 28-84.

Kaufmann, Hans: 30 Jahre 911, in: Christophorus Porsche Magazin No. 241, March 1993, p. 29-64.

Kay, John: Foundations of Corporate Success, Oxford University Press, New York 1993 (Preprint).

Kelly, Anthony: The Changing Cycle of Engineering Materials, in: Interdisciplinary Science Reviews, Vol. 19, No. 4, p. 285-297.

Komarek, Peter et al.: Hochtemperatur-Supraleitung, Hoffnung auf eine neue Technik, panel discussion protocol, in: Bild der Wissenschaft 4/1989, p. 108-118.

Koyanagi, T.: NEC, IBM latest combatants in computer war, in: The Japan Economic Journal, 28 October, 1989.

Krasnoff, B. and Mandell, M.: How High-Tech Products Can Achieve Profitable Longevity, in: High Technology Business, Jan. 1989, p. 18-21.

Krubasik, E. and Stein, L.: Reducing time-to-market boosts the bottom line (part 4), in: Electronic Business, Vol. 15, 1 May, 1989, p. 57-60.

Krugman, Paul: Competitiveness: A Dangerous Obsession, in: Foreign Affairs, Vol. 72 No. 2, March/April 1994, p. 28-44.

Kumpe, T. and Bolwijn, P. T.: Manufacturing: The New Case for Vertical Integration, in: Harvard Business Review, Vol. 66, March/April 1988, p. 75-81.

Lane, Neal F.: What is the future of research? The science policy of the USA, in: Interdisciplinary Science Reviews, Vol. 20, No. 2, 1995, p. 98-103

Lanus, D.: Globale Sättigung und wenig wirklich Neues, in: Japaninfo, Vol. 11, 5 February, 1990, p. 7-9.

Lashinsky, Adam: Far-flung Kanebo struggles to par losses. Broad diversification leaves firm with no core of expertise, in: The Nikkei Weekly, 2 January, 1995.

Levinson, Marc: Cutting Edge? If you're a critic of Clinton's controversial technology policy, rest easy. There's much less to the plan than meets the eye, in: Newsweek, 8 March, 1993, p. 34-36.

Lewis, G.: Is the Computer Business Maturing? in: Business Week, 6 March, 1989, p. 68-78.

Lewis, Robert: Science and Industrialisation in the USSR, Industrial Research and Development 1917-1940, University of Birmingham, 1979.

Littlewood, Bev and Strigini, Lorenzo: The Risks of Software, in: Scientific American, Nov. 1992, p. 38-43.

Lopez, Virginia C.: Aerospace employment trends, 1962-1995, in: Aerospace America, July 1995, p. 14-16.

Ludsteck, Walter: Nur eine Handvoll Firmen kann noch mithalten, in: Süddeutsche Zeitung, 16/17 January, 1993 (Ludsteck, 1993 I).

Ludsteck, Walter: Unterwegs zu neuen Dimensionen, Die Telekommunikation wandelt ihr Gesicht, in: Süddeutsche Zeitung, 27/28 February, 1993 (Ludsteck, 1993 II).

Lund, Robert T. and Denney, Wm. Michael: Opportunities and Implications of Extending Product Life, Massachusetts Institute of Technology Working Paper CPA-77-9, presented at the Symposium on Product Durability and Life, National Bureau of Standards, Gaithersburg, Maryland, November 1-3, 1977.

Lundgreen, Peter; Horn, Bernd; Krohn, Wolfgang; Küppers, Günter; Paslack, Rainer: Staatliche Forschung in Deutschland 1870-1980, Campus Verlag, Frankfurt/New York, 1986.

Masuko, Takashi: Besieged NTT carrying on with basic research program, in: The Nikkei Weekly, 9 November, 1992 (Masuko, 1992 I).

Masuko, Takashi: China most favored by software firms, in: The Nikkei Weekly, 10 August, 1991.

Masuko, Takashi: NTT bets its future on R&D; $ 2.3 billion to fund high-tech quest, in: The Nikkei Weekly, 21 March, 1992 (Masuko, 1992 II).

Matsufuji, Masatsugu: Cheaper Toshiba HDTV stirs market, in: The Nikkei Weekly, 22 February, 1993, p. 11.

Matsumoto, Motohiro: R&D costs criticized. Analysts question skyrocketing spending, in: The Japan Economic Journal, 11 August, 1990.

Matsuo, Hirofumi: Komatsu bulldozes into new businesses, in: The Nikkei Weekly, 23 January, 1995.

McCreadie, J.: Why technology change is the curse of the laptop class, in: Electronic Business, 6 February, 1989, p. 70-72.

McCutchen, Charles W.: Peer Review: Treacherous Servant, Disastrous Master, in: Technology Review, Oct. 1991, p. 27-40.

McGrath, Michael E. and Romeri, Michael N.: The R&D Effectiveness Index: A Metric for Product Development Performance, in: Journal of Product Innovation Management, Vol. 11, p. 213-220.

McIntyre, P. H.: Market Adaption as a Process in the Product Life Cycle of Radical Innovations and High-Technology Markets, in: Journal of Product Innovation Management, Vol. 5, June 1988, p. 140-149.

McLeod, Thomas L.: Industrial Research and Development, in: The New Encyclopædia Britannica, Chicago 1979, Vol. 15, p. 739 et seq.

Meeks, Fleming: Watch out, Motorola, in: Forbes, 12 September, 1994, p192.

Mergler, Axel: Mißklänge in der digitalen Videowelt, in: Süddeutsche Zeitung, 14 March, 1996.

Meyer-Krahmer, Frieder: Freie Fahrt für Innovatoren, in: Bild der Wissenschaft 12/1994, p. 100-101.

Michaelis, Anthony R. and Schmid, Roswitha: Wissenschaft in Deutschland, Niedergang und neuer Aufstieg, Paperback published by Naturwissenschaftliche Rundschau, Stuttgart, 1983.

Ministry of International Trade and Industry: Issues and Trends in Industrial /Scientific Technology - Towards Techno-Globalism, Government Publication Office, Tokyo 1992, # BI-80, 72 pages [MITI, 1992].

Mitsusada, H.: Carmakers shift sales projections into high gear, in: The Japan Economic Journal, 9 December, 1989.

Mitsusada, Hisayuki: Machine tool makers innovate to recuperate, in: The Nikkei Weekly, 25 January, 1993.

Mizuno, Y.: Firms curb spending as cost of capital climbs, in: The Japan Economic Journal, 2 March, 1991.

Morishita, Kaoru: Stock-price manipulation alleged, in: The Nikkei Weekly, 27 February 1995, p. 21.

Mowery, David C. and Rosenberg, Nathan: Technology and the Pursuit of Economic Growth, Cambridge University Press, Cambridge 1989.

Munich Reinsurance: Weltkarte der Naturgefahren (World Map of Natural Dangers), in-house publication, Munich 1988.

Naegele, T.: Now It's Time to Fix the Sky, in: Electronics, April 1989, p. 92-97.

Naide, Akira: NEC aims to outdo Sharp over LCDs, in: The Nikkei Weekly, 30 August, 1993.

Nairn, Geoff: Switch to hot wire, in: Financial Times, 17 October, 1995.

Nakamoto, Michiyo: At the Sharp End, in: Financial Times, 10 September, 1993.

National Research Council, Division of Engineering and Industrial Research: Executives and Bankers Look at Research, New York, 1930.

Neher, J.: Firms Pamper R&D in Bid to Go Global, in: International Herald Tribune, 16 December, 1991.

New Grolier Multimedia Encycolpedia, CD-Version 4.03, Grolier Electronic Publishing, Danbury, CT, USA 1992.

Nishioka, Kazuhiko: From Alchemy to Science of Language, in: The Nikkei Weekly, 26 October, 1991.

O'Toole, T.: Interview with Vice President J. D. Quayle, in: Aerospace America, May 1991 p. 6-7.

O'Toole, Thomas P.: Color LCD makers stepping up output, in: The Nikkei Weekly, 27 September, 1993 (O'Toole, Thomas P., 1993 I).

O'Toole, Thomas P.: Epson out to regain share with cut-price PC line-up, in: The Nikkei Weekly, 6 September, 1993 (O'Toole, Thomas P., 1993 II).

OECD: OECD Proposed Guidelines for Collecting and Interpreting Technological Innovation Data (Oslo Manual), Paris, 1992.

OECD: OECD Science and Technology Indicators, Resources Devoted to R&D, Paris, 1984.

Ohmae, Kenichi: Japanische Strategien (German version of: The Mind of the Strategist, McGraw-Hill, 1982), Mc-Graw-Hill, Hamburg, 1986.

Ohmae, Kenichi: Managing Innovation and New Products in Key Japanese Industries, in: Research Management, Vol. 28, No. 4, July/Aug. 1985, p. 11-18.

Okino, Seiji: Less is more: Japanese automakers attack engineering costs, but fear quality could suffer, in: Automotive Industries, Vol. 175 No. 3, March 1995, p. 81-82.

Oldag, Andreas: Vom Segen der Bio-Technologie, in: Süddeutsche Zeitung, 11 Jaunary, 1996.

Onishi, Yasusuki: Seiko Epson gets serious about cost-price ratios, in: The Nikkei Weekly, 16 August, 1993.

Ota, Takashi: War games and weapons: Australia leaves the bunker, in: The Nikkei Weekly, 25 May, 1994.

Patton, Robert: Seiko-Epson challenges NEC in Japan's domestic PC market, in: Electronics, 28 November, 1994 Vol. 67, No. 22, p. 5.

Pearson, Ian and Cochrane, Peter: 200 Futures for 2020, in: British Telecommunications Engineering, Vol. 13, January 1995, p. 312-318.

Petroni, G.:Who Should Plan Technological Innovation?, in: Long Range Planning, Vol. 18, No. 5, 1985, p. 108-115.

Pfeiffer, W. et al.: Technologie-Portfolio-Methode des strategischen Innovationsmanagements, in: Zeitschrift Führung und Organisation 5-6/1983, p. 252-261.

Phelps, R.: Cutting the Lifecycle, in: Systems International, Dec. 1987, p. 35-38.

Pierer, Heinrich von: Zeitwettbewerb - der Weg ist das Ziel, in Siemens Zeitschrift No. 2, March/April 1993, p. 3-5.

Plumpe, Gottfried: Die I.G. Farbenindustrie AG, in: der Schriften zur Wirtschafts- und Sozialgeschichte, Vol. 37, Duncker & Humblot, Berlin, 1990.

Porter, Michael E.: How competitive forces shape strategy, in: Harvard Business Review, March-April 1979, p. 137-145.

Postman, Neil: Das Technopol, Die Macht der Technologien und die Entmündigung der Gesellschaft, S. Fischer Verlag, Frankfurt/M 1992.

Potter, A. A.: The Federal Government and Research, in: Electrical Engineering, May 1939, p. 205 et seq.

Quarantelli, E.L.: Future Disaster Trends and Policy Implications for Developing Countries, Preliminary Paper #199, Unversity of Delaware Disaster Research Center, 1994, 47 pages.

Rack, Helmut and Schwarzer, Ursula: Der große Irrtum, in: Manager Magazin 7/1992, p. 74-82.

Raelin, J.A. and Balachandra, R.: R&D Project Termination in High-Tech Industries, in: IEEE Transactions on Engineering Management, Vol. EM-32/No. 1, February, 1985, p. 16-25.

Reche, K.: Über die Entwicklungsarbeit und die Forschung der Siemens & Halske AG, in: Siemens Zeitschrift Vol. 17, March 1937, No. 3, p. 111 et seq.

Ricca, M. N.: Can Anyone Make a Profit in the PBX Market?, in: Business Communication Review, Sept./Oct. 1988, p. 33-36.

Roberts, Edward B.: Benchmarking the Strategic Management of Technology - I, Sloan WP # 3746, Massachusetts Institute of Technology, 1994, 33 pages.

Roberts, Edward B. and Meyer, Marc H.: Product Strategy and Corporate Suceess, in: IEEE Engineering Management Review, Vol. 19 No. 1, Spring 1991, p. 4-18.

Rosenau, Milton Jr.: Faster New Product Development, American Management Association publ., New York, 1990.

Rosenberg, Nathan: Inside the Black Box, Cambridge University Press, 1982.

Rosenberg, Nathan: Why Technology Forecasts Often Fail, in: The Futurist, July-August 1995, p. 16-21.

Ross, Ian M. et al. (National Advisory Committee on Semiconductors): A Strategic Industry at Risk, Report to the President and Congress, Washington D.C., Nov. 1989.

Roussel, Philip A.; Saad, Kamal N.; Erickson, Tamara, J.: Third Generation R&D. Managing the Link to Corporate Strategy, Harvard Business School Press, Boston, 1991, 192 pages.

Rubner, Jeanne: Den Wettlauf gewonnen, in: Süddeutsche Zeitung, 14 November, 1991.

Rudzinski, K.: Der Aufwand für Forschung und Entwicklung, in: Frankfurter Allgemeine Zeitung, 11 October, 1967.

Saito, H.: 4M Dram Production Augurs Further Advances, in: The Japan Economic Journal, 3 February, 1990.

Schäfer, G.: Wahl der Waffen, in: highTech, No. 3/1990, p. 122-128.

Schmelzer, H. J.: Zeit ist Geld, in: Bild der Wissenschaft 2/1990, p. 102-103.

Schröder, Barbara: High-Tech-Chemie auf neuen Wegen, in: Süddeutsche Zeitung, 10 November, 1994.

Schwanhold, Ernst, MdB et alii: Verantwortung für die Zukunft - Wege zum nachhaltigen Umgang mit Stoff- und Materialströmen, Zwischenbericht der Enquête-Kommission "Schutz des Menschen und der Umwelt - Bewertungskriterien und Perspektiven für umweltverträgliche Stoffkreisläufe in der Industriegesellschaft" des 12. Deutschen Bundestages, Economica Verlag, Bonn 1993.

Seitz, Konrad: Die japanisch-amerikanische Herausforderung, 4th ed., Bonn Aktuell, München 1992.

Senge, Peter: The Fifth Discipline, Doubleday, New York 1990.

Shane, H.G.: University of the Air. Interview with Lord W. Perry, in: The Futurist, July/Aug. 1989, p. 25-27.

Shimura, Y., Director of Kogyo Chosakai Publishing in Asahi Shinbun, quoted in: Japaninfo, Vol. 11, No. 6, 30 April, 1990, p. 5-6.

Shiraki, Midori: Prescription for drugmakers: More R&D, in: The Nikkei Weekly, 23 May, 1992.

Shulman, Seth: The National Labs Unplugged? in: Technology Review, October 1995, p. 15-17.

Singh, Karan: AD2000 - An Early Maturity for the East, in: Interdisciplinary Science Reviews, Vol. 18, No. 2, p. 101-102.

Smith, Preston G. and Reinertsen, Donald G.: Developing Products in Half the Time, Van Nostrand Reinhold, New York 1991.

Smith, S.: Leaders of the Most Admired, in: Fortune Magazine, 29 January, 1990, p. 22-28.

Solla Price, Derek de: Science Since Babylon, Yale University Press, 1975.

Sommerlatte, Tom: Heiße Vabanque-Spiele, in: highTech 11/90, p. 8.

Sougiannis, Theodore: The Accounting Based Valuation of Corporate R&D, in: The Accounting Review, Vol. 69, No. 1, p. 44-68.

Staal, Frits: Concepts of science in Europe and Asia, in: Interdisciplinary Science Reviews, Vol. 20 No. 1, 1995, p. 7-19.

Stalk, George Jr. and Hout, Thomas M: Competing against Time. How time-based competition is reshaping global markets, The Free Press/Macmillan, New York-London 1990.

Stalk, George Jr. and Webber Alan M.: Japan's Dark Side of Time, in: Harvard Business Review, July/August 1993, p. 93-102.

Star, Steven and Urban, Glen: Competitive Marketing Strategy, in: MIT Management, Spring 1989, p. 16-19.

Statistische Jahrbücher für das Deutsche Reich (German Statistical Yearbooks), 1923 through 1941/42.

Stifterverband für die Deutsche Wissenschaft: Aus Wissenschaft und Wirtschaft, Vol. 1966.

Sudhoff, Karl.: Der deutschen Naturforscherversammlungen Werden und wachsende Bedeutung in ihrem ersten Jahrhundert, in: Wissenschaft und Industrie, Vol. 1, No. 3, 15 September, 1922, p. 34-35.

Sullivan, Aline: Pharmaceutical Stocks Swallow Some Bitter Pills, in: International Herald Tribune, 6/7 March, 1993.

Swoboda, Frank: Motorola hunts for qualified workers. Electronics giant hit by shortage of people who can adapt to technological changes, in: The Japan Times, 23 May, 1994, p. 7.

Takahashi, Kazufumi, Defense firms zero in on private sector, in: The Nikkei Weekly, 30 January, 1995. p. 15.

Takaki, Shinji and Yoshida, Chikara: Fickle consumers puzzle researchers, in: The Nikkei Weekly, 26 July, 1993.

Teece, D. J.: Capturing Value from Technological Innovation: Integration, Strategic Partnering and Licensing Decisions, reviewed version of: Profiting from Technological Innovation, in: Research Policy, 1986 Vol. 15, No. 6, no page numbers.

Tenbrock, Christian: Brüchiger Erfolg. Die Konkurrenz macht Verluste - Boeing schreibt vorerst noch schwarze Zahlen, in: Die Zeit, 12 October, 1990.

Tenenbaum, David: The Greening of Costa Rica, in: Technology Review, October 1995, p. 42-52.

Tepper, J.: Meilenstein oder Overkill, Die neue Generation der 486er, in: Frankfurter Allgemeine Zeitung, 20 March, 1990.

Tickell, Crispin: The Future and its Consequences, in: Interdisciplinary Science Reviews, Vol. 19 No. 4, 1994, p. 273-279.

Toffler, Alvin and Toffler, Heidi: Getting Set for the Coming Millenium, in: The Futurist, March-April 1995, p. 10-15.

Tsukagoshi, Shinya: Kanebo to spin off textile business, in: The Nikkei Weekly, 11 December, 1995.

Tucci, Christopher L. and Cusumano, Michael A.: Benefits and Pitfalls of International Strategic Technology Alliances, Sloan WP # 3706-94, Sloan School of Management, MIT, 1994, 38 pages.

Urban, Glen L.; Weinberg, Bruce; Hauser, John R.: Premarket Forecasting of Really New Products, Sloan Working Paper # 3689, Massachusetts Institute of Technology, 1994, 27 pages.

Urban, M.: Hoffnung auf die Forschung - Angst vor der Technik, in: Süddeutsche Zeitung, 25 February, 1993.

Volk, H.: Halbwertzeit des Wissens, in: Süddeutsche Zeitung, 10 February, 1993.

von Braun, Christoph-F.: Die Beschleunigungsfalle in der Praxis, in: Zeitschrift für Planung 1991, No. 3, p. 267-289 (von Braun, 1991 II).

von Braun, Christoph-F.: Die Beschleunigungsfalle, in: Zeitschrift für Planung 1991, No. 1, p. 51-70 (von Braun, 1991 I).

von Braun, Christoph-F.: Innovation und Qualität. Freunde oder Feinde? in: QZ. Qualität und Zuverlässigkeit, Vol. 40, 1995, p. 248-249.

von Braun, Christoph-F.: The Acceleration Trap in the Real World, in: Sloan Management Review 1991, Vol. 32 No. 4, p. 43-52 (von Braun, 1991 III).

von Braun, Christoph-F.: The Acceleration Trap, in: Sloan Management Review 1990, Vol. 32 No. 1, p. 49-58.

von Braun, Christoph-F.; Fischer, Hartmut G.; Müller, Anja E.: The need for and the issues involved in integrated R&D planning in large corporations, in: International Journal of Technology Management, Vol. 5, No. 5, 1990, p. 559-576.

Waldegrave, William MP: To Communicate Across Disciplines, in: Interdisciplinary Science Reviews, 1994, Vol. 19, No. 2, p. 117-120.

Waller, David: Siemens sets up separate internal fund management arm, in: Financial Times, 14 January, 1993.

Weiss, Jiri: Firms active in R&D at U.S. universities, in: The Nikkei Weekly, 18 July, 1994.

Wheelwright, Steven C. and Clark, Kim B.: Revolutionizing Product Development. Quantum Leaps in Speed, Efficiency and Quality, Free Press New York, 1992.

Wiener, H.: MIPS and Reality, in: Datamation, Vol. 32, No. 1, 1 January, 1986, p. 91-95.

Wintermann, Jürgen H.: Forschungs-Milliarden flüchten ins Ausland, in: Die Welt, 16 April, 1993.

Winton, Neil: Gates see accelerating personal computer market, Reuters Financial Report, Paris, 4 September, 1995.

Yip, G. S.: Gateways to entry, in: Harvard Business Review, Sept.-Oct. 1982, p. 82-95.

York, Herbert: Race to Oblivion: A Participant's View of the Arms Race, Simon and Schuster, New York 1970.

Yoshikawa, Hiroyuki: Japan's future prosperity depends on innovation, cultivation of new industries, in: The Nikkei Weekly, 27 June, 1994.

Young, Alison: What Goes into R&D? in: The OECD Observer No. 183, Aug./Sept. 1993, p. 34-38.

Zachary, G. Pascal and Yoder, Stephen Kreider: Order From Chaos: Computer Industry Divides Into Camps Of Winners and Losers, in: The Wall Street Journal, 28 January, 1993.

Zell, Rolf-Andreas: Goldene Zeiten, in: Bild der Wissenschaft 7/1994, p. 40-45.

Zick, Michael: Stiefkind Wissenschaft, in: Bild der Wissenschaft 7/1993, p. 42-45.

Index

Numerics

A

B

C

M

T